The Poetry of Men's Lives

The

University

of

Georgia

Press

Athens

and

London

The
Poetry
of
Men's
Lives

An

International

Anthology

Edited by

Fred Moramarco

and Al Zolynas

For Louise,
with best
wishes,

Al Zolynas

Credits for previously published works appear on pages 393–406,
which constitute an extension of the copyright page.

© 2004 by the University of Georgia Press
Athens, Georgia 30602
All rights reserved
Set in Ehrhardt by Graphic Composition, Inc., Athens, GA
Printed and bound by Edwards Brothers
The paper in this book meets the guidelines for permanence and
durability of the Committee on Production Guidelines for
Book Longevity of the Council on Library Resources.

Printed in the United States of America
08 07 06 05 04 C 5 4 3 2 1
08 07 06 05 04 P 5 4 3 2 1

Library of Congress Cataloging-in-Publication Data

The poetry of men's lives : an international anthology /
edited by Fred Moramarco and Al Zolynas.

     p. cm.

  Includes index.

  ISBN 0-8203-2351-9 (hardcover : alk. paper) — 0-8203-2649-6
(pbk. : alk. paper)

  1. Poetry—Male authors. 2. Poetry—20th century.

  I. Moramarco, Fred S., 1938– II. Zolynas, Al, 1945–

  PN6109.8.P64 2004

  808'.81'0081—dc22   2004007884

British Library Cataloging-in-Publication Data available

CONTENTS

The Middle East

Europe

Africa

South America

North America

Oceania, Australia, and New Zealand

IDENTITIES: CULTURAL, PERSONAL, MALE

Asia

Europe

Africa

MEN AND WOMEN

MYTH, ARCHETYPES, AND SPIRITUALITY

POLITICS, WAR, REVOLUTION

POETS AND POETRY, ARTISTS AND ART

BROTHERS, FRIENDS, MENTORS, AND RIVALS

WORK, SPORTS, AND GAMES

Oceania, Australia, and New Zealand

ACKNOWLEDGMENTS

A book of this kind is by its very nature a collaborative effort. First and foremost we would like to thank the translators, who usually labor quasi anonymously, without whom we obviously would not have been able to even conceive the idea of an international anthology of men's poetry in English. Their names are listed on pages 391–92, and they are the "producers" of this book as much as we are. Of course we thank as well the poets who continue to make poetry a necessary art in a technological age. So many factors mitigate against the writing of poems in our time, especially in countries with difficult economic or political situations, that it is nearly a miracle that writers continue to find the words to express their personal and public worlds.

We want to thank the several editors who have moved this book along in various stages. Karen Orchard, who was enthusiastic about the idea of a men's poetry anthology a dozen years ago when she ushered our first anthology, *Men of Our Time,* into the world, was equally enthusiastic about our new project. Her successor, Barbara Ras, got behind the "international" notion of this book from the start, and Nancy Grayson's continuing enthusiasm and support for the project kept us on track and keenly focused on our goal. In addition Jacqueline Vaught Brogan and C. K. Williams read the original manuscript, made many insightful and original suggestions, and then read the manuscript again for clarity and coherence. They very much helped shape this book, and it would be a very different book without their editorial acumen. And we were fortunate to have the keen editorial eyes of Mindy Wilson and Jon Davies to prepare the final draft for publication.

Both San Diego State University and Alliant International University made many resources available to us at various stages of our labors. We are deeply grateful for that support. A special thanks to David Robinson, an MFA student at SDSU, who oversaw the enormous job of getting permissions to reprint many of these poems and handled the correspondence for us.

Finally, our wives, Arlie Zolynas and Clarissa Moramarco, were indispensable for a number of reasons—for their insightful feedback and suggestions on the project at its various stages, and, most importantly, for their ongoing love and support of two sometimes harried and hassled editors.

INTRODUCTION

This gathering of poems reflects the inner lives of men throughout the world, inner lives shaped by many influences: culture, heredity, personal experience, values, beliefs, wishes, desires, loves, and betrayals, just to mention a few. The internal self is what generates the poetry of men's lives; as the American poet Philip Levine once said, poetry may be many things, but first it is "the inside of one person talking to the inside of another." At least that's the conception of poetry we value most as editors, and that is the sort of poetry you will find in these pages.

Unlike *Men of Our Time*, an earlier anthology of male poetry that we edited in 1992, this book has nothing to do with the "men's movement" or with any collective set of views men share on a group of issues. *Men of Our Time* had been limited to poetry in the United States and reflected a good deal of the energy many American men were generating in the early nineties through national and regional men's conferences and gatherings. We had been discussing the possibility of creating an international sequel to *Men of Our Time*, and when we were invited to read some poems from it at a conference on men and masculinity in Sevilla, Spain, we discovered a new *worldwide* interest in exploring masculinity and its cultural manifestations. The Sevilla conference, attended by scholars from a wide range of countries, encouraged us to expand our vision to a global context. How did poetry written by men throughout the world reflect cultural norms of masculinity, maleness, and manhood as well as what we intuited were important changes taking place in the lives of men everywhere—both internally and externally? So while the men's movement that inspired *Men of Our Time* is history now, a continuing interest in gender-based men's issues has taken hold in various academic disciplines.

In the more than a decade since we edited *Men of Our Time*, a substantial literature, both in the scholarly and popular press, focusing on gender has emerged, especially exploring distinctions between men and women in the contemporary world. This literature, which includes books like Susan Faludi's *Stiffed*, Deborah Tannen's *You Just Don't Understand Me: Men and Women in Conversation*, Warren Farrell's *The Myth of Male Power*, Christina Hoff Sommers's *The War against Boys*, David Deida's *The Way of the Superior Man: A Spiritual Guide to Mastering the Challenges of Women, Work, and Sexual Desire*, and Ken Wilber's *The Eye of Spirit: An Integral Vision of a World Gone Slightly Mad*, is redefining and reconsidering notions of masculinity and maleness. Most of these books have suggested that men *as a class* have been unjustly blamed for all of the world's evils. For example, in her popular 1999 book *Stiffed*, Susan Faludi argues that America in the late twentieth century experienced a "masculinity crisis" and speaks of the "betrayal" of American men by the reduction and diminishment of men's roles in the culture. She discovers a striking metaphor that underscores this diminishment: "Symbolically speaking, what the fathers really passed on to their sons was not the GI ethic but the GI Joe 'action figure,' a twelve-inch shrunken-man doll whose main feature was his ability to accessorize." More strikingly, Faludi, who is also the author of *Backlash*, an early nineties title that did its own share of male bashing, recognizes the impact of several decades of hostility toward men in the culture, citing two psychologists who have observed firsthand the collateral damage of the women's movement: "By provoking mothers to denigrate their sons, feminist attitudes can 'create boys that are either murderous or suicidal.'"

Virtually all of these books deal primarily with American men, but very recent titles dealing with other countries and cultures suggest that this reconsideration is becoming an international phenomenon. Books like *The "Man Question" in International Relations*, edited by Marysia Zalewski and Jane Parpart; *Machos, Mistresses, Madonnas: Contesting the Power of Latin American Gender Imagery*, edited by Marit Melhuus and Kristi Anne Stølen; and *Men and Masculinities: Key Themes and New Directions*, by Stephen Whitehead, are all part of this expansion. Although we've heard a great deal about misogyny from feminists over the years, two Canadian authors, Paul Nathanson and Katherine K. Young have evoked its male counterpart in their *Spreading Misandry: The Teaching of Contempt for Men in Popular Culture.*

Ken Wilber, who has been called the "Einstein of consciousness" and the deepest and broadest contemporary philosopher alive today, has taken on the question of gender definition throughout his many books (see especially *Sex, Ecology, and Spirituality: A Brief History of Everything* and *The Eye of Spirit: An Integral Vision of a World Gone Mad*). In an attempt to synthesize the best thinking on the subject, he uses the work of feminists like Carol Gilligan and Judy Heifitz and comes to the following conclusion (necessarily oversimplified here): men and women are, in fact, not merely "socially constructed," though society and culture play major roles in how we view and relate to and express gender. In *The Eye of Spirit*, Wilber writes: "There are . . . two flagrant errors that are constantly being made in the study of sex and gender. The first (common with conservatives) is to assume that all gender issues are totally determined by sex differences (so that biology is destiny). The second (common with liberals) is that all sexual differences are merely culturally constructed (so that biology can be ignored). Both of these stances are profoundly distorted, and almost always driven by ideology." Wilber argues for a more integral approach that combines biology and culture and recognizes the value of both the female and male, feminine and masculine spheres. In that sense, our anthology is not intended to provide material that reveals men—that is, the male gender—as "hegemonic," "patriarchal," or inherently "dominant," but rather shows them to be one half of the human species, driven by both biology and the shifting patterns and evolution of culture. So we're emphatically *not* trying to promote men at the expense of women. What we are saying, and hopefully demonstrating through the evidence of these poems from all over the world, is that neither men nor women can be put into ideological categories without severe and damaging consequences for all of us.

One of the reasons it is important to pay attention to men's poetry in particular is that men are notoriously reticent about openly expressing their feelings. Because poetry is a kind of index of those feelings, through it we can discover revelations about how men feel about their families, their lovers, their relationships, their sexuality, their childhood, and many other aspects of their lives that they are often reluctant to talk about publicly. Men's poetry has become more expressive about personal matters and more unguarded about public matters. The poetry in this anthology tells us a good deal about who men are and what they are feeling and thinking at this particular juncture of world history. In this sense, these poets are surrogates or representatives of men in general. By inclination and training, they are capable of articulating the feelings many men are unable to express.

We decided early on that this would be an English-language anthology because to include the poems in their original forms would double the size of the volume, force us to limit our selection of poems, and require a vast knowledge of the world's languages. This decision meant relying on translations and translators for all the non-English-writing poets. Although Robert Frost has famously written that "poetry is what gets lost in translation," we don't agree. At least we believe it does not *necessarily* get lost. In fact, translation has become more and more of an art form in itself, as the excellent work done by the many translators on whom we relied illustrates.

As we began gathering poems, it quickly became evident some nations have had a lot more of their poetry translated into English. From our vantage point as U.S. editors, it was much easier to find and obtain poems from some places than others. For example, we could readily identify important contemporary male poets in France, Russia, and Israel whose work was being translated and published in English; it was not so easy to find their counterparts in countries like Saudi Arabia or Afghanistan—to mention two countries that have been at the center of world attention—or in countries like Nepal or Uruguay that have not. Despite our best hopes, it became obvious that we would not be able to include *all* of the world's nations. (According to the U.S. State Department, there are 192 independent nations.) However, we were determined to make this collection as international as possible—a "worldcentric" anthology that did not privilege any single region or cultural perspective. Ultimately we were able to include 295 poems by 253 poets from nearly one hundred countries, with wide representation from each of the broader geographical areas of the world: Asia, the Middle East, Europe, Africa, South America, Central America and the Caribbean, North America, and Oceania, including Australia and New Zealand. As a practical matter, we particularly felt that the fifty most populous nations in the world should be well represented, since they make up over ninety percent of the world's total population. Nearly one-third of the world's population lives in only two countries—China and India—and over half of our planet's inhabitants live in only ten countries: China, India, the United States, Indonesia, Brazil, Pakistan, Russia, Bangladesh, Nigeria, and Japan. All of these are represented in our anthology.

We experimented with many different ways of organizing this anthology and ultimately decided that some combination of thematic and geographic organization would best convey both the *international* quality of the poetry here, as well as provide comparisons and contrasts among the ideas, feelings, and themes of each poem. As we began to group the poems, most seemed related to the stages of a man's life, his identity, his relationships, his work, and his political and religious convictions and experience. We then further sorted the poems into the following categories. Obviously, many overlap, and many poems are about more than a single subject; nonetheless, we felt that readers would find these divisions useful:

Boyhood and Youth
Families
Identities: Cultural, Personal, Male
Men and Women
Myth, Archetypes, and Spirituality
Politics, War, Revolution
Sex and Sexuality
Poets and Poetry, Artists and Art
Brothers, Friends, Mentors, and Rivals
Work, Sports, and Games
Aging, Illness, and Death

Within these thematic categories we arranged the poems by the broad geographical regions mentioned above.

Men's poetry in the world today can provide us with real insight into a great variety of male experience. For example, the "Men and Women" section includes poems that explore similarities and differences in male-female relationships throughout the world. Is Israeli Yehuda Amichai's "Ideal Woman" "put together . . . from all his desires" similar to or different from Romanian Virgil Mihaiu's "Ultimate Luxury

Woman" "locked up in a black display cabinet"? Are those differences or similarities cultural or individual?

Not surprisingly, the largest thematic category is men's search for their identities. This search has, of course, been a theme of much of the world's great literature, from Odysseus and Oedipus to Ivan Ilych and Holden Caufield. As Edward Dahlberg has noted, this is a life-long search that ends for many men without clear resolution: "At eighteen I set out to discover who I was. At thirty I thought I knew, and at fifty I knew I would never know." Where does a man's identity spring from, and where does it reside? The answers are not so simple. While men's identities are clearly tied to families, culture, sexuality, work, and personal history, these take highly distinctive and individual forms of expression. Some poets emphasize how much of their identities are shaped by their culture and nationality. For example, Nobuo Ayukawa writes:

I'm Japanese
so I hate saying
& hearing
the word *love*

reflecting the traditional Japanese reticence to express emotions openly. He contrasts this reticence with his perception of the West's almost indiscriminate expression of emotion:

Westerners say *I love you*
out of habit
they might even say *I love you*
instead of *good morning*
but the purity of the words is lost
& love is just a formality.

What makes this exploration of cultural identity especially interesting is that by the end of the poem, Ayukawa is to some degree standing outside the strictures of his own culture and offering a critique of it:

Locked in taboo, in the heart
the *ai* [love] in my Japanese *love*
is still a virgin.

Even though he recognizes the limitations imposed by his culture, Ayukawa, like many men in many cultures, is unable to transcend those limits.

Much male poetry reflects ancient and ongoing images of masculinity and its various dimensions. Stories such as Samson and Delilah, where male strength is pitted against female guile; creation myths, which attempt to explain human origins; fairy tales, which often reflect on male and female roles; and tales of male initiation and of the trials and tribulations of heroes all serve as sources for many contemporary male poets. American poet Stephen Dunn gives us a fresh take on the journey of Odysseus; Italian Primo Levi and Spaniard Jose Manuel del Pino revisit the Biblical story of Samson and Delilah; Romanian Mihai Ursachi's "A Monologue" explores the role of the powerful male leader throughout history, and Canadian Howard White's "The Men There Were Then" takes a tongue-in-cheek look at male nostalgia for larger-than-life heroes.

Politics, war, and revolution have been perennial themes in literature written by men, and contemporary world poets continue this tradition. The depth of pain and anguish reflected in poems on these themes is particularly striking. Poetry from all regions of the world that have recently suffered or are currently suffering from man's inhumanity to his fellow man demonstrate the depth of that tremendous suffering and its universality. Whatever one's individual politics, the ability to recognize the humanity of one's own adversaries is deeply affecting. The Israeli Admiel Kosman, for example, reminds us in "Games" that corpses have no nationality:

Here at the end of games,
we will break the circles open,
and then we will
all descend the hills
in bags,
the officers and the soldiers too.

One especially interesting category of themes surprised us: "Poets and Poetry, Artists and Art." We were fascinated to see how many male poets paid tribute to one another, either by acknowledging a debt of influence, paying a compliment to a fellow poet, or "speaking back" to another poet, commenting on his particular take on a subject or theme. Sometimes these connections are cross-cultural, as in Norwegian Jan Erik Vold's tribute to the eighteenth-century Japanese painter Hokusai or Scottish poet Donny O'Rourke's celebration of American Nelson Algren's tough-guy prose. And sometimes they are within a culture, such as the Canadian Simon Thompson's direct response to fellow Canadian Leonard Cohen's famous lyric "Suzanne." The tone of these poems ranges from the near adulation of a neophyte for his master-teacher to the friendly banter of peers who may have different attitudes toward the same subject. Both extremes of tone are emblematic of male interactions, the way men kid as well as admire and compete with one another.

We intend this book to embrace a wide audience, not just readers of poetry or academics with narrow literary specializations. And certainly not just men. We particularly hope the book will reach a wide audience of women, who may find it helpful in deepening their insights and understanding of what makes men who they are. Although it may be a broad generalization, Gail Sheehy's comment in *Understanding Men's Passages* is striking: "Men don't understand women, but at least they know it. Women don't understand men, but they *don't* know it." We hope this book might help bridge the distances between the stereotypes men and women have of one another. We also think that psychologists, sociologists, anthropologists, historians, gender studies scholars and students, political scientists, as well as those interested in the humanities and literature will find the book useful, stimulating, and provocative. It may be "difficult to get the news from poems," as William Carlos Williams points out, but "what is found" in these poems has the power to take us deeper into the male psyche than the transitory events of the day.

The Poetry of Men's Lives

Boyhood and Youth

Little boy who grew like a desire, show it to me!
—James Sacré

The passage from childhood to adulthood is not easy for men or women, but young men face some unique challenges. They often internalize what being a man means in any given society and find themselves falling short of social expectations. In many of the world's cultures, the dictates of "manhood" remain surprisingly uniform. Men are supposed to be strong, courageous, uncomplaining, protective, stoic, and able to provide in cultures as diverse as South Asia and Latin America. Boys, of course, are not able to live up to these expectations and often feel intimidated by them. In many modern societies traditional rituals acknowledging the transition from boy to man have vanished, leaving a kind of ache in a boy's soul as he searches for his masculine identity.

Many of the poems here record and reflect that ache. The Irish poet Ciaran Berry finds a symbol of boyhood in the image of an impotent ram, which a boy must ritualistically kill before he can come of age. He writes of the pain of being belittled by classmates and mocked by teachers. The Brazilian Carlos Drummond de Andrade hears the sound of a boy crying in the night as the expression of a universal male angst that suggests both man's compassion for and his contribution to the world's suffering. The Pakistani Shuja Nawaz writes of the burden of vengeance passed down from generation to generation of males in that society. And another Pakistani, Taufiq Rafat, evokes the physical pain of circumcision at the tender and impressionable age of six, while the French poet James Sacré writes of a whole series of boyhood traumas including cruel games, the anger of "mommy and daddy," and the death of relatives.

But not every boyhood is steeped in pain and trauma. Tender and nostalgic moments are evoked here too. The Japanese poet Anzai Hitoshi captures the surprise and excitement of a young man's first shave. The Dominican Norberto James speaks of the power of childhood dreams. And the Frenchman Jean-Pierre Rosnay recalls his boyhood as a time when almost anything seemed possible.

These poems about boyhood and youth describe how the foundations of men's lives are shaped throughout the world in different cultures with different values. They speak of a distinctly male prelude to the burdens, responsibilities, pleasures, achievements, and failures of adulthood.

Asia

Anzai Hitoshi

Anzai Hitoshi (1918–94) was born in Japan, where he worked as a reporter and served as chairman of the Japanese Modern Poetry Society. The speaker in "New Blade" witnesses an important moment of initiation in the life of his young son—the attempts at a first shave. When the boy accidentally draws blood, the poet asks if something is "broken" in the young man. If so, what is the celebration that even the birds are singing about?

NEW BLADE

My son   his hands unsteady
Uses a new razor-blade
Seeing that he is masquerading as an adult for the first time
He thrusts out his elbows as if it is a ceremony or something
He is careful not to look to either side
At his temple   a bead of blood no longer than the tongue of a small bird
Trickles down wipe and wipe though he may
He is a little   surprised
What inside him has been broken?
His naked back   like a tree with its bark peeled off
Is glistening brightly
My son does not appear to hear it but
Around the young bark
The birds all together   are singing
He does not appear to see it but
Inside the mirror the tide is swelling.

translated by Leith Morton

Shuja Nawaz

Shuja Nawaz was born in Chakri Rajgan, Pakistan. A journalist, he has worked for the *New York Times* and as a newscaster and producer for Pakistan Television. He has also translated Punjabi poetry into English. Here he shows us an "initiation" into the kind of tribal maleness that requires sons to avenge the murders of their fathers. Inevitably and predictably, such a tradition simply fuels the cycle of vengeance through the generations.

THE INITIATION

From the day he could talk, the son asked
about his father and got no answer.
He learned to grow up alone and stood
by himself at prayers, solitary
as the heliograph posts in the Khyber Pass.
The high mud walls of his fort-like house
echoed the barren language of the hills.
And each year's questions were laid to rest
like a still-born child, unlamented.

Till at fifteen someone slapped his face
with word of his father's unavenged murder.
That night he took out the family rifle,
received blessings from his mother and left.

He saw the killers come as silhouettes growing
from the bank of a moon-lit field. Hurriedly,
he mumbled God's name three times and dropped
all three with a skill mastered over centuries.

Next day, when the wailing rose from the other
village, the elders saw the rifle he carried
and pointed him out as Sherdil Khan's son.

Taufiq Rafat

Taufiq Rafat was born in Sialkot, Pakistan. He was educated in Dehra Dun, Aligarh, and Lahore. He is credited with revolutionizing Pakistani poetry written in English. All art requires distance, says Simone Weil, and perhaps that's what saves this poem from lapsing into the gruesome or into self-pity. A circumcision performed on a six-year-old boy is a harsh dose of reality that shortcuts his "innocent" desire for beauty and romance and prepares him for the pain of this world.

CIRCUMCISION

Having hauled down my pyjamas
they dragged me, all legs and teeth,
that fateful afternoon, to a stool
before which the barber hunkered
with an open cut-throat. He stropped it
on his palm with obvious relish.
I did not like his mustachios, nor
his conciliatory smile. Somehow
they made me sit, and two cousins
held a leg apiece. The barber
looked at me; I stared right back,
defying him to start something.
He just turned aside to whisper
to my cousin who suddenly cried
"Oh look at that golden bird,"
and being only six I looked up;
which was all the time he needed
to separate me from my prepuce.
"Bastard, sonofapig," I roared,
"sister-ravisher, you pimp
and catamite," while he applied
salve and bandaged the organ.
Beside myself with indignation
and pain, I forgot the presence
of elders, and cursed and cursed
in the graphic vocabulary
of the lanes, acquired at leap-frog,
marbles, and blindman' s buff.
Still frothing at the mouth they fetched

me to bed, where an anxious mother
kissed and consoled me. It was not
till I was alone that I dared
to look down at my naked middle.
When I saw it so foreshortened,
raw, and swathed in lint, I burst
into fresh tears. Dismally
I wondered if I would ever
be able to pee again.

          This
was many many years ago.
I have since learnt it was more
than a ritual, for by the act
of a pull and downward slash,
they prepare us for the disappointments
at the absence of golden birds
life will ask us to look at
between our circumcision and death.

Europe

Mario Benedetti

Mario Benedetti was born in 1920. A political activist, he has lived in Argentina, Peru, and Cuba and presently divides his time between Uruguay and Spain. "The Magnet" underscores the fundamental fact that passing on knowledge from one generation to the next is the essence of teaching. An older man seems to ward off death by taking the time to teach a boy the mysteries of a magnet.

THE MAGNET

Solitude is turning dark
the wind insisting at day's end
I'm tired as after a dream

and though I would like to be with friends
I drink my wine from a wrinkled glass

small knuckles bang on the door
it's Nelson a five year old neighbor
asking if he can play with the magnet
I don't want to disappoint him I say yes
and he begins to discover its truth

he goes away learned and frowning
the wind urges but with different rhythm
I finish the wine without getting anxious
and slowly stretch out my stiff arm
toward the magnet that waits in its mystery

translated by Richard Zenith

Ciaran Berry

Killing an impotent ram, bombing a school at which he was humiliated, smoking his first
cigarette, joining the IRA—all are signs of manhood for a young man coming of age in to-
day's still troubled Ireland. Ciaran Berry was born in Dublin in 1971. He grew up in Con-
nemara and northwest Donegal and currently resides in New York City. In "Uascán" he
captures the rites of passage he experienced in his native land. This sad and troubling poem
reveals something about outmoded notions of masculinity and the psychic costs of killing.

UASCÁN

Always under your father's feet:
size eleven Doc-Martens, steel toe-caps,
their quickstep over gravel, grass, tarmac
not waiting for you—four years young,
legs drowning in hand-me-down Wellingtons,
behind him running, fast as you're allowed,
tripping over cow-pats, whimpering

until he turns, threatens the back of his hand,
then disappears over wall, ditch, rusty gate.

In school the master mocks you for your stammer,
the *and . . . and . . . ands* that clamour round your tongue
even when you know the answer.
Your smart-arsed classmates are no better,
they hate you for your shite-caked shoes,
the clothes that used to fit your sister:
Hey Peadar, are you feared of water?

And so you plan to bomb the school
after you've joined the I.R.A.,
you call yourself *Kalashnikov*
among the dens and forts you share
with a three-legged dog called Dick,
your sole sidekick, a pure-bred mongrel
with whom you fight and win your boyish wars
against bushes, briars, the odd mad bull.

———————

The ould boy keeps black-faced sheep,
breeds them to sell at the local mart; first
there's an *uascán* born every odd year,
an impotent ram—the most useless thing—
they're shot or beaten dead with sticks,
thrown on the bog, left to the birds.

When you're thirteen, he hands you a roughish stone,
sends you to kill your first *uascán,*
says it'll make you a better man
or at least give you something to talk about.
You follow it around the field, a slow trot
at first, then sweat, face drizzle-wet,
feet tripping over cow-pats until you corner it,
bring the stone down into the dark matter of its skull.
To celebrate this little death,

he hands you your first full cigarette,
says there might be a bit of spark in you yet . . .

But you hang yourself with a halting rope
and he's left to lower you from the tree.

Ussin Kerim

Ussin Kerim (1927–84) lived and worked in Bulgaria. The speaker of his poem "Mother" finds that though he still carries the "stone of grief" over the loss of his mother in boyhood, he is losing his ability to dream her into physical form.

MOTHER

Poor mother, my martyr,
you didn't get to raise your first-born son . . .
I ask the earth and the earth is mute:
where are you buried, Mother?

No trace, no place, no grave.
So when dusk falls my faithful
grief and I sit down to weep
like an old couple: at least we have

each other. I simmer with thirst
and day by day miss your warm hands.
My youth was washed away by a vile flood,
but this stone of grief endures.

I love to remember
playing with the other kids
and women whispering,
"He looks just like his mother."

Sometimes when black night had come
and I was launched on the white sea of dreams

you'd be there, alongside,
your steady hands, the salt, the foam.

You'd rock me in your lap,
you'd mop my tears with your lips,
and I'd subside from toss to lull,
as still as water in a cup.

I'd lay my head on your shoulder
and the earth would answer me,
though now you don't, though now you're mute
though I still cry out, "Mother!"

translated by William Matthews

Ivan Matanov

Ivan Matanov was born in 1952 in Bulgaria. He is a graduate of the University of Sofia in Pedagogy and the author of three collections of poetry. As Freud reminded us, sex and death are inextricably linked. Nowhere is it more painfully and mysteriously so than in the mind of a six-year-old boy trying to make sense of his parents' lovemaking.

STILL I SEE IN FRONT OF ME

the six-year-old boy
driven out of his room,
out of the house,
outside!
All alone on a Sunday afternoon,
with one eye glued to the keyhole,
the other tightly shut
with horror
as he watches how
two sweating centaurs,
two enormous monsters
are fighting inside,
he watches the love-game
of his parents

whom he loves,
who love him,
who have to live
yet in a minute
will fall
dead
on the bed.

translated by Lyudmila Kolechkova

Valeri Petrov

Valeri Petrov was born in 1920 in Sofia, Bulgaria. He has been a war correspondent, journalist, radio editor, diplomat, and translator. He has translated all of Shakespeare's plays into Bulgarian. In this poem an old man imagines responding to the children in the street calling their playmate—whose name is the same as the poet's—to come out and play.

A CRY FROM CHILDHOOD

Why must it come just now to trouble me,
This sudden, shrill, and dreamlike cry
Of children calling "Valeri! Valeri!"
Out in the street nearby?

It is not for me, that distant childhood call;
Alas, it is for me no more.
They are calling now to someone else, my small
Namesake who lives next door.

Though such disturbances, I must admit,
Are troubling to my train of thought,
I keep my feelings to myself, for it
would be comical, would it not,

If, from his high and studious retreat,
A gaunt old man leaned out to say

"I can't come out" to the children in the street,
"I'm not allowed to play."

translated by Richard Wilbur

Peter Redgrove

Peter Redgrove has taught science at Cambridge, has worked as a research scientist and
scientific journalist, and is regarded as one of England's most influential and original poets.
His numerous awards include The Queen's Gold Medal for Poetry. He has produced
twenty-four volumes of poetry, nine novels, and fourteen plays. In "My Father's Trap-
doors" the speaker is mystified by his father's magician-like disappearing acts but ulti-
mately locates his father naked, without all the paraphernalia of the magician; he in fact
finds his father within himself.

MY FATHER'S TRAPDOORS

I.
Father led me behind some mail-bags
On Paddington Station, my grief was intense,
I was a vase of flowing tears with mirror-walls,

He wore a hard white collar and a tight school tie
And a bristly moustache which is now ashes
And he took me behind the newsprint to kiss me hard,

The traveling schoolboy,
And his kiss was hungry and a total surprise.
Was it the son? Was it the uniform?

It was not the person, who did not belong
Not to father, no.

II.
He drove a hole-in-one. It flew
Magnetized into its socket. He'd rummy out

While all the rest shuffled clubs from hearts.
He won always a certain sum on holiday

At any casino; called it his "commission."
He could palm cards like a professional.
He had a sideboard of cups for everything

From gold and tennis to public speaking.
He took me to magic shows where people
Disappeared and reappeared through star-studded

Cabinets with dark doors, and magicians
Chased each other through disappearance after disappearance.
He sat down in front of my dead mother's mirror

And disappeared himself, leaving
Only material for a funeral.

III.
I looked behind the dressing-table
Among the clooties of fluff and the dust,
I looked under the bed and in the wardrobe

Where the suits hung like emptied mourners,
I looked through the shoes and the ironed handkerchiefs
And through a cardboard box full of obsolete sixpences,

I looked in the bathroom and opened the mirror,
Behind it was aspirin and dental fixative,
I looked through the drinks cabinet full of spirits,

And I found on the top of the chest-of-drawers
Where there was a photograph of my dead mother,
My living self and my accident-killed brother,

A neat plump wallet and a corroded bracelet watch

And a plate with one tooth which was hardly dry,
And I looked down the toilet and I turned

All the lights on and I turned them off,
But nowhere in the bedroom where he sat down
And fell sideways in a mysterious manner

Could I find how he did it, the conjurer
Had disappeared the trapdoor.

IV.
It was easy to disappear me.
He was doing it all the time.
I did not return that bristly kiss.

On my fourth Christmas there were so many toys
I disappeared into them thoroughly,
There was a silver crane on my mother's counterpane

It was faulty but I did not want it returned,
I have reappeared and so has it,
Nearby and grown-up in the Falmouth Docks,

And there was a conjurer's set
With ping-pong balls that shucked their shells
From red to amber, amber to green,

With a black-white wand that would float,
And half-cards and split rings as tawdry
As going up on the stage among the trapdoors

And meeting Maskelyne close-up, his cuffs were soiled—
White tie and tails should be spanking clean,
My father's would have been, and I hoped

The conjurer would not kiss me,
It would disappear me.

V.

He could wave his wand casually
And I would reappear elsewhere;
Once in bed at ten cuddly with mother

He waved a wand in his voice
And I got out of the silken double-cabinet
For ever.

VI.

The rough kisses come round the door.
I give rough kisses myself, I am as bristly.
I am not a woman or a little boy.

And I can frighten her or make her disappear
Temporarily so she has to go to find herself
Again in the mirror somewhere;

But having learned this I am careful not to do it.
I do it less than I did.
I did not ask for this bearded equipage.

VII.

It has taken me a long while
To appreciate this wedding-tackle at its worth.
My father gave it to me like a conjuring-set.

I do not use my wand to disappear you,
I am rather too fond of disappearing it myself,
But I also use it to empower us both,

It is the key to a wonderment openness
Like turning inside-out harmlessly
Among lights, turning

Over in bed into someone else.

VIII.

The conjurer in his soup-and-fish

Vanishes into his cabinets,
His rival reappears, they cannot bear

To be together on the stage
Not while they're dressed in their power
Of black whiteness with starched bows

And cuffs that make the hands flash
While explaining here's a new trick:
The Chinese Cabinet.

It is a silk tent with a front door
As black and tall as Downing Street.
This must be a special trick, shall I expect

Mr. Major to ride out on a white horse?
Three people with slant eyeliner have erected it,
They are dressed as spirits who seem

Of the one sex which is both sexes,
And this cabinet is not coffin-like,
No, not at all, what coffin

Would be painted with sun, moon, and stars?
A Grand Mandarin with a little drum comes in,
And throws an explosive down as conjurers will

So that the tent shivers and collapses—
Yes, it is a wardrobe that has disappeared all the clothes
The white tie and tails, the sponge-bag trousers, the soup-and-fish,

For someone is coming through stark naked
And it feels good to him
For he is laughing and the mandarin bows as if proud of him,

He who touches everywhere for all clothes are gone,

Why, he's in the buff and happy as Jesus save that
His lean rod is floating out just as it should,

Floating like my own, pleased to be like him.

Jean-Pierre Rosnay

Jean-Pierre Rosnay was born in Lyon, France, in 1926. He was a teenaged fighter in the
Resistance during World War II. Since the 1960s he has published six books of poetry and
three novels. The speaker of "Piazza San Marco" recalls a time in his youth when the world
seemed fresh and full of possibility, when poverty was something to be laughed off, when
the beautiful places of the world were at his feet.

PIAZZA SAN MARCO

for Elyane Simon

Imagine for yourself what was in my heart
I was in Venice for the very first time
Piazza San Marco
With a thousand lire in my pocket
About a thousand lire
The pigeons were drunk on music
You know Venice better than I do
You know the Italians
Their music their pigeons
I was totally adrift
At nine o'clock it suddenly occurred to me
That I hadn't eaten since the day before
The day before I had an orange for lunch
I stop a woman
She keeps on going
I'm lucky I bump into another
She laughs I laugh
But even before I have a line
Ready in my mind
I remember I'm in Italy
And don't know the language

I catch a pigeon by the wing
It claps me on my hat and flies off
Imagine for yourself
What was in my heart
I was in Venice for the very first time
With a thousand lire in my pocket

translated by J. Kates

James Sacré

James Sacré was born in 1939 in the French village of Cougou. He has published over thirty
books of poetry and is considered one of France's leading poets. He has been awarded major
prizes for poetry in France and is currently Doris Silbert Professor in the Humanities at
Smith College in the United States. These shards of real or invented memories from his in-
fancy and boyhood evoke the early eroticism and raw emotions of first experiences.

A LITTLE BOY, I'M NOT SURE ANYMORE

If you really think about it, nothing so childish or nice in those vanished years. The
whole bunch of us, don't we know most of our actions were mean, all the nasty will
for me to live instead of you, the cruel games played even in the caresses we gave
one another. And the indifference of the sky carrying you away in its storms, dust
and straw childhood a whole flight of little demons in a big fart of the wind. Of
course life smells bad. Got to get used to it.

You end up remembering things that might not have happened someone told them
to you old woman in the village over there you think you can see her lovely face
now welcoming you into the world Mommy had left you all alone at the end of the
field in a little baby carriage, almost nothing but it's like suddenly words were given
to you with the other person and the vastness of the ample world. . . . Did
childhood begin with the first memory we have? And did you leave it behind when
you stopped wearing short pants? No one will ever tell you. The old woman in the
village didn't know either.

Mommy Daddy getting mad a lot life's not easy, still smiles sometimes, pleasure of having the family all together, uncles aunts, long cherry-picking days, the black ones from below Aubraille flat baskets, Daddy walking on his hands, but gotta go back to work in the fields tomorrow, the same crumpled-up anger thrown at the other one, Mommy Daddy like life like death a little boy still not understanding it. You think so? Mommy Daddy are going to die, you'll have known what?

Games with weenies and doody, weewee for fun, sister is your age, a cousin, neighbor's kids in the fields, alone too, the whole adventure of how to be and do it with others with oneself for pleasure, is that happiness? A question of loneliness and silence by yourself or with others, isn't that unhappiness? Little boy who grew like a desire, show it to me!

Uncle Ernest died a few days ago there he is still carrying you away not sure where anymore or how he took care of my feet all bloody you musta slipped on the rocks of the oyster bed, somewhere on the Ile de Ré, we used to sell crates of Foussais apples there, cheeses, nighttime trip in a van before dawn, sometimes my uncle would stop to sleep a minute, now he's asleep for good what am I really thinking of, the night goes on; am I still the same little boy?

One day like the first disturbing thrill. And nothing's simple anymore. The neighbor brings you home from school in his fast horse cart. There you are sitting uncomfortably between his legs, continual jerking of the cart with benches, something swelled a little against you under the fabric of his thick corduroy pants. When was the first time I thought back to all that? The memory still does me good. The whole village for a long time, like a peasant who can't say things good. Neither can I now. Like a disturbing thrill in the words.

A little boy walks along with his dog in front of him, passes behind the most familiar trees then a few uneven fields all thorny brush, big flowers latch on to you, walking along not knowing why or where but not a long time and no problem going back suddenly the barn and the big straw pile again the dog like time hasn't budged what d'you remember now, Mommy yakking and you laughing at her worrying you couldn't see why?

So there'll be no end to it, memory, here's a bit to hold words together it's really just two or three gestures, a fit of anger astonishment you're not too sure anymore, you stretch the words, add a color, exaggerate, you make flimsy scarecrows that don't scare anybody, little poems of straw and rags, time has eaten all the cherries: what're you looking in since you can't even find the pits?

Probably nothing that complicated let's not get carried away a childhood like lots of others restrictions desires looking after the cows going to school Daddy getting mad, reality drama, Mommy making up problems not to see the real ones, they showed you everything hid everything: no point complicating things, you don't understand more or less than they did; yes you did watch the cows, and school does go on. So watch out, make sure your poem doesn't cheat.

A good little boy, or not, you're not sure what you'd like to have been anymore, maybe neither one nor the other but those unexpected things you did (hard to remember, now that everything's cluttered up with fear or pretension) the dolls that truly kept you company, the games of fishing out grown-ups' secrets, you forget it all right away, then anger like a fit of real anger in the rough immediacy of the world, and knowing how to follow a big cloud all the way to nowhere, after school, and that meant bringing the cows back home. Neither goodness nor wickedness in your mind, totally unaware of what was growing up.

That feeling often, you're not sure anymore, childhood's where? What're you learning? Nothing exactly right, really, so many memories you could hook onto, these blocks of writing here like so many light motors, two per page, waving like trees in the old days, you run after them, little word machines to not tell, indifference and the pleasure of moving forward, wouldn't that be childhood recaptured? Nothing, yes writing like you'll never know where it comes from. Or is it gone? Another book here ahead of you: how does time cross over?

Writing's like leaving traces—you're makin a mess, Mommy says, watch what you're doin! Something like a real memory: maybe not the best one, nor the first nor the most intense, but something's going away leaving a little boy out there way ahead, his big dog leading him where to? The wonder of the world and death along

with it. The poem like a trace of what's to come. Memory like a tomorrow: I can't
recognize much of anything.

translated by David Ball

South America

Carlos Drummond de Andrade

Carlos Drummond de Andrade (1902–87) was a major Brazilian poet. His work, deeply
influenced by modernism and by a growing sense of Brazilian national identity, gave rise to
a uniquely Brazilian aesthetic. Drummond founded the modernist journal *The Review* in
1925. Much of his poetry captures some of the paradoxes of masculinity in Latin American
cultures. For example, the boy in this poem becomes a symbol of human suffering. What is
the boy crying about? Why can't anyone do anything about it?

BOY CRYING IN THE NIGHT

In the warm, humid night, noiseless and dead, a boy cries.
His crying behind the wall, the light behind the window
are lost in the shadow of muffled footsteps, of tired voices.
Yet the sound of medicine poured into a spoon can be heard.

A boy cries in the night, behind the wall, across the street,
far away a boy cries, in another city
in another world, perhaps.

And I see the hand that lifts the spoon while the other holds the head,
and I see the slick thread run down the boy's chin,
and slip into the street, only a thread, and slip through the city.
And nobody else in the world exists but that boy crying.

translated by Mark Strand

Central America and the Caribbean

Norberto James

Norberto James is one of the outstanding young poets of the Dominican Republic and founder of a group called La Isla. "I Had No Books" celebrates the "tireless love of life" rather than the things one accumulates in it. The poet draws strength, as many men have, from the solitude experienced in boyhood.

I HAD NO BOOKS

I had no books
no bicycle.
All the poetry of the days
I captured
in the diffuse colors
of borrowed pencils.
Mine was
the early age of sadness
the ancient solitude of man
the warm nights of the port
the sea salt
the breeze
and a tireless love of life
and the music that makes it possible.

My dreams
didn't have sufficient protection
and like a whirlwind of leaves
many desires tumbled and strayed.
(I would taste tender almonds in my mouth
for many hours.)
Anguish
was an inescapable inherited sign,
solitude

a permanent frame
for rising joy.

translated by Beth Wellington

Mervyn Morris

Mervyn Morris was born in 1937. A widely published Jamaican poet, critic, anthologist, and essayist, he has championed the poetry and literature of the Caribbean. He is professor of creative writing and West Indian literature at the University of the West Indies. The following poem captures a moment of transformation when a young boy's deeper identity is revealed to him after he defies warnings and transgresses a boundary.

THE POND

There was this pond in the village
and little boys, he heard till he was sick,
were not allowed too near.
Unfathomable pool, they said,
that swallowed men and animals just so;
and in its depth, old people said,
swam galliwasps and nameless horrors;
bright boys kept away.

Though drawn so hard by prohibitions,
the small boy, fixed in fear, kept off;
till one wet summer, grass growing lush,
paths muddy, slippery, he found himself
there at the fabled edge.

The brooding pond was dark.
Sudden, escaping cloud, the sun
came bright; and shimmering in guilt,
he saw his own face peering from the pool.

Families

Whose story then? Whose history shadowed
or foreshadowed, if not mine?
—David Bottoms

While the meaning of family life is constantly being reconsidered and reconfigured, a belief in the ancient bonds of "blood ties" still penetrates deeply into the psyches of most men. Men's relationships with their fathers, mothers, brothers, sisters, sons, and daughters, as well as "significant" aunts, uncles, cousins, grandparents, and so on form the basis for a good deal of men's poetry. Sometimes those poems reflect a deep sense of caring and commitment, and sometimes they reflect the ambivalence that often characterizes familial connections.

Of course we can be touched by poems of unconditional love, such as Israeli poet Yehuda Amachai's "A Flock of Sheep near the Airport," which expresses a father's feelings for his son, or Jan Erik Vold's "Thor Heyerdahl's Mother," which reminds us how vital a mother's love is in shaping her son's ambitions and dreams, or Jim Daniels's "Falling Bricks," which demonstrates the depth of a father's protectiveness toward his daughter.

But because we live in a time when the phrase "dysfunctional"—at least in the West—has become a household word in relation to families, it's not surprising that many of these poems are more conditional in their expression of affection, and sometimes openly hostile. Shaun Levin writes about the discomfort he feels when his mother visits; Michael Donaghy's longing for a "present" father is palpable in "Inheritance"; Ismael Hurreh's "Pardon Me" uses bitter irony to address how a son internalizes his father's sense of disappointment; and the father figure casts a long shadow in Jayanta Mahapatra's poem of that name.

We have a tendency, in the Western world particularly, to romanticize family connections, but as Stephanie Koontz points out in her aptly titled *The Way We Never Were,* family life has always been a mixed blessing. These poems speak to both the deep ties many men feel to their family heritage as well as the burdens imposed by that heritage. They are poems about protective fathers and overbearing fathers, about tender and loving mothers and smothering mothers, about loving siblings and disconnected siblings. They reveal aspects of male relationships with their families that are not often openly expressed outside the family context. They are about the sunshine of family life as well as the shadows that are cast over the light and warmth of our domestic haven.

Asia

Nobuo Ayukawa

Nobuo Ayukawa (1920–86) was a founding member of the *Arechi* (Waste Land) group in Japan. He is a translator of Eliot's *The Waste Land* and during the years following World War II, emerged as Japan's preeminent modernist poet. "Sister, I'm Sorry" registers some of the guilt and regret of a surviving sibling who cannot justify his own life against the great loss of potential that his sister's death represents.

SISTER, I'M SORRY

March 27, 1947

When the unforgettable sad face comes to mind
(me, who escaped from death!)
beautiful sister,
it is you
spooning milk down your thin throat,
hiding alone in a lonesome grave.
Though you never say a word,
is the hide-and-seek of love and death fun
in the end?
With inconsolable regret
I thought of your breasts that never matured,
the mole on your cheek that would have seduced many men.
Your childlike smile, hidden in shadow,
softly caresses my mind,
starving from earthly desire.
Sister, you were pure.
Are you really living in the dark underground
on your own?

Your breasts and that charming mole,
why should I remember them now?
Before the ring of your future
sparkled with blue light
the pendulum swings.
Sister, why did you say good-bye to life
in sweet baby talk?
Even now,
I wipe fatigue from my glasses
and dream of a lonely room
where no one exists.
Sister,
about our bet that I would live
with hunger, thirst, and a weary face:
It is I who lost it.
I, having failed to die,
what shall I do
with tomorrow's sunset
at my back?

translated by Oketani Shogo with Leza Lowitz

Yu Jian

Yu Jian was born in 1954 in Kunming, China. He graduated from the Chinese Department of Yunnan University and in 1984 founded *They,* an underground poetry magazine to which many New Generation poets contributed. In his poem about a son's obligation to follow in his father's footsteps, the narrator's ambivalence is not revealed until the very end. The son recalls his father's compliance in Mao's cultural revolution, his conformity, his timidity in the face of social and cultural intimidation, and finds himself a man, exactly like his father, "hard working simply dressed immaculate." Is there a subtext of resentment in the poem, a desire that his father had bequeathed him a more individualistic legacy?

THANK YOU FATHER

Twelve months a year
poppy flowers bloom in your pipe
A warm family they never divorce

never look for trouble never borrow money never
    laugh aloud
quiet as mice cleaner than a hospital
The ancestors' virtue smooth as pebbles
never bleeds In the flooding century
its designs become more simple
As a father you brought home bread and salt
At the long black table you sat in the middle
The seat that belongs to emperors professors and leaders
Your sons sat at your sides they were not negotiators
but your golden buttons made you shine
From your seat you stroked us your eyes full of love
like a stomach warm and persistent
teaching me how to be a man
You used to have stomachaches
When you were in pain your sons became beetles
    helpless insignificant

We were together from morning to night but I never
    saw your back
I didn't see your resumé till I grew up
"active and hard working warm and honest amiable and
    easy to approach
respects authority never complains never leaves early"
Once you told me you liked football when you were young
as well as dancing especially the two-step
I was startled as if you were talking about a sea lion
I knew as a child that you were a good person These days
there are more bad guys than good guys on the streets
When those heathens were arrested exiled
    and gone forever
you walked out of the park and became a bridegroom

In 1957 you became a father
As a good person Father how hard your life was
confess denounce inform
after you'd done all these you went home with
    your suitcase
At night you couldn't sleep always listening carefully

or getting up   to examine our diaries and dreams
as seriously as the Gestapo
Your own children were like tigers   they worried you
Any impertinent remarks might implicate relatives
You stood in line till midnight to buy coal and exchange the
        rationed cooking oil for milk
You traveled to Shanghai   enduring the hardship
        to buy us clothing;
You made friends with doctors   drivers   and guards
Experienced and astute   always flexible   smooth
in the dark age   a time of turmoil   you brought me
        up like this
and got me an identity card
Finally I grew up   not an easy job   Father   I've become a
        man   exactly like you
hard-working   simply dressed   immaculate
As a baby I looked like a hard luck case
I might have lost my sanity and died of encephalitis
or been crushed under a truck while crossing against
        a red light
or been misled by hoodlums and sent to prison
or been addicted to drinking   drugs   gambling
        or got AIDS
But Father   I'm involved in none of these
        not even masturbation
I don't travel far away from my parents
I study hard and progress every day
go to bed at nine-thirty   do my laundry on Sunday
I remained a virgin till 28 and passed the physical
        before my wedding
Three-bedroom apartment   living with parents
        children all fine
The family sits around the dining room table
        as warm as spring
This is not an easy job   my captain
my white-haired father   not an easy job

  translated by Wang Ping and Ron Padgett

Jayanta Mahapatra

Jayanta Mahapatra, a physicist as well as a poet, was born in 1928 in Cuttack, India, where he still resides. During 1976–77, he was a member of the University of Iowa's International Writing Program. He is also editor of the literary journal *Chandrabhaga*. "Shadows" explores the father's far-reaching shadow and the son's struggles to internalize its effects while keeping them distinct from who and what he feels he is.

SHADOWS

Shadows can never open their mouths.
They don't talk politics. Or love.
Do I have a shadow I have lived in?
Do I have one which regards me
with cold contempt? Or one that accuses me?
I think my shadow ruined me a long time ago.
As a boy I remember the time my father threw
those shadows of his on the walls of our house,
the rage and greed and the bruised infidelities,
like birds and animals, with his clever hands—
and silence stood between us, father and son.
How do I come out of the shadows,
those that want to be with me,
shrouding my face like a mask,
when I know I am doing the right thing
for the wrong reasons?
As long as they give me life, I tell myself.
This shadow of mine
lives in the middle of a breath,
a patient, flaming butterfly
that will keep on flitting near my memory.
The chill of words it gave me through closed lips
is now more than sixty years old.

Wang Xiaolong

Wang Xiaolong was born in 1955 in Hainan and is considered a poet of the "Newborn Generation." He lives in Shanghai where he runs a video company. Xiaolong's poem is interesting for its suggestion that the father's pervasive boredom was a by-product of his being smart and unchallenged in a system that encouraged mediocrity and passive complicity over any attempts to stand out and contribute.

IN MEMORIAM: DEDICATED TO MY FATHER

a bunch of winecups stand on the dining table
one must be yours
I knocked against a drawer
out came the letter you forgot to mail
that pair of old shoes is moored under the dry bed
thinking hard
the razor keeps a few hairs of your rusty beard
why did everything become the past so quickly
when I blow out the match
I raise my head and there you are
smoking in the mirror
every morning you sat there
feeling bored
you were smart
therefore you were incompetent
every time you got mad you were actually scolding yourself
your skin was dark
and had large pores
when a sad flock of wild geese brushed past your eyes
autumn was gone

translated by Michelle Yeh

The Middle East

Yehuda Amichai

Yehuda Amichai (1924–2000), born in Wurzburg, Germany, was Israel's best-known contemporary poet. The final image below captures something of a father's deep devotion to his son, as well as his gratitude and relief at finding him safe in the world. While the narrator says "his feelings always come in twos," this feeling is absolutely singular.

A FLOCK OF SHEEP NEAR THE AIRPORT

A flock of sheep near the airport
or high voltage pylons beside the orchard:
these combinations open my life
like a wound,
but they also heal it.

That's why my feelings always come in twos.
That's why I'm like a man who tears up a letter
and then regrets it,
gathering the pieces and pasting them together
with enormous effort—sometimes
for the rest of his life.

But once I went looking for my son at night
and found him in an empty basketball court that was lit
by a powerful floodlight. He was playing by himself.
And the sound of the bouncing ball
was the only sound in the world.

translated by Chana Bloch

Yair Hurvitz

Born in Tel Aviv in 1941, Yair Hurvitz was part of a group known as "the Tel Aviv poets," the generation which succeeded Yehuda Amichai. Hurvitz died at the age of forty-seven, at the height of his powers, of the heart disease that plagued him from childhood. In "An Autobiographical Moment," the silence of a dead father becomes a potent form of communication for the son—though we are left to wonder exactly what the father says "without lips."

AN AUTOBIOGRAPHICAL MOMENT

Now my father always has to come to terms
with his other language where time is no barrier,
but when he was forced to give up the simple words
I heard many sounds. I could not believe
I was crying so I went out to a place
where I thought I would meet my father, a place
where I could not believe I would never meet him again.
At that noon hour there were benches and bodies
that belonged to them by right of poverty, but my lack
was different when the trees did not seem like trees,
perhaps more like heavy sculptures then,
when I said to him words he could not add to
and that he continues to say
without lips until this
very day.

translated by Lois Bar-yaacov

Shaun Levin

Shaun Levin immigrated to Israel from South Africa as a young boy. He taught at Tel Aviv University and began publishing in Hebrew in 1992 in Israeli literary journals and newspapers. He currently lives in London where he teaches creative writing and runs a gay men's writing workshop.

WITH YOUR MOTHER IN A CAFÉ

On an afternoon when you're sitting
with your mother in a café on Shenkin Street
during an especially hot Tel Aviv summer

you'll hear those voices screaming:
"You are unloved and ugly;
you always have been."

Those are the voices that hide
the core of your being and keep you
from entertaining your real desire.

That morning, when you were grading papers,
sitting in your study listening to Elgar's Enigmas,
the muslin curtains brushing against
the rosemary and lobelia on your windowsill,
she called to ask you to take her for coffee—

her desire begging to swallow yours,
make it cotton candy in her mouth—

that was the moment you wished
you had a lover, a reason
to say to her: "I am not alone."

You're not getting any younger!
There's more to life than constant rejecting,
fending off the advances of mothers.

Think to yourself: What shall I do today,
now that I want nothing but love?
Open the door and walk out into the sun,
the wax of your wings will not melt.
Let sweat trickle down your back,

spread like ink on your blue silk shirt.
Say hello to the neighbours you think ignore you;

keep your heart open even when
the woman from whom you came needs
your company for those hours in the middle of the week.

Europe

Martin Crucefix

Martin Crucefix was born in Wiltshire, England, in 1956. His books include *Beneath Tremendous Rain* (1990), *At the Mountjoy Hotel* (1993), and *A Madder Ghost* (1997). The moment a son becomes a father is a moment indelibly pressed into many men's psyches. "Pietà" records that moment, as the world around the new father slips away into background noise for this colossal event.

PIETÀ

We pack a radio to relax

—becomes a blithe soundtrack
over suffering,
stopped only by The News
that has us screaming at politics,
its greed and earthly powers
an irrelevance
to the *pietà* we will make
after hours of pain
and mystery and the dancing

keep upright, keep on the move

as if the pain's a blow-fly

we might chase to earth
and destroy once, for all

while I spray water to cool
and with each gasp
feel your temperature rise,
your body beginning
to gape like a bear trap,
all chains and razor teeth
and absence of control

as light freshens the window
showing it still going on,
so many days since last night
when I read Dick Francis
for the first time in my life
waiting for contractions

and you sink with your back to me,
slung limp from my arms
like the impossibility of flight,
hair wet with the effort
and damp with my weeping
at the ghastly calculation
of this thing

where *pax, stop, enough, enough*
have no virtue at all,
only gas and air,
rasped by a diver
who is herself the sea,
out of which is drawn the core
a soaking-scalped purplish boy.

Michael Donaghy

Michael Donaghy was born in the United States but has lived in London since 1986. He has been awarded the prestigious Whitbread Prize for Poetry and is a Fellow of the Royal Society of Literature. His collected poems, *Dances Learned Last Night,* was published in 2000. In "Inheritance," a poem about an absent father who cherished his work more than his family, the speaker barely suppresses his bitterness.

INHERITANCE

My father would have cherished an heir,
but he remained unmarried.

Science was his mistress, and after science,
my mother. But we were provided

with a collection of seashells
second only to the emperor's.

I regret I will not live
to see the final specimen auctioned.

It is the jewel in the diadem,
A sulphur nautilus,

Wound like the spring of a gold watch.
My mother would not part with it in life.

When he died I saw his name
In the *Journal of Marine Genetics.* Sharp,

peach-coloured spikes of coral
are named for him.

Franco Fortini

Franco Fortini was born in Florence in 1917 to a Catholic mother and a Jewish father. He has occupied the Chair of Literary Criticism at the University of Siena since 1976 and has written many collections of poetry and criticism. "The Seed" considers the passing of heritage from father to son and questions whether this truly provides consolation for our mortality.

THE SEED

The paper bags fall to the ground
the leaves of the towering magnolia
shimmer like doves. Under the cedars
the afternoon light is deep.
I see the tall cruel acid grass
and the questioning reappears
with the gusts of wind, bows its head
is split apart reappears but no say the blackbirds
strutting or standing still.

My father
would grow sentimental about his own death
listening to the allegretto of the Seventh.
In the corners where in March there's rubbish
with great weeping the children bury
the birds fallen from the nest. But the music
ignores us and speaks alone
with its horns and trumpets
between these sweating walls.
In place of him there's me
or my son or nobody.

The flowers are all just scenes of irony.
The wound now will never heal.
With this shame I shall go down
Into the basements of the clinics,
and with resentment.
It is not yet July—

Not yet warmed the seed is dry
absolved.

translated by Paul Lawton

Tonino Guerra

Born in 1920, screenwriter Tonino Guerra has collaborated with many of Italy's most im-
portant filmmakers, including Federico Fellini and Michelangelo Antonioni. He has writ-
ten more than fifteen volumes of poetry and fiction, mostly in the dialect of his native
Santarcangelo di Romagna in the province of Forli. He captures the isolation of life in a
small, decaying, rural Italian town in "Canto Three" from his collection *Abandoned Places*.
The poem also examines the complex relations between brothers as the speaker, obviously
more worldly and ambitious than his sibling, expresses concern and perhaps a bit of envy
that his brother might be content with so little.

CANTO THREE

My brother works at the telegraph office in the station
where no trains have passed in forty years;
they took away the tracks during the war
when they needed iron for the cannons.

He sits there and waits. But no one ever calls
and he doesn't call anyone. The last telegram
to arrive came from Australia,
addressed to Rino from Fabiòtto who's six feet under.

The day that I went to look for him, my brother
was under the iron shelter
with his hands in his pockets, sitting in the middle of an aria
being chirped pizzicato by birds flying off in the distance.

The track where the trains used to pass
is covered with weeds. Now, a chicken is coming down toward us
and passes without even turning its head to look back.

translated by Adria Bernardi

Seamus Heaney

Born in Ireland in 1939, Nobel laureate Seamus Heaney is one of the world's most honored poets. His recent modernization of *Beowulf* has already become a classic. In this elegiac sonnet, the speaker remembers the pure simplicity, the primal and unrepeatable intimacy of working side by side with his mother peeling potatoes. The poem captures the dynamic tension between all young males and their mothers—and of a particular son and a particular mother.

IN MEMORIAM M. K. H.

1911–84

When all the others were away at Mass
I was all hers as we peeled potatoes.
They broke the silence, let fall one by one
Like solder weeping off the soldering iron:
Cold comforts set between us, things to share
Gleaming in a bucket of clean water.
And again let fall. Little pleasant splashes
From each other's work would bring us to our senses.

So while the parish priest at her bedside
Went hammer and tongs at the prayers for the dying
And some were responding and some crying
I remembered her head bent towards my head,
Her breath in mine, our fluent dipping knives—
Never closer the whole rest of our lives.

Alan Jenkins

Alan Jenkins is deputy editor of the *Times Literary Supplement*. He has published four collections of poetry and lives in London. This Proustian recollection centers on the awkwardness between a mother and a son having dinner on the anniversary of his father's death. Instead of a madeleine biscuit, however, the memory-evoking object is a pair of chopsticks that recalls the masts of his father's model ships and the piano duet that evokes family life in other times.

CHOPSTICKS

She struggles with her chopsticks, and I watch her slyly
as she mounts a two-pronged attack on a mound
of noodles, or pincer-prods a shrivelled prawn around
its dish of gloop. I watch her as she shyly
sets down the chopsticks and picks up a spoon.
Chicken and cashews, sweet-and-sour pork; no shredded beef—

It's too difficult, what with my teeth—
and special fried rice. Dinner will be over soon.

Ten years to the night since he died, and I concentrate
on fashioning from my chopsticks a mast
like the masts on the model clipper ships he built
and rebuilt and rebuilt and rebuilt
hour after hour, night after night, working late
threading cotton through the tiny balsa blocks—a stickler for detail—
to make the rigging shipshape on the imagined past
into which, in his little room, he'd set sail . . .

Someone's singing. *So merry Christmas, and a happy New Year*
and I tap out the beat with my chopsticks; *Is everything all right?*
You're very quiet. Everything's fine, mother, let me sip my beer
and remember how we sat with him—ten years to the night—
how we sat with him till it was nearly dawn
and watched him try to breathe,
the white bed between us, and him on it, and grief
no easier now there's a tablecloth, a plate with one sad prawn;

remember how I sat at the piano with my sister
to play our duet—"Chopsticks"—over and over, *ad nauseam,*
and start Christmas day. The clipper ships
still have pride of place in the sitting-room, the museum
where I'll sit for a "nightcap" among his prints and pipes,
and pour myself another scotch from his decanter and watch
the late film while my mother dozes and my sister,
miles away, plays "Chopsticks," for all I know;
where I'll sit and think of ten years gone and her two cats gone,

gone with the Christmas dinners, my grandmother and great-aunt,
with the endless Sunday mornings, Billy Cotton on the radio
and the endless Sunday lunches of roast beef,
gone with half her mind and all her teeth;
she watches me as I place my chopsticks together. *Go on,*
finish up that last prawn. But I can't.

Lyubomir Levchev

Lyubomir Levchev was born in 1935 in Troyan, Bulgaria, and is arguably Bulgaria's pre-
mier living poet. He has written more than fifty books. The young speaker of "Cronies" is
heartened by a leaf falling on his shoulder, a seemingly friendly gesture from the world of
nature, though his mother misreads his pleasure.

CRONIES

Last night as I was returning home alone,
someone tapped me on the shoulder
as a good friend might.
Pleased, I turned around.
Nobody was there.
But on my shoulder glowed
the ruddy palm
of a single
giant
weighty
chestnut leaf . . .

. . . all that evening I was happy.
So my mother, glowering at me
from under heavy eyebrows, railed away:
"You've been wasting time with cronies again!"

translated by Theodore Weiss

Karl Lubomirski

Karl Lubomirski was born in 1939 in the Austrian Tyrol and grew up in Innsbruck. He is a member of both PEN Austria and Liechtenstein and has published more than a dozen books. He lives in Milan. "Mother" is more intriguing for what it leaves out than what it reveals: the exact nature of the son's relationship to his mother. The implications of the word *everything* seem enormous.

MOTHER

On lonely
sunny afternoons
when nothing happened
everything
happened

translated by Renate Latimer

Stein Mehren

Stein Mehren was born in 1935 in Norway and studied philosophy at the University of Oslo. This poem reveals how a long-dead mother still works her magic in a man's psyche. He carries her inside him, "a fetus in my memory," and she retains the power to help heal him years after her death.

MOTHER, WE WERE A HEAVY BURDEN

Mother, we were a heavy burden for you
fatherless sons as we were
Suddenly you set us down one day
and turned away in death

First you became a pale being
mild, motherly seen from this side of death
Then you sank into darkness, became smaller

and smaller, as if you curled up
within the womb of memories, still clear

Now, when the days darken around me
I can feel you, glowing, far far
inside me, as though I carry you
a fetus in my memory, and at any moment
might give birth to you, a child of my broken childhood

translated by Olav Grinde

Alexander Shurbanov

Alexander Shurbanov was born in 1941 in Sofia, Bulgaria, and teaches English and American literature at Sofia University. He has published four books of poems and two of prose and is an acclaimed translator of classic English poets. In "Attractions," a father marvels at how his younger son imitates his older brother, striving to be more mature before his time. The father, from his distant and adult perspective, is powerless to communicate to this son the value of the boyhood he is trying to outgrow.

ATTRACTIONS

What's the attraction of age that makes
my younger son follow the elder
at every step,
trying to copy him
in everything, even at the risk of looking ridiculous?
But no, he won't be left behind
in games,
in his story,
in his haircut, even in stature—
he'll even stand on tip-toe
to be level with him . . .
What's he afraid of?
Why won't he stay
where he is now?
How can I tell him

that his present spot
is sunniest of all?

translated by Ewald Osers

Marin Sorescu

Marin Sorescu (1936–97) was born in Romania. The author of some ten books, he was well known as a poet, novelist, playwright, and essayist. Here a father gives his son advice that is at once archetypal and cryptic, and the son tries to follow it as best he can.

BALLS AND HOOPS

My father, the juggler at the circus,
Was urgently summoned far into the night
And has left me
To take his place.

"Everything you see around you
Is just balls and hoops,"
He told me. "Don't forget this:
Balls and hoops.

"The trees are green hoops.
You must spin them quickly about your hand, very quickly,
In order that they not suddenly lose
All their leaves.

"The clouds are blue hoops.
You spin them with the tip of your toes
And the restlessness of your heart.

"Women are hoops, too.
They must be beautifully slipped in,
Between clouds and smoke.

"As for the balls,
Be very careful not to drop the red one,

Or you'll find yourself in pitch darkness,
And don't toss the black ball too high,
For all our species
Is bound to it by oath."

The game is fun.
I master it the best I can,
My world of balls and hoops.
But, look, it's become very late,
And Father, the juggler,
Must no longer be coming back.

translated by Adam J. Sorkin and Lidia Vianu

Jan Erik Vold

Jan Erik Vold was born in Oslo in 1939. He is a dedicated translator, critic, editor, and poet who has published numerous editions of works by Scandinavian writers. This poem celebrates the unconditionally loving mother who supports a son in his schemes, no matter how harebrained. Thor Heyerdahl, of Kon Tiki fame, is not the first accomplished famous man to enjoy the special gift of a mother's unqualified support.

THOR HEYERDAHL'S MOTHER

Thor Heyerdahl, a stolid
and quiet
Norwegian, had these
ideas

which he wanted
to
verify—so he built himself a raft
of balsa wood

in the manner
of the ancient

Incas, he wanted to sail
across

the ocean. Not many people thought
he was going to make it
but his mother
thought

so, she sent
a telegram: Let us know
when
you get there. And he got there.

translated by the poet

Andrew Waterman

Andrew Waterman was born in London in 1940 and has taught literature at the University of Ulster for over thirty years. He has published several collections of poems and is also a translator of Rainer Marie Rilke. "Birth Day" celebrates the transformative moment in a man's life when he becomes a father, an experience that men in most western societies have been able to witness firsthand only since the late 1960s.

BIRTH DAY

1
The waters have broken. Now your body's slow
convulsions irreversibly begin.
Packing, I finger-lift a slat of blind:
low roofs sleeping, tree-traceries
rising like dreams, faint watermarks on night.

2
Admission seems a languid dream
of birth inverted: sunken entry lipped
with flexing doors, a lift ascending through
dormant entrails to the labour ward . . .
My overshoes squeak on aseptic floor

around the candid trolley-bed where you
are laid; dawn graying past your pane.

3
You are subdued to process,
an intravenous drip tamped to your wrist;
divested of your clothes, belongings, watch,
almost of me beside you. Shifts
of nurses, midwives, come and go, abstracting
to ink on paper your identity;
while, irrevocable hourglass,
above you the translucent glucose-drip-bag
decanting sheds its luminousity.
You cry, "I can't bear this" as yet again
the shark's-tooth jag of a contraction shows
ticking through the monitoring-machine.
Like metering needles your gold earrings shaking.

4
"Bear down . . ." Your palm grips mine,
your body opening like petals and
ah! The bloodied head emerging,
a wriggled slither and, suspended there
as if a tiny astronaut connected
by the umbilical's rich purple coil
to life support, "You have a son,"
the doctor says. Steel cuts the link. Adrift,
lost to the close dark amniotic warmth,
his spasm gulps wide world's thin air.
Brute fact miraculously born.

5
The fallen world rolls over into night.
Two army vehicles splash through lamplit rain,
miniskirts throng a disco. Things
ongoing register again.
My "Goodnight" left you hazed on a ward bed;
and you, our Rory, ankle name-tagged, parked
one in a row of wheeled transparent cots:

beautiful accident, success
in lieu of whose unique incipience
like failed intentions cells in millions died.
You are fallen on history's brink. Unthinkable,
"one bomb no bigger than a cricket-ball"
could shrivel Belfast, gunmen, parents, all
who have been babies. Meanwhile
my mind with doubled vision now pursues
my own childhood paths among
green forest, and I sense
my first loved books reopening their wings.
Half-conscious at a crossing I come to,
I carry myself with novel care,
like a cup trembling to overbrim.
Frail lighted streets diverge into wet dark.
The world rolls hurtling you beyond my sight.

Karol Wojtyla

Not many men write poems about their sisters, so when we came upon this touching poem
by the Polish poet Karol Wojtyla, who may be better known to you as Pope John Paul II, we
were pleased to include it. The word *sister* here clearly has much more resonance than it
otherwise might.

SISTER

1.
We grow together.
Growing upwards: propped by the heart, green space
moves towards the burdens of wind suddenly cast
onto leaves.
Growing inwards: not growing but learning
how deep your roots thrust,
how much deeper—

We move about in the darkness of roots
thrust into our common soil.

From here I compare the lights above:
the reflex of water on the banks of green.

2.

No ready footpaths for man.
We are born a thicket
which may burst into flames, into the bush of Moses,
or may wither away.

We are always having to clear the paths,
they will be overgrown again;
they have to be cleared until they are simple
with the mature simplicity of every moment:
for each moment opens the wholeness of time,
as if it stood whole above itself.
You find in it the seed of eternity.

3.

When I call you sister
I think that each meeting
contains not only the communion of moments,
but the seed of the same eternity.

translated by Jerzy Peterkiewicz

Andrea Zanzotto

Andrea Zanzotto was born in 1921 in Treviso, Italy, and is the author of five books of poetry
and a book of prose. The subject here is the maternal influence that shapes the whole of an
Italian man's life. The adult speaker addresses his mother "from a new height" but ulti-
mately cannot come to a clear resolution as to whether that lifelong mother worship is nur-
turing or damaging.

FROM A NEW HEIGHT

I

Again, mother, I turn to you,
don't ask the truth of me,
nor this closed

last green I did not know
for so many years and which May now fleeing
offers to me; to my polluted
mind, my shattered peace.
Mother, whence my speaking to you,
why do you keep silent like the high green
the rich nihil,
that impends, exalts, where
beautifying flowers and icy winds
open after the terror—and you, sky,
do you still adapt me to myself,
to the mirror that evolves into tomorrow?
But whence, from what viscera of yours
the dark gurgle of rivers,
from what obsession those grasses
that for centuries
you impose on me, wretched?
Love to you, voice to you, or silence
Melted like snows like rays
Scraped from nothing: I rise and this groan
that binds, this flower that sprinkles
fields and lips with red, this door
that motionless crumbles
into dog days and waters . . .

And as from a new height,
my soul does not remember you—
in dreams of
steps, in impervious astenias,
between mild smoke and deep-dug gardens
there under the lake, there in the overflowing
dew, still
inherited by the eye
still rising at the sad
touch of dawn . . .

II
A sense that does not move to an image,
a color detached from an idea,
an unwitnessed anxiety

or a peace perfect but precarious:
is this the I you gave me, mother, that now
I scarcely recognize, not word
not shape not shadow?
To truth—to the black seethe of mountains—
with tears still unsated,
still saved for a day from the dragon's sting,
I return and I don't know
I don't know how to keep silent.

I understood nothing, then,
of the greedy groping of beasts
insects, flowers and suns,
nothing appeared to me of the work
whispered and strewn there
in the fields; shrivelled in the nest
neither did sweat appear to me,
others' watchful
combustion, and I alone
I, transcended in a fierce speaking void,
brow to brow did I attain myself?
The warm hand still strokes the fruit.
In the side-street child and workman.
Lively the eyes' light in the depths.
Was this mine and did I never know, never see?
Did I still not rejoice not weep for you?
Mother your face was unknown to me but not the anxiety
always multiplying
in each crease in every good in all
your revealings to me,
but not the irreparable love
which from you, monster or spirit, enfolds
and warms me aridly.

   translated by Ruth Feldman and Brian Swann

Africa

Ismael Hurreh

Ismael Hurreh was born in Hargeisa, in the northern region of Somalia. Educated at the University of New Mexico, he teaches in Mogadishu. Parents' expectations nearly always weigh heavily upon sons, regardless of culture. In "Pardon Me," the speaker seeks his father's pardon for not measuring up and especially for not adopting his father's values. In the final lines, almost as an afterthought, he asks his mother's pardon as well.

PARDON ME

pardon me father if I am a disappointment to what you
expect of me

                                 pardon me father

if I cannot slaughter other tribesmen
if I do not say my prayers in the morning
if I turn my back on some of your advice

                                 because father

although your blood runs in my veins
although I too have been a nomad
although I've slept under roofless huts

                                 eyeing the moon

and raising my hands to God
and envying His might
time has unfolded many strange sheets
and spread them between us
time has uprooted me
time has transplanted me to grounds
where prayer is of no use,
and mother pardon me for digging your bones out

(your bones that were buried here)

                                        pardon me

if I had forgotten that you were buried here.

South America

Narlan Matos-Teixera

Narlan Matos-Teixera was born in 1975 in Bahia, Brazil. He won the prestigious Xerox Award of Brazilian Literature for a collection of his poetry. "My Father's House" recognizes the powerful influence a father has over his son's outer and inner lives. For most men, there is no final exit from the father's house.

MY FATHER'S HOUSE

In my father's house
each door is a labyrinth
(twenty in all)
Each door opens
a memory a secret
I'm inside the house
The house is inside me
I see phantoms of myself
forms of myself
I thought were dead
come to life again
scary as Lazarus
when he climbed from the sepulchre
I'm sure
I'll never escape from here
Alive

   translated by the poet and Al Zolynas

North America

David Bottoms

David Bottoms's first book was chosen by Robert Penn Warren as winner of the 1979 Walt Whitman Award of the Academy of American Poets. Bottoms is the author of four other books of poems, as well as two novels. In "Bronchitis," the sound of his daughter's wheezing interrupts a father's reading of a Civil War history. When he returns to the book and reads of a young girl killed by an errant shell, he is startled by the terribleness of the event and by the injustice that surrounds us.

BRONCHITIS

I

Rough sleep from the room across the hall.
Mouth open, my daughter breathes the little noise of wheels
on dry axles. I've cut the ceiling fan
to hear her, but rain intrudes against the house,
along with something quieter
and more disquieting,
some muffled trudge
like soldiers crossing our soggy yard,
ghosting cannons east again toward Kennesaw.

I mark my page with a postcard
and delay General Sherman on his blaze to the sea.
Shadow faces on the curtains grimace
and sneer, a burlesque of hysteria,
but nothing as cadaverous
as history. The truth is,
my eyes tend to tire and blur.

Cough and ragged wheeze, and outside
in the driveway
the wind rakes the lid of a garbage can.

All the loose uncertainties of fatherhood grate
in the joints of my chair.

2

A bloated rail yard, hardly more,
yet miserably strategic . . .
Off to the north cannons booming on Kennesaw, sullen
and dull, like heavy luggage tossed from a train.
Shouting in the houses, haste of foot traffic
and nervous horses, wheels
and mules stirring the streets into dust,
everything flying into wagons, the roads clogging,
the sky clogging.

Then after days, an odd silence—
the Federals flanking east of the mountain, crossing
the Chattahoochee. Skirmishes dying into siege.
The first shell whistling into the city
kills a three-year-old girl
playing with her dog in the street.

Under the traffic light
at Ellis and Ivy,
I've tried to gauge some vague geography lifted
from books. That was the crossroads,
but which was the corner the house sat on?
Two parking decks, Wachovia Bank,
a hot dog vendor,
a sidewalk gallery of African art—

3

I think of her sporadically, shell crater and spaniel,
powder stench, geyser of dust settling
as her mother staggers
onto the porch—
and I wonder whose story this is. I don't know,
only imagine the color of her eyes or hair,
or what she might have weighed
on the feed-store scales,
or what piece of ground they laid her in.

I don't even know the name on the stone
they must've placed at her head.

Neither, it seems,
does the man who wrote the history,
who mentions her only as a footnote in the abstract
strategies of war.
Whose story then? Whose history shadowed
or foreshadowed, if not mine?
Or yours?

The book lies open on my lap.
The postcard is from a friend in Washington—
cherry blossoms on the White House lawn.
A blizzard, he writes,
is pounding the city, the homeless
have invaded the monuments and galleries.

Jim Daniels

Jim Daniels is the director of the Creative Writing Program at Carnegie-Mellon University. He draws heavily on his working-class Detroit background in his five books of published poetry. The father in "Falling Bricks" tries to protect his daughter from the treacheries of the world but realizes that despite his best efforts he can never make her completely safe.

FALLING BRICKS

My daughter sings under a brick arch
of the abandoned house next door,
her stage for an audience of stones
and weeds. Her voice through glass
high and griefless, higher than it
might ever go, the sky endless
pure blue without credit cards
or betrayal.

Who can you trust? I'm making a list
of things to do—it helps me

keep control. I fold up the list
and toss it in the trash with a piece
of broken glass. When she is tired,
my daughter clutches my neck
as if it were a rope to save her.

The song has more than one name
if we have to put a name on it,
write it down—three songs
intermingled and strung together
seamlessly, like I imagine our lives
should be—mine, hers, and down
the line.

Above her, the bricks
are loosening. I should not
let her sing there, but she is perfectly
framed like a saint in an altar.
I hold my own neck like that,
to imagine the comfort she takes.
My skin is loosening there.
Oh, my beautiful child,
do not trust me.

Philip Levine

Philip Levine was born in Detroit in 1928. Educated at Wayne State University, he is professor emeritus of English at California State University in Fresno. Here Levine—sparked by an old family photograph—imagines his parents as young adults setting out on their lives, not knowing what the future holds, "the whole weight of the rain to come."

CLOUDS ABOVE THE SEA

My father and mother, two tiny figures,
side by side, facing the clouds that move
in from the Atlantic. August, '33.
The whole weight of the rain to come, the weight

of all that has fallen on their houses
gathers for a last onslaught, and yet they
hold, side by side, in the eye of memory.
What was she wearing, you ask, what did he
say to make the riding clouds hold their breath?
Our late August afternoons were chilly
in America, so I shall drape her throat
in a silken scarf above a black dress.

I could give her a rope of genuine pearls
as a gift for bearing my father's sons,
and let each pearl glow with a child's fire.
I could turn her toward you now with a smile
so that we might joy in her constancy,
I could bury the past in dust rising,
dense rain falling, and the absence of sky
so that you could turn this page and smile.
My father and mother, two tiny figures,
side by side, facing the clouds that move
in from the Atlantic. They are silent
under the whole weight of the rain to come.

Walt McDonald

Walt McDonald was born in 1934 in Texas. A former Air Force pilot and professor at the
Air Force Academy, he is the author of eighteen collections of poems. He has been Texas
State Poet Laureate and is now retired from Texas Tech University. In "Crossing the
Road," a younger brother remembers an incident in which his older brother saved him from
embarrassment. Despite the older brother's decisive and competent action as a protector at
home, he could not shield himself from danger later in life.

CROSSING THE ROAD

What's a boy to do, both shoes caught in the tar,
the road past our house turning to street,
and me, a chicken trying to reach the other side.
Men burly as uncles swore and shook their shovels,

laughing. My mother waited on the porch,
drying her hands in her apron. My big sister teased,
her gawky girlfriends howled, and someone screamed
Tar baby! I swear I tugged, cursing the only words

I had learned, squashed down in July asphalt
like a bug, like Captain Marvel in the comics
turned into a tree, unable to budge. And of all days,
on my birthday. Carl would see me soon, and Mary Jane,

all kids I knew pointing on the curb and dancing.
Like God roaring up on his motorcycle, my brother
dismounted and stared. Tucking a Camel in his lips,
he lit and flipped the match away, came strolling down,

fists doubled, snorting smoke, not smiling.
Massive, towering above me, he jerked me up
without my shoes and hauled me like a sack of oats
back to the grass, his own boots ruined.

I remember him that way, not the box of belongings
they brought from Okinawa, not the flag Mother hung
in the window for all cars to see speeding past
the four-lane street, pounding my sneakers down.

W. S. Merwin

W. S. Merwin was born in New York City in 1927. He is the author of more than fifteen books of poetry, the translator of some twenty, and the recipient of numerous prestigious awards. He lives and works in Hawaii. This poem considers the distance between a father and son—their obvious love for each other and their inability to express it.

YESTERDAY

My friend says I was not a good son
you understand
I say yes I understand

he says I did not go
to see my parents very often you know
and I say yes I know

even when I was living in the same city he says
maybe I would go there once
a month or maybe even less
I say oh yes

he says the last time I went to see my father
I say the last time I saw my father

he says the last time I saw my father
he was asking me about my life
how I was making out and he
went into the next room
to get something to give me

oh I say
feeling again the cold
of my father's hand the last time
he says and my father turned
in the doorway and saw me
look at my wristwatch and he
said you know I would like you to stay
and talk with me

oh yes I say

but if you are busy he said
I don't want you to feel that you

have to
just because I'm here

I say nothing

he says my father
said maybe
you have important work you are doing
or maybe you should be seeing
somebody I don't want to keep you

I look out the window
my friend is older than I am
he says and I told my father it was so
and I got up and left him then
you know

though there was nowhere I had to go
and nothing I had to do

Leonard Nathan

Leonard Nathan was born in 1924. He has published more than twenty books and is a win-
ner of multiple awards, including a Guggenheim Fellowship. He is retired from teaching at
the University of California, Berkeley. "Circlings" presents a situation with haunting im-
plications: a long-departed son desperate to return home is cast as an endlessly circling
wolf, unrecognizable to his aged parents.

CIRCLINGS

Father dozes with a book of heroes
open on his lap. Mother stitches
darkness into the quilt. Outside, a wolf
paces the snow around their tiny house,
thinking in ever-tighter circles, thinking
if he, if he could only tell them, if he

could tell them that, despite this unruly hair,
these yellow teeth, he is their son returned.

But he foresees their eyes, widened now
with horror, when he opens his mouth to speak
and all he can do is snarl, whimper, howl,
and the door slams shut and he resumes
his ever tighter circling—no end
it seems to leaving home, to coming home.

Jonas Zdanys

The Lithuanian American poet Jonas Zdanys was born in New Britain, Connecticut, in 1950. A graduate of Yale University and the State University of New York, he is one of the most prolific translators of Lithuanian poetry into English. Here the speaker acts as intermediary between his father and his own children, who never knew their grandfather. The speaker has protected his children by leaving out the more gruesome and shameful details of his father's difficult life, but he reveals the truth in this poem, which the children presumably will read one day, when they are mature enough to share their father's tough compassion.

THE ANGELS OF WINE

He died before my children were born and I tell them about him sometimes, when I tell our family's stories—uncle and godfather, raw-boned and visionary, alcoholic son and failed father, in the end a weak reed no one leaned upon, who struggled with his gloom and self-loathing and was caught in a trap he laid for himself in the teeth of the wind.

He would listen to me in moments of clarity, drawing a breath as if waiting to speak then letting it out in a sigh and waiting for me to talk myself out. He would nod when I said that life is not something that was waiting for us around the corner but was here and now, and then would ask me for money for a bottle of sweet wine, too tired and shaky to invent another lie. It was not for his thirst, he would say, but because with it everything grew remote and the stars in the sky began to swim and the horizon expanded again.

Once he said he thought we gave birth to our death, like something lifting inside us, like the tunnel where he thrashed and choked and could not breathe because there was no light. That's how they found him early one morning as the sun touched the edges of his room: the artery in his liver spilling his life out into something scarlet and black, his nose burrowed between the thighs of the woman he lived with like a small lost dog looking for the place he'd come from and where he wanted to return.

I think of him like that but do not tell my children the details of his final story: lying in the dark in a pool of his own blood, not knowing what was rolling over him as a veil of grayness covered his eyes, perhaps dreaming one last time of the daughter he had abandoned or the grandchildren he would never see or the angels that would come to him with the wine in the dead of night.

Oceania, Australia, and New Zealand

Dimitris Tsaloumas

Dimitris Tsaloumas was born on the Greek island of Leros in 1921. He has lived in Melbourne, Australia, since 1952. He began to write in English in the 1980s and has since published five collections of poetry. "A Song for My Father" explores the power of a father's words, however enigmatic, to wilt the speaker's "soul with frost."

A SONG FOR MY FATHER

My father speaks in riddles,
"Your life's been blessed," he says,
his voice somewhat sad
through the dusk-pale incense.
"At your age I was dead,"
Not so impenetrable
Perhaps. But this, on lips
Parched by years of dust:
"There are no waves for sound
this side of truth. Besides,
I no longer wish to hear
your reckless music"—
this wilts my soul with frost.
Why should any song
disturb what must be immutable?

Or this, weary now
With all the distance, que-
rulous: "Don't pace the night.
The stars you name burn holes
in our firmament.
Watch out for leaks of darkness."

Dimitris Tsaloumas

The Greco-Australian poet Dimitris Tsaloumas captures a poignant moment in "Old Snap-
shot" as an elderly father looks at an old photo of his daughter, apparently long gone and
out of touch. There is an almost Lear-like sense of loss and regret in this poem, in the old
man's wistful hope that his daughter has flourished, which of course he cannot know.

OLD SNAPSHOT

A mere child dog-eared
in my wallet
eyes open wide
at some surprise of sorrow
the fading tint cannot
assuage

My catalogue of wrongs
records no harsh rebuke
no punishment I could now
redeem

I think of you daughter
Flickering thoughts
in a place of draughts

There are no letters

she must have long crossed
this sad child's reverie
into the sunny landscapes
of her youth

Identities: Cultural, Personal, Male

I felt like an ethnic top
To be worn once and thrown away
—Harris Khalique

I resemble everyone
but myself
—A. K. Ramanujan

You're not a man until you've died like one
—Husein Tahmiščić

Identity—everyone has one . . . or two or three or a dozen. And these disparate identities are not necessarily in harmony with each other at all times. But that discord gives each man's life its particular bluesy twang and helps make him unique. Men, of course, have a variety of "male" identities that seem to cut across whatever labels their cultures assign them. In compiling this anthology, we did not find many examples of cultures that had not bought into the notions of maleness familiar to us in the West—autonomy, independence, strength, virility, to name the obvious traditional values. Mythically speaking, these values are expressions of the warrior archetype, an archetype that historically has had some ascendancy for males, especially young males, throughout most cultures.

Husein Tahmiščić, a poet from Sarejevo, is clear about what is expected of men in his culture and, arguably, in any culture to date: sacrifice, even of one's own life. "You're not a man until you've died like one," he tells us. Of course, not all men are soldiers, but all have had to engage their warrior archetype at times in their lives when energy and reserves have to be summoned to "get the job done."

Men identify themselves as lovers, too. Frank Aig-Imoukhuede from Nigeria bemoans the Western value of "one wife for one man," much preferring his traditional culture's acceptance of polygamy. Nobuo Ayukawa, a Japanese poet, draws attention to a particular cultural value when he tells us the phrase *I love you* is not one he feels comfortable saying out loud, that he feels it actually cheapens love to express it verbally. His identity then is both culturally shaped and encompassed by a larger identity that acknowledges the possible limitation of the taboo in which he feels trapped.

When Jamaican poet A. L. Hendriks asks "Will the Real Me Please Stand Up?" he is giving voice to the heart of the existential question of identity—what is it? His poem follows an extended metaphor of the poet stripping himself down to the very bone, though carefully saving his genitalia (for their "aesthetic" value). Stripped of all but his sexual identity, the poet anticipates finding himself again, which, interestingly enough, he hopes to do through writing. Dennis Brutus, the exiled African poet, shows us what happens to a man's identity when he has been forced to leave his homeland and make his way in strange new cultures: he feels like an "alien in Africa and everywhere," though occasionally he glimpses his true identity in his inner self. In a similar vein, Harris Khalique, a Pakistani-born poet residing in London, feels objectified by a flirting woman who tells him how much she likes "Bright South Asians," showing us how much our own sense of identity can be violated when reduced by someone else to easy identifiers. Indian poet A. K. Ramanujan illustrates how slippery the question of who and what we are can be when he sees himself briefly reflected in a passing shop window as the "portrait of a stranger . . . signed in a corner / by my father."

If Pound was right and poets or artists do have more sensitive antennae than other mortals, one of the things they seem able to detect is change in the cultures in which they find themselves. Alan Brownjohn, an older poet from the United Kingdom, keenly feels the passing of his role as a "gentleman." With his hats and fountain pens, his old-fashioned public politeness, he feels about as needed as the old "city tram." Contrast his view to Leseko Rampolekeng's, a young poet from South Africa who, writing a raplike poem, welcomes us to the "new consciousness" of a chaotic postmodern world of "derearranged senses."

Through the many points of view and cultural influences at work, the "poetry of men's lives" nonetheless collectively underscores a strong sense of male identity. Despite the paradoxes of masculinity—its strength and vulnerability, its callousness and sensitivity, its violence and tenderness—men seem to be men, the world over.

Asia

Nobuo Ayukawa

Nobuo Ayukawa (1920–86) was a founding member of the *Arechi* (Waste Land) group in Japan. He is a translator of Eliot's *The Waste Land* and, during the years following World War II, emerged as Japan's preeminent modernist poet. "Love" is a clear and compelling expression of the power of culture to shape our attitudes—what we can say and what we can't. Ayukawa gives us insight into the Japanese male's silence about love and the dignity and purity of that silence.

LOVE

I'm Japanese
so I hate saying
& hearing
the word *love*

I've never told
a woman
I love you
and I've never been told
I love you
by a woman
but I consider myself lucky.

If the words *I love you* had spilled from my mouth,
I would have been ruined by now.
The liar's forked tongue
could not have withstood
the addition of one honest tongue.

Westerners say *I love you*
out of habit
they might even say *I love you*
instead of *good morning*

but the purity of the words is lost
& love is just a formality.

Different customs &
different feelings
are inevitable &
even though foreign influences abound
I can't make words of love my own.
If I had,
I would have been ruined by now.

Words of love
that mean nothing
scare me even now,
& I don't know how to act.
Even if everything is taken from me, I couldn't complain.
Even if everything is given to me, I couldn't complain.
In the face of this inexplicable contract
there's nothing to do but keep my mouth shut.

Locked in taboo, in the heart
the *ai** in my Japanese *love*
is still a virgin.

translated by Oketani Shogo with Leza Lowitz

*Japanese for *love*.

Xue Di

Xue Di was born in Beijing in 1957. Since shortly after the Tienanmen Square Massacre in 1989, he has been a fellow in Brown University's Freedom to Write Program. In this strange, surrealistic evocation of a man's youth and his projections about the future, the speaker seems trapped between a motherland "he can't take with him" and a future that is hollow and unknown. The poem reminds us that nostalgia can distort truth, because the past is not really how we remember it.

NOSTALGIA

A man looks back on the land as it
rises. He sees youth as
nails hammered into the dust. Motherland
is the land he can't take with him.
Parents distant, decrepit. Wall
collapsing. Home is a
hunk of meat on a hook.
Childhood a butcher knife raised, wooden handle
decaying memory. A man
looks forward to the land as it rises
the hollows running primly.
As the stranger turns his head, herds
of animals are mating. The man
lonely, nostalgic
hears screams, and again
rising from below, screams.

translated by Wang Ping and Keith Waldrop

Sunil Gangopadhyay

Sunil Gangopadhyay was born in 1934 in Faridpur, Bangladesh. He now lives in Calcutta.
A prolific writer and literary prizewinner, Gangopadhyay has published more than two
hundred volumes of poetry and fiction. In the following poem, he makes literal the post-
colonial dilemma of being between worlds searching for an identity.

FROM ATHENS TO CAIRO

Inside the aircraft, I take off my necktie, unfasten my seat belt, and stand up.
"Where is everyone?" I shout.
Two air hostesses, their faces fluffy like cotton wool, come running—
Then over my head and below are the Mediterranean sky and silver sea,
            in between them blue clouds and dragonflies.
Behind me Europe at dusk burns in roaring flames,
            Before me the East is swathed in darkness.
My voice rough, I say, "Where have you been,

I wanted a drink half an hour ago,
besides I am hungry—"
The two young women, dolled-up girls, laugh embarrassedly.
Amid all that fire and darkness such feminine laughter
sounds inconsequential; their body lines, shapes are nothing to the eye.

In the sky over the Mediterranean, I am suddenly free of all bondage,
                                        simple and honest.
Europe burns behind me, before me lie the black ashes of the East,
In between them, I, lone Indian, son of an emperor.
I want to cry out and tell the whole world,
            I am hungry, I am hungry
            I can bear it no more,
            I am poised ready—
                    to tear, masticate, and devour.

translated by Nandini Gupta

Liu Kexiang

Liu Kexiang was born in Taizhong in central Taiwan in 1957. He received his B.A. in jour-
nalism from the Chinese Culture University and is now assistant editor in chief of the liter-
ary supplement of the *China Times*. "Choice" captures the ideological conflict confronting
many young Taiwanese men. How politically engaged should they be? The narrator would
prefer to settle in a border town but is caught up in the anxiety of the age. Is he Chinese?
Taiwanese? Neither? Both?

CHOICE

This is an age of anxiety
Rebellion and escape are likely to occur
Once I gave up my job
And traveled alone on the west coast
Observing waterfowl
I drifted from one seashore to another
I did not meet any friends of my age
Just saw schoolchildren picnicking
Or once in a while, old men fishing by the sea
Tonight, as in former journeys

I am leaving the city
I want to come back, to imitate the silent crowd
As long as I engage in work that stays away from politics
What I most fear is to
Castigate the ruling power, as I did before
And then, like a young rebel wandering
In search of truth,
Switch from one political magazine to another
Over an ideological conflict

A few days ago, when I passed through the far south
An old classmate from college hugged me
And introduced me to his wife
His child called me uncle
That night, like now, I could not sleep
It is a worrisome, complicated life
I am thirty years old, single
And flutter with the cataclysmic changes of the times
I can forget them only by traveling
Tonight I continue to feel exhausted
I would like
To settle down in a border town
Yet how reluctant I am

translated by Michelle Yeh

Harris Khalique

Harris Khalique was born in Karachi, Pakistan. He was educated in Urdu and in English and has a degree in mechanical engineering. A great many Pakistanis live in the United Kingdom, but have they really been assimilated into British culture? The speaker of "In London" feels like a specimen rather than a human being—the same feeling of objectification about which women have often complained.

IN LONDON

Defiant flirtation
Never puts me off
But when she said

"Bright South Asians
Have always struck my sight
I've never been close to one
What are you doing tonight?"
I felt like an ethnic top
To be worn once and thrown away
A balti dish never tried before
From the newly opened Indian take-away.

Kim Kwang-kyu

Kim Kwang-kyu was born in Seoul, the Republic of Korea, in 1941. He is a professor of German language and literature and a translator of German poets, including Heinrich Heine. Here, Kwang-kyu defines a particular man by what he is not. After that, there's not much left. The poem asks a question central to the definition of masculinity: Is manhood a totally socially defined phenomenon or is there something essential in it?

SKETCH OF A FETISH

He is no common man
definitely not an ordinary man
Far more lenient than a common man
far crueller than an ordinary man
he is not some meek kind of man
who endures hardship patiently
deliberately hiding his tears
He is not a man who gazes at the moon
longing for days gone by
Nimbly seizing the ball
like a goalkeeper before a tense crowd
he is not a man who works all day
and then goes home in the evening
He is not the kind of man who keeps to his lane
for fear of the traffic patrols
He is not a man who speaks in words
as he takes over all the best expressions
producing an urn of white silence

He is not someone who gazes
at the endlessly rolling waves
and fathoms the ocean's heart
He is not a man who hastens
onwards at dawn firm in the conviction
that yesterday's I is alone believable
He is not the kind of man who lowers his head
and silently follows after
Taking up sacred burdens beyond his power
and marching on and on
he is definitely not an ordinary man
not a common man
in short not a man at all

translated by Brother Anthony

Fei Ma

Fei Ma was born in 1936. He is known as one of the Bamboo Hat poets who writes in both Japanese and Chinese. This resonant poem suggests the slow motion progress of a drunk, describing a state of mind and body as well as a way of life. Years seem to pass between steps, or episodes, of an alcoholic's life. But why does he seem to be walking toward his mother?

A DRUNKARD

Walking a short lane
into a bending,
Entwining
Sad intestine
of a thousand miles;

Step on left,
Ten years passed,

Step on right,
Another ten years.

Oh, mother,
I am trying hard
To walk
toward you.

translated by Dominic Cheung

A. K. Ramanujan

Attippat Krishnaswami Ramanujan (1929–93) was born in Mysore, India. The author of
more than fifteen books, he taught for many years at the University of Chicago. His awards
include the Padma Shri and a MacArthur Fellowship. In this miniature self-portrait, the
pervasive influence of father on son becomes evident in even the most subtle ways, espe-
cially in the son's search for an identity he can claim as truly his own.

SELF-PORTRAIT

I resemble everyone
but myself, and sometimes see
in shop-windows,
        despite the well-known laws
        of optics,
the portrait of a stranger,
date unknown,
often signed in a corner
by my father.

Suchart Sawadsri

Suchart Sawadsri is a Thai poet, dramatist, editor, and lecturer. Here a man who had few
intimates in his life feels completely isolated after their deaths. Now, though still "difficult,"
"failed," and "severe," he seeks a closeness that will allow him to risk intimacy and break
through the seemingly solid wall of the self.

IF YOU COME CLOSE TO ME

I'm a person who is difficult
to understand.
But if you come close,
maybe not so difficult.

I've got only my mother
and a few books
and a few cats.
I'm a man.

I've got only myself.

One of my cats died yesterday.
I buried it near my mother's urn.

I'm a severe man,
a failed poet.
I'm difficult,
but not now,
not if you come close to me.

translated by Kathryn Rhett and the poet

Nguyen Quang Thieu

Nguyen Quang Thieu was born in 1957 near Hanoi. He attended Hanoi University and
studied in Cuba for a number of years. He has published books of poetry, novels, short sto-
ries, and stories for children. In this excerpt, he deals with the pain of being a sensitive male
during a time when masculinity is expressed primarily through warrior-type attributes.
The poem deals too with the fear of his father's authority, the loss of his mother, and the
birth of his daughter, as well as with the passage of time and with spending much of his life
having "groped in smoke."

FROM "ELEVEN PARTS OF FEELING"

I
My heart beats in the first spring,
On the vanished paths of my childhood.

A human call is running
Along the edges of sleeping grass;
I am hurting with my first hurt.

I hide a sexless love behind
The flap of a schoolboy's shirt.

On a day when my mother's shadow
Has disappeared, I cry in silence.
Hens peck at the pocked face of dusk.

Let me kneel
And silently
Throw things away.
My eyes have been under the spell of love
Since the days when my hair was not yet grown.

II
As coffee cools
Its color darkens.
My thoughts are wet,
My thoughts are dry.

A cigarette has been burning since I was fourteen;
My father's whip cuts the cigarette smoke in pieces.
An angry day is fixed in my mind with tears,
Though I cried just once, and now my eyes are dry.

Smoke fills my lungs;
A watersnake creeps through my throat.

Where is my father's whip?

Where is my father's whip?

All my life I have groped in smoke.

.   .   .   .

VI
It's not fever imprisoning me,
It's not weakness imprisoning me.
The winter window opens without a sound.

I meet my mother when she was seventeen—
The teeth of a worn wooden comb bite her hair.

I meet my father when he was twenty—
Pieces of green wood break from his axe
With the laughter of fire.

The winter window opens without a sound.
The shirt of my newborn daughter flies by—
It's the mocking laughter of time.

.   .   .   .

VIII
    Father!
I called out, and then I was ill.

Solitude grew up with me.
I cried often, in silence—
I didn't need to cry behind my fingers.
I loved wildly, running from sadness and pain—
No mark is left by wet kisses,
No dust rises from falling onto the bed.

A dog's teeth graze one side of time,
Warm ashes cover the other.
Something is wrong;

I tremble with fear, hearing
Your heavy breath early this morning.

　　Father!
I wronged you once, long ago, when I lied.
But I wrong you for the rest of my life
Telling you the truth early this morning.

　　translated by Martha Collins

Tenzin Tsundue

Tenzin Tsundue was born in Himachal Pradesh in 1975. He has a degree in English literature from Loyola College in Chennai. Some of his poems have been published in the *Indian Literary Panorama* and the *Sunday Observer.* Tsundue's poem explores men's powerful need to have a fixed identity. Traditionally, young men have gotten their identities through life-transforming initiation rites. Men forced to leave their homelands often experience uncomfortable feelings of disorientation, while their children, raised both in a new cultural environment and within the values and practices of their parents' culture, feel a double or split identity.

MY TIBETANNESS

Thirty-nine years in exile.
Yet no nation supports us.
Not a single bloody nation!

We are refugees here.
People of a lost country.
Citizen to no nation.

Tibetans: the world's sympathy stock:
Serene monks and bubbly traditionalists;
one lakh and several thousand odd,
nicely mixed, steeped
in various assimilating cultural hegemonies

At every check-post and office,
I am an "Indian-Tibetan."

My Registration Certificate,
I renew every year, with a salaam.
A foreigner born in India.

I am more of an Indian.
Except for my chinky Tibetan face.
"Nepali?" "Thai?" "Japanese?"
"Chinese?" "Naga?" "Manipuri?"
but never the question—"Tibetan?"

I am Tibetan.
But I am not from Tibet.
Never been there.
Yet I dream
of dying there.

Ko Un

Ko Un was born in Kunsan, the Republic of Korea, in 1933. He is probably the most prolific contemporary Korean writer, having published well over a hundred volumes of poetry, fiction, essays, translations, and drama. The poet remembers his boyhood experiences with a Japanese schoolmaster whose punitive ways and prejudice against "peninsula people" is critiqued within the context of relations between Japan and Korea.

HEADMASTER ABE

Headmaster Abe Sudomu, from Japan:
a fearsome man, with his round glasses,
fiery-hot like hottest pimentos.
When he clacked down the hallway
in slippers cut from a pair of old boots,
he cast a deathly hush over every class.
In my second year during ethics class
he asked us what we hoped to become.
Kids replied:
"I want to be a general in the Imperial Army!"
"I want to become an admiral!"
"I want to become another Yamamoto Isoroko!"

"I want to become a nursing orderly!"
"I want to become a mechanic in a plane factory
and make planes
to defeat the American and British devils!"
Then Headmaster Abe asked me to reply.
I leaped to my feet:
"I want to become the Emperor!"
Those words were no sooner spoken
than a thunderbolt fell from the blue:
"You have formally blasphemed the venerable name
of his Imperial Majesty: you are expelled this instant!"
On hearing that, I collapsed into my seat.
But the form-master pleaded,
my father put on clean clothes and came and pleaded,
and by the skin of my teeth, instead of being expelled,
I was punished by being sent to spend a few months
sorting through a stack of rotten barley
that stood in the school grounds,
separating out the still useable grains.
I was imprisoned every day in a stench of decay
and there, under scorching sun and in beating rain,
I realized I was all alone in the world.
Soon after those three months of punishment were over,
during ethics class Headmaster Abe said:
"We're winning, we're winning, we're winning!
Once the great Japanese army has won the war, in the future
you peninsula people will go to Manchuria, go to China,
and take important positions in government offices!"
That's what he said.
Then a B-29 appeared,
and as the silver 4-engined plane passed overhead
our Headmaster cried out in a big voice:
"They're devils! That's the enemy!" he cried fearlessly.
But his shoulders drooped.
His shout died away into a solitary mutter.
August 15 came. Liberation.
He left for Japan in tears.

translated by Brother Anthony, Young-Moo Kim, and Gary G. Gach

Liang Xiaobin

Liang Xiaobin was born in Anhui province in 1956. He has published several poetry collections, including the prizewinning *Xuebai de qiang* (The snow-white wall). The speaker here tries to regain entry to his country by "following the trail of the heart." The reader gets the impression that the nation—the all-pervasive State—is not supportive of his introspective inclinations.

CHINA, I'VE LOST MY KEY

China, I've lost my key.

That was more than ten years ago.
I ran wildly along the red boulevard;
I ran to the deserted suburbs and shouted in glee.
Then
I lost my key.

The spirit, the spirit of hardship,
Will wander no more.
I'd like to go home,
Open the drawer, and leaf through my childhood album;
I'd also like to see the fresh green clover pressed between the pages.

Besides,
I'd like to open the bookcase door
And take out the poems of Heine.
I want to go on a date
And raise the book in my hand
As a signal of love
Sent to the azure sky.
None of these
Wonderful things
Can be done.
China, I've lost my key.
It is raining again.
Key,
Where are you lying?
I fear storms have corroded you,

You must be all rusty.
No, I don't think so.
I will search obstinately
Hoping to find you again.
Sun,
Have you seen my key?
May your rays
Warm it.
I am walking in a field,
I am searching, following the trail of the heart.
I am pondering
All that was lost.

DECEMBER 1979

translated by Michelle Yeh

Europe

Wolfgang Bächler

Wolfgang Bächler was born in 1925 in Augsburg, Germany. For many years he lived in France. In "A Revolt in the Mirror," the speaker is fed up with society's endless demands. All of his natural actions are modified, which is why adverbs are so prominent in the last two lines of the first stanza. They signal his turn toward rebellion against his very proper image in the mirror.

A REVOLT IN THE MIRROR

Sick of the mask he slips into every morning,
weary of the decal of hollow security,
weary of standing his ground, of putting his shoulder
to the wheel, of getting into trouble and bubble,
weary of warming up, bridling up,
showing off and, over and over again, of adapting,

adjusting himself correctly, neatly, adroitly, collectedly,
staidly, engagingly, shrewdly, astutely,

he tore his tie from his chest
and tailored it into a doll's apron
for his daughter, cut his hat
into parallel ribbons for his little son,
made his veins swell and flexed his muscles
till his cuffs burst
and his collar button splintered.

Then he landed a flourish of left and right hooks on the chin
of his mirror image and aimed precision low blows
at its stomach, its spleen and its liver,
stepped on the broken pieces, stamping
and crushing them, and, satisfied,
licked the blood off his fists.

translated by Reinhold Grimm

Alan Brownjohn

Alan Brownjohn (b. 1931) is a prolific British poet whose *Collected Poems* appeared in 1988. "In a louts' age," Brownjohn writes, "A gentleman seems an anomaly," and surely the very word *gentleman* seems more and more antiquated, used only ceremoniously as in "Ladies and Gentlemen." Yet a few such men endure, and the speaker in this sonnet likes to think he's one of them.

SONNET OF A GENTLEMAN

How often have I courteously uncrossed
My legs to let someone in a tram pass by,
Only to kick him on the shins, thus lost
The whole point of the gesture! Some of my
Best efforts go for nothing . . . In a louts' age
A gentleman seems an anomaly,
Apt to incur bewilderment, even rage,
When his decency goes wrong.

But truthfully,
To be gracious, charming, courtly, open doors
For ladies, raise one's hat, use fountain pens
Rather than biros—all this is a cause
Requiring no apologia or defence,
And in my heart of hearts I know I *am*
Helpful, and needed; like the city tram.

Robert Crawford

Robert Crawford teaches at the University of St. Andrews in Scotland and is the author of four collections of poetry, most recently, *Spirit Machines* (1999). He is coeditor, with Simon Armitage, of the *Penguin Book of Poetry from Britain and Ireland Since 1945*. The eager lad who raises his hand "erect as a spear" in the last stanza of this poem seems to be displaying as much masculinity as the Latin lover the narrator becomes. Can the poem be read as an ironic take on the idea that masculinity and femininity are purely social constructs?

MASCULINITY

At our school sexes were colour-coded
Blue for a boy and blue for a girl;
A different shade, though, more skyish
On the soft, hard woolen blazer.

Evenings we'd lie up in our rooms
Learning masc. and fem. declensions,
Mensa, mensae. Our diningroom table
Had squat, chunky, rebarbative legs

Unlike those of my lithe first girlfriend
Who crossed hers when she came to tea.
That term I became her Latin lover,
My whole world zinging with testostericity,

All I touched shocked by another language—
Trees, ships, houses, roads

Masculine or feminine, caressed
And confused, the way next term Greek

Gendered things just a little differently,
Maybe because it was older.
It took me years to understand
Erotic grammar and the answer given

By the boy at the back who raised his hand
Erect as a spear, "Please, sir, please,
Masculinity's not much to do
With sex. It's all about gender."

Igor Irtenev

Igor Irtenev was born in 1947. He is the author of ten books of poetry and currently a magazine editor in Moscow. How ironic is the word *ideal* in the third line of this bitterly political poem from "the New Russia"? How important is autonomy and freedom to a drunk, homeless vagrant? How is his manhood defined?

UNTITLED

to A. Eremenko

At the Pavelets radial-line station
Amidst Ionic columns
Stood an ideal man
Drinking Troinoi* cologne.

Of diminutive stature.
A face like flint.
Decisively dressed, and simply.
Underpants. Galoshes. A belt.

Everything about him had a significance
I'd never known,

And somewhere music pealed
And children fell in their sleep.

And he stood
(of the masculine gender . . .
(in his singular form . . .
unpreconceived autonomy
burned on his brow.

translated by Mark Nowak and Patrick Henry

*Troinoi was a very cheap Soviet cologne. It contained a lot of alcohol, making it a favorite of down-and-out alcoholics, especially during the dry years under Gorbachev.

Dmitry Kuzmin

Dmitry Kuzmin (b. 1968) is a philologist, editor, translator, and the founder and head of Vavilon, the all-Russian Union of Young Writers. His work has been translated into English, French, and Polish. In the following poem, a lover's response to his haircut leads the narrator into an extended meditation on their relationship and on homosexual relationships in general. The poem also explores aging and the possibilities for happiness within the current Russian social context.

UNTITLED

Our hairdresser friend
clipped your hair above the forehead
just the way the rave kids wear it,
you immediately started whining—
no clothes to match this haircut,
a full closet of shirts but nothing one could wear to work
and the skin on the face is no longer
the way it should be to match such a haircut
silly to show up at work with such a haircut
a haircut like this should go off club hopping
and it's too late for us, the clubs,
these idiot DJs make us puke
and so do the kids who fashion their lives after Araki's and Van Sant's characters,
sorry for them all but what's the use,

some overdose and croak at abandoned construction sites, others go into business,

you can't be of any help to either the former or the latter,

and we are home together every evening

each doing his thing

looking at each other from time to time, compassionate

I master the basics of web design,

you put photos into albums,

you still have long hair there,

perhaps right there one doesn't notice

dryness of skin, wrinkles, shadows under the eyes,

but then, during this vacation, you didn't get up early,

half a year passed, it seems more than that,

one can't understand, time seems to fly

just yesterday we met in the subway, and now it's our seventh year together,

and the certainty about tomorrow, and the day after tomorrow,

if, of course, this obscene country doesn't blow up in a big way,

if the police don't fuck us over the residence permits,

if they don't move from looks to something menacing,

the imbeciles in leather jackets that hang out in our stairway,

and I too now have bad skin under my eyes,

but to hell with it, this isn't the meaning of life,

by the summer, if you want, you can let your hair grow,

they promise new arrivals at the vintage store,

show me, a professor asks, a happy gay person,

this, the professor says, tougher to find than a cheerful corpse,

corpses are not our business, so what shall we tell him?

a) here we are, open your eyes, you fucked-up idiot!

b) show us a happy person period.

translated by Vitaly Chernetsky

Michael Longley

Michael Longley was born in Belfast in 1939 and was educated at the Royal Belfast Academical Institution and Trinity College, Dublin, where he studied the classics. He has won the prestigious Whitbread Prize for Poetry. He currently lives and works in Belfast. In "Self-Portrait," the speaker becomes deeply connected to his ancestors and emerges as a rough-hewn poet who sings "with the vocal chords of the orang-outang."

My great-great grandfather fell in top hat and tails
Across the threshold, his cigar brightly burning
While the chalk outline they had traced around his body
Got up and strolled through the door and became me,

But not before his own son had wasted a lifetime
Waiting to be made Lord Mayor of the Universe.
He was to choke to death on a difficult word
When a food particle lodged against his uvula.

I came into being alongside a twin brother
Who threatened me at first like an abortionist
Recommending suicide jumps and gin with cloves.
Then he blossomed into my guardian angel.

Peering back to the people who ploughed the Long Field
My eyes are bog holes that reflect a foreign sky,
Moustaches thatch my utterance in such a way
That no one can lipread the words from a distance.

I am, you will have noticed, all fingers and thumbs
But, then, so is the wing of a bat, a bird's wings.
I articulate through the nightingale's throat,
Sing with the vocal chords of the orang-outang.

Cees Nooteboom

Cees Nooteboom was born in 1931 in the Netherlands. He is primarily known as a novelist and travel writer. An "uncollected man in converse with himself" is the subject of this poem of fragments and reflected images. The metaphysics of identity may be intriguing, but the narrator experiences the immediate world and his own identity as a series of temporary and disconnected fragments. If our identity is so fragmented, who is the "someone" who experiences it?

MIDDAY

It takes so little:
An afternoon of burnished hours
that will not fit together
and himself broken up by himself,
sitting in various chairs
with almost everywhere a soul or a body.

In one part of the room is night.
In another, time past, vacation and war.
On the ceiling the sea touches the shining beach,
and no hand that controls all this,
no equerry, no computer,
only forever the same self, selfsame he,
someone, somebody scattered,
the uncollected man in converse with himself,
dreaming and thinking
present, invisible.

Someone who was going to eat and sleep later.
Someone with a watch and shoes.
Someone who left.
Someone who was going to leave.

Someone who stayed on for a while.

translated by Herlinde Spahr and Leonard Nathan

Vittorio Sereni

Vittorio Sereni (1913–83) was born near Lago Maggiore in Italy and is widely regarded as the best Italian poet of the generation after Montale. He published some half-dozen volumes of poetry. In "Each Time That Almost," the poet reflects on an Italian's typical ties to his region and small town, even though he may have long ago left it behind him.

EACH TIME THAT ALMOST

in secret I come back to Luino
on the lakeside piazza
spurting from a shop runs
someone to embrace me
mumbling my mother's name.
An elder brother of his years ago
did the same
and as then now suddenly
blossomed from a wall of clay
backwards along the chain
of the dead a hand is clutching out at us.

translated by Marcus Perryman and Peter Robinson

Vittorio Sereni

Albert Camus famously remarked that there is only one question worth answering: "Is life worth living?" Vittorio Sereni's poem embodies this question. A killer has been stalking the narrator; the killer turns out to be himself.

FIRST FEAR

Every corner or alley, every moment's good
for the killer who's been stalking me
night and day for years.
Shoot me, shoot me—I tell him
offering myself to his aim
in the front, the side, the back—
let's get it over with, do me in.
And saying it I realize
I'm talking to myself alone.
                            But
it's no use, it's no use. On my own
I cannot bring myself to justice.

translated by Marcus Perryman and Peter Robinson

Olafs Stumbrs

Olafs Stumbrs (1931–96) was born in Latvia. A refugee from World War II, he emigrated to the United States and settled in Los Angeles, where he took part in the Beat poetry movement. In "Song at a Late Hour," Stumbrs considers the Baltic male's propensity to strengthen his soul by retreating into the deepest cave of the self. If we retreat far enough into ourselves, will we then be safe? Bounded in our nutshells, will we then be rulers of infinite space?

SONG AT A LATE HOUR

Sometime at night you'll look for me
in the mole's narrow burrow,
but I'll just chuckle softly
and hide at the deepest end.
 I'll look up at you;
  you'll stand black against the stars
  but be unable to reach me in that darkness—
  neither your pain, nor your palm.
And I'll whisper to the mole: "Landlord
do you see? That's my soul—
returned at last
when this burrow has become all and plenty."

 translated by Inara Cedrins

Husein Tahmiščić

Husein Tahmiščić was born in 1931 in Sarajevo. He studied philosophy and literature at Sarajevo University. He is an essayist, critic, poetry editor, radio dramatist, fictionist, and writer of children's literature. Having spent the years since World War II in Prague, he returned to Sarajevo in 1996. The message of this poem is clear: whether given up in heroic sacrifice, by standing up for the oppressed, or in fighting in a war, your life is expendable, for a greater good, to be sure, but expendable nonetheless.

YOU'RE NOT A MAN IF YOU DON'T DIE

(on hearing the news of the death of Velimir Stojanović)

Let me tell you the shortest story
Let's shut our ears to those vampire professors
Let me tell you what the poets *really* meant
— *You're not a man if you don't die*

Let me read your palm and quiz your heart
Let's not applaud when they fiddle with the truth
Let me wash your eyes with light from the restless sky
— *You're not a man if you don't die*

Let me take down the seventh heaven and offer it to you
Let's not go willingly down any more garden paths
Let me put a candle in your head, open the door of the night
— *You're not a man if you don't die*

Let me bring peace to your innocent skull
Let me dust your sleep with dreams of icing sugar
Let me show you amazing vineyards that ripen and glow
— *You're not a man until you've died like one*

translated by John Hartley Williams

Ulku Tamer

Ulku Tamer was born in 1937 in Turkey. He is a graduate of the Institute of Journalism at Istanbul University. He has published poetry and translated over a hundred books into Turkish. The buried, rusting dagger of the following poem is clearly a symbol of something, but the reader is left to speculate just what that something is. The postponed dreams of a people? The rejection of violence? Or the ongoing influence of the past on the present?

THE DAGGER

Back in the fall we had buried our dagger
In this courtyard covered with square tiles.
That dagger was both precious and sharp.

Its handle must have melted away by now
Looking like the mossy hair of the herdsmen.

The blood of worms and hawks must be clinging
Onto its skeleton lying in the ground.
Spilling all over the blood-tiles of the yard
The blood of the hawks that sent their flight
Deep down in the form of a disheveled line.

The sea has lit the lamps on its streets.
The dagger received its only defeat from us.
Out of the land of its spouts it gazes at night,
At birds that cling to their wings as they fall.
We received our final defeat from the dagger.

For some reason it frightens the gray silence
Of a beggar's voice and the mountaineers' sky,
It frightens the faces of rope-hearted seamen
Who cross the seas each with a panther on its back:
That noise which the dagger makes while rusting.

translated by Talat Sait Halman

John Powell Ward

John Powell Ward was born in Suffolk, England. He has published a number of books of
poetry and has been the editor of *Poetry Wales.* Several decades of attacks on white middle-
class males as the cause of most of the world's woes have taken their toll on the men who,
through no fault of their own, happen to fit that description. Here Ward "confesses" his
sins of class and gender and hopes to move ahead in life in spite of them.

IN THE BOX

Father, I have sinned and I confess
For I am white, male, and middle-class and

Was brought up in the south-east of England.

Wretched I turn desperately to you asking what

To do with these appalling errors. I have
Tried living in Canada five years and (oh shame,

Shame) in Wales twenty-five, running a cockney
Stepney youth club, stopping my offspring

(Both male too god forgive me) from yuppie-talk and
Bringing home their ghastly Oxbridge friends, I

Even give a percentage to selected charities.
Every day I deprave myself just the same,

And now know not where to turn. The worst
Aspect is this nauseating guilt-complex which

Makes me ape people's accents, pretend to like
Music-murder on the streets and all the time

Really just avoiding women, patronizing blacks and
Releasing aggro on youth and equals. God, it festers,

Old plants lose their blossoms (OK like men
Other parts, which in my case don't reach I

Guess), they turn brown and a nasty smell and die
God. God. Did I really think all those Tory things

In those earlier years, and am stuck with them as
If no good feeling, no love, ever moved me? I come to

You for forgiveness, yes, but for guidance too in my
Years left, such as may be granted. The millennium

Comes nearer, the planet's population groups realign
Casually, cautiously and creatively, and old material

Declines as it should and must. Forgive my reactionary

Demeanour; it is a mere stuck groove and a worn

Lazy failure to rotate on the poor axis of flesh.
Life, as always, goes. I've had mine. Forgive, father.

Hugo Williams

Hugo Williams was born in Windsor, England, in 1942 and grew up in Sussex. He has been a journalist, a travel writer, a TV critic, and a poetry editor. In 2000 he won the T. S. Eliot Prize for *Billy's Rain*. In the Western world, the relationship between a man and a necktie can be complicated. The tie is an article of male apparel that almost always has symbolic weight. Most businessmen can't wait to get it off after a day's work, but some men make friends with their ties—like the poet here who turns that relationship into a parable about the things men pass on to one another, including the importance of learning to be yourself.

MAKING FRIENDS WITH TIES

His khaki tie was perfectly knotted in wartime.
The tail was smartly plumped.
The dent became a groove
where it entered a sturdy, rectangular knot,
never a Windsor.

This groove came out
in exactly the same place all his life,
never in the middle,
but slightly to the left.
"You have to get it right first time,"
he told me, my first term at school.
"Otherwise you go raving mad."

I was so impressed by this
I didn't listen in class.
I made friends with peoples' ties, not them.
One day when I was drunk I told him,
"I don't like the groove!"
His face softened towards me for a moment.
"Don't you, dear boy? Well, I'm *delighted*."

Africa

Frank Aig-Imoukhuede

Frank Aig-Imoukhuede was born in 1935 at Ebunabon, near Ile-Ife, Nigeria. He attended Igbobi College and University College, Ibadan. Here the poet playfully describes, in pidgin English, the conflict the speaker feels as he moves from a tribal to a more modern culture, with the attendant value shifts. Monogamy, for some men as well as for some cultures, is not a natural state of affairs.

ONE WIFE FOR ONE MAN

I done try go church, I done go for court
Dem all day talk about di "new culture":
Dem talk about "equality," dem mention "divorce"
Dem holler am so-tay my ear nearly cut;
     One wife be for one man.

My fader before my fader get him wife borku.*
E no' get equality palaver; he live well
For he be oga† for im own house.
But dat time done pass before white man come
Wit 'im
     One wife for one man,

Tell me how una‡ woman no go make yanga§
Wen'e know say na'im only dey.
Suppose say—make God no 'gree—'e no born at all?‖
A'tell you dat man bin dey crazy wey start
     One wife for one man.

Jus' tell me how one wife fit do one man;
How go fit stay all time for him house
For time when belleh done kommot.

How many pickin', self, one woman fit born
      Wen one wife be for one man?

Suppose, self, say no so-so woman your wife dey born
Suppose your wife sabe book, no'sabe make chop;
Den, how you go tell man make'e no' go out
Sake of dis divorce? Bo, dis culture na waya O!
      Wen one wife be for one man.

    borku—plenty   †*oga*—master or Lord   ‡*una*—variation of "your"
    §*yanga*—vanity, pride, and perversity   ‖She has no children.

Dennis Brutus

Dennis Brutus was born in Harare, Zimbabwe, in 1924. Exiled from South Africa in 1966, he is now professor emeritus of Africana studies at the University of Pittsburgh. Part of a man's identity is nearly always tied to nationality and ethnicity. The long history of colonialism in Africa has made those identities less clear cut than they once were. Brutus expresses this conflicted sense of identity in a poem where he sees himself as alien everywhere except, perhaps, in his own being.

I AM ALIEN IN AFRICA AND EVERYWHERE

I am alien in Africa and everywhere:

in Europe, outside Europe I stand and assess them
—find French racial arrogance and Teuton superiority,
moldering English humbug:

and in Africa one finds
chafing, through bumbling,
at the restraints of restraint,
brushing impatiently through varied cultures
in fruitless search of depths:
only in myself, occasionally, am I familiar.

PARIS–ALGIERS

Jonathan Kariara

Jonathan Kariara's poetry, stories, and plays have been widely published. He is managing editor of the eastern African branch of Oxford University Press. The leopard in the Muu tree, hovering near the hearth and home of the narrator, is surely symbolic. But symbolic of what? The speaker notices the leopard "watching my women" and considers him a kind of elder alter ego. Does the leopard represent some aspect of masculinity?

A LEOPARD LIVES IN A MUU TREE

A leopard lives in a Muu tree
Watching my home
My lambs are born speckled
My wives tie their skins tight
And turn away—
Fearing mottled offspring.
They bathe when the moon is high
Soft and fecund
Splash cold mountain stream water on their nipples
Drop their skin skirts and call obscenities.
I'm besieged
I shall have to cut down the Muu tree
I'm besieged
I walk about stiff
Stroking my loins.
A leopard lives outside my homestead
Watching my women
I have called him elder, the one-from-the-same-womb
He peers at me with slit eyes
His head held high
My sword has rusted in the scabbard.
My wives purse their lips
When owls call for mating
I'm besieged
They fetch cold mountain water
They crush the sugar cane
But refuse to touch my beer horn.
My fences are broken
My medicine bags torn

The hair on my loins is singed
The upright post at the gate has fallen
My women are frisky
The leopard arches over my homestead
Eats my lambs
Resuscitating himself.

Leseko Rampolekeng

Leseko Rampolekeng was born in Soweto in 1965. He attended the University of the
North, where he studied law. He has published two volumes of poetry and recorded his
work with musicians. He is largely an oral poet. The rhythms of rap music have certainly
influenced contemporary poetry; some would say it is poetry. Obviously written to be per-
formed, this poem welcomes us to a "new consciousness" that satirizes all the delusional
foibles of contemporary society but at the same time, gathers them in a warm and generous
human embrace.

WELCOME TO THE NEW CONSCIOUSNESS

Welcome to the new consciousness
we utilise everyone

some fertilise the soil
some are food for lies & lice
some's only toil is to BE pigsties
some sit in the power tower
some shit in a flower shower
some cower from hate's gleam in the street
while some meet the NEW DREAM with a scream

the war is done the gore is won
there's something for everyone for some the sun
for some the moon
for some (perhaps the wise)
both the sun & the moon rise
some take acid moon trips
& some are microwaved in slave ships

some spin in space
while some make the pace of the human race

some hermaphrodites in the light
are eunuchs in the dark
some dicks are sticks some are ticks
some are sick getting their kicks
when the weak lick them slick
some lynch erections
some have ejaculations for lunch
& some count on cunt & cum
while some just read palms & psalms
for a sum of things to come

some are the storm
some the worm
some are only calm
tongue—deep in a bum

some play the death-game
some are too lame for the shame
of this sham-change
some are just deranged small change
while some cringe & some whinge
some are things to give joy
to the uncouth
some are just toyi-toyi boys
throw stones by day
& sow moans by night

some are hypochristians
some are wine-drunken catholics
taking a tumble on the bible
casting a coy look at the prayer-book
while some live in rotten sperm & jackal laughter
some strip to their souls
& show the holes
& some burrow like moles
& if you're hip

you can hop to the lop
jump into the mine
& PUMP UP on the drum & bass line

some perverts work on the nerves
some just work on their relatives
some make music
some speak the lyrics
of violence
in tongues of silence

WELCOME to the new consciousness
of derearranged senses
we utilise everyone

Léopold Sédar Senghor

Léopold Sédar Senghor (1906–2001), one of Africa's greatest poets, was born near Dakar in Senegal. One of the originators of the idea of negritude, Senghor led an active and committed political life, which eventually led to his election as the first president of Senegal. Here he contrasts an African's loyalty to his heritage with his need to defend himself against "the arrogance of fortunate races." He keeps his heritage hidden, which impacts upon his expression of masculinity.

TOTEM

I must hide him down in my deepest veins
The Ancestor whose stormy skin
Streaks with lightning and thunder
He is the guardian animal I must hide
Lest I burst the dam of scandal.
He is my loyal blood demanding loyalty,
Protecting my naked pride against myself
And the arrogance of fortunate races . . .

translated by Melvin Dixon

Ahmed Tidjani-Cissé

Ahmed Tidjani-Cissé was born in 1947 in Conakry, Guinea. He is a professor of African dance and director of an African ballet troupe in Paris. This sad poem embodies the essence of exile: how one grows disconnected from one's homeland despite political action on its behalf; how things continue to change both at home and abroad; and how sometimes it just simply becomes too late to ever return to one's roots.

HOME NEWS

"My dear son I am well thanks be to God
I pray for you day and night."

"My dear brother it's my sad duty to announce
the death of our beloved mother
Which occurred last Sunday
after a short illness."

"My cousin I've grown a lot
send me some trousers and new shoes."

"My love, it's now ten years I've been awaiting you
What's keeping you there in the white man's land
think of the trouble you cause us
by such a long absence."

"My dear friend our country's changing
into a huge shanty-town.
No-one can eat his fill except . . .
Send me a tape-recorder."

"My dear son it is I your father
I beg you to return to your land
if not you will not have even
the sorrow of recognizing my tomb."

"My dear nephew, I must tell you
of your father's death

we all hope you'll be able to attend
the forty-days' wake."

"My dear . . ."
A tear yesterday when the postman passed
Anxiety today in awaiting his return
The abyss of sadness envelops me
When I have no news from home
My soul shrivels a little
When home news tumbles over me.
The other day I made a fleeting boat
Full of home news.
I set it in the water at the wharf of Exile-Overseas.
I went to attend its arrival
at the landing stage of Loneliness-under-Hope.
My boat landed some secret passengers for me
Next day the postman's prophetic hand was
stretched towards me.

"My dear friend, your brother was arrested
last week in reprisal
for your political work against the government
Your family is left without a head
Send me a shirt and a neck-tie."

translated by Gerald Moore

South America

Juan Carlos Galeano

Juan Carlos Galeano was born in the Amazon region of Colombia in 1958 and moved to the
United States in 1983. His poetry, translations, and essays have been published in journals
in Latin America, the United States, and Europe. He teaches Latin American Poetry at
Florida State University. In "Eraser," he develops an intriguing metaphor about "erasing"
the past to create room for the future. But how much of it can we erase without obliterating
our identity? And can we distinguish between erasing places and people?

ERASER

to Roberto Fernández

The man who needs space in his mind for important things
rubs a giant eraser on his forehead every night.

He erases many thoughts of his homeland, and every day he wakes up
with fewer square miles of memories.

His parents tell him to erase carefully, not to get so carried away,
that one day he may end up erasing them, too.

The man assures them that he has had a lot of practice, that he only erases
the lands and things that aren't important.

He says that he knows how to strip the trees of their leaves and let
the houses and people go untouched.

translated by Delia Poey

Central America and the Caribbean

A. L. Hendriks

A. L. Hendriks was born in Jamaica and educated there and in England. He has published five books of poems and has been president of International PEN, Jamaica Centre. He now lives in England. The search for identity seems a common enough preoccupation of all modern human beings, male or female. What gives this poem its male perspective is the speaker's strong identification with his "sex-parts." After he has stripped all away and discarded even his bones and guts, they remain, hidden away—for their aesthetic value only, of course.

WILL THE REAL ME PLEASE STAND UP?

As soon as i saw i was naked
i put on mother's dress
but it smelled of pain
and had holes where vanity had poked through

so i tried on father's coat
but it was too small for me
his ego being dwarfish

my brother's jacket
almost fit
but he had need of it

the circus was in town
a clown! that's it i thought, a clown!
but i didn't like the laughter, it got me down,

tin-hat, wig of judge, robe of priest,
tried them all, for a while at least.

Animals seemed simply suited
so i concocted a beast to clothe in:
the elegant tights of a black panther
jerkin of a chameleon
and the hood of a Capuchin monkey
but the one i loved
said i was so beautiful
no one would undress me to go to bed with

something kinetic being needed
i appeared like a flock of white birds
circling over a green field

but the other i loved
said birds and fields were reminiscent of scarecrows

or Leda's bestialism
and was i sure i wasn't unsympathetic to homosexuals.

Therefore i decided to undress completely,
i unrolled my skin,
it came off neat as a banana,
carefully unstrapped my backbone and my guts,
stripped the pink flesh from the creamy bones
and threw them along with the bag of organs into the north wind
however secreting the sex-parts in my pocket,
not for utility
but because of their sculptured aesthetic,
the tactile and visual values, you understand.

Now i am carefully scanning
that relentless closed-circuit
which cameras and screens
every   thing
and when i pick me out
I will write again.

Evan X Hyde

Evan X Hyde is a poet from Belize. Here he relishes and celebrates his mixed racial and
ethnic heritage. He claims it as a source of strength and pride despite the opposition of the
"racial purist."

SUPER HIGH

I'm the son of a buccaneer
and a black woman
I'm the son of a Spanish man
and a Carib woman
I'm the son of a Creole man
and an Indian woman
I'm the son of an English
Soldier

and a mingo whore
I'm the son of love
I'm the son of sex
I'm the son of violence
Damn you, racial purist
I am Belize

I am the shining sun
I'm black, sucker
I'm gold and brown
and white and yellow
and bad
I'm the burning sun
fool
I'm cooking and
I'm smoking
I'm going to eat your head off
crush your ribs
kick out your seed
son of a bitch
you gon find out.

Derek Walcott

Derek Walcott, Nobel laureate (1992), was born in 1930 in Saint Lucia, the Lesser Antilles. He has been a journalist, playwright, drama critic, and professor of poetry. He has taught at the University of Boston and continues to divide his time between the United States and Trinidad. "Love after Love" may not be a "male poem" in any narrow sense, yet the poet is getting at something profound about the possibility of a return to a truer, deeper self. Interestingly, the return is made possible by the arrival of the lover-stranger, the one who has known you better than you have known yourself.

LOVE AFTER LOVE

The time will come
when, with elation
you will greet yourself arriving

at your own door, in your own mirror
and each will smile at the other's welcome,

and say, sit here. Eat.
You will love again the stranger who was your self.
Give wine. Give bread. Give back your heart
to itself, to the stranger who has loved you

all your life, whom you ignored
for another, who knows you by heart.
Take down the love letters from the bookshelf,

the photographs, the desperate notes,
peel your own image from the mirror.
Sit. Feast on your life.

North America

Robert Bly

Robert Bly's work has influenced men all over the world. Born in Minnesota in 1926, he travels widely but always returns to his Midwestern roots. "The Man Who Didn't Know What Was His" raises the central questions of identity. Do men define themselves by their possessions? The families they belong to? Their likes and dislikes? Take away all that, and what's left? Maybe something very surprising, according to this poem.

THE MAN WHO DIDN'T KNOW WHAT WAS HIS

There was a man who didn't know what was his.
He thought as a boy that some demon forced him
To wear "his" clothes and live in "his" room
And sit on "his" chair and be a child of "his" parents.

Each time he sat down to dinner, it happened again.
His own birthday party belonged to someone else.

And—was it sweet potatoes that he liked?—
He should resist them. Whose plate is this?

This man will be like a lean-to attached
To a house. It doesn't *have* a foundation.
This man is helpful and hostile in each moment.
This man leans toward you and leans away.

He's charming, this man who doesn't know what is his.

Philip Dacey

Philip Dacey was born in 1939 in St. Louis, Missouri. He has published seven collections of poetry and along with David Jauss has edited the anthology *Strong Measures: Contemporary American Poetry in Traditional Forms.* He lives in the countryside outside Lynd, Minnesota. The epigraph of "Four Men in a Car," with its implication of threat and male disposability, seems to capture some of the backlash of feminism and the evolving men's movements. With some irony, Dacey reverses traditional roles: women are out in the world and engaged; men are relegated to the curious domestic domain of a car interior, where they are ineffectual and struck dumb, though curiously at peace—or pacified? Are they trapped, isolated without their women? What makes the sight of four men in a car "the ugliest thing in the world"?

FOUR MEN IN A CAR

The ugliest thing in the world is the sight of four men in a car.
—David Bailey, photographer, quoted in *American Photographer,* September 1988

We sit in the womanless car,
maleness twice-squared, going nowhere.

Two in front and two in back,
in the Jill-less car, Jack, Jack, Jack, and Jack.

We know how ugly we are,
but what can we do? We live here.

The truth is none of us can drive,

though our horsepower is impressive.

It may be a meeting's our goal,
or a game, or something illegal,

but it's all the same. The deadest end.
So we tell jokes. You know the kind.

Outside the car the women walk
and run and leap or make such talk

as prompts their hands to fly about
in ways ours, cramped inside, cannot.

Close, but not too, we don't move much;
it's accidental when we touch.

Oh, there's nothing as ugly as we,
four men in a car, not five or three.

To breathe, we roll our windows down,
and then we roll them up again.

Pier Giorgio Di Cicco

Pier Giorgio Di Cicco (b. 1949, Italy) has lived in Montreal, Baltimore, and now Toronto, where he has worked as a bartender and editor. Among his collections are *The Tough Romance* (1979). A lot of men, feeling bashed and battered by several decades of feminist anger, will relate to Di Cicco's poem. There is a sense of exhaustion over the endless arguments about men and women that see individual differences in sociological terms. Are men condemned to spend their entire lives feeling like oppressors?

MALE RAGE POEM

Feminism, baby, feminism.
This is the anti-feminist poem.
It will get called the anti-

feminist poem. Like it or not.
Dedicated to all my friends who
can't get it up in the night,
accused of having male rage during the
day. This is for the poor buggers.
This is for me and the incredible boredom
of arguing about feminism, the right
arguments, the wrong arguments, the
circular argument, the arguments that stem
from one bad affair, from one
bad job, no job—whatever; fill in the
blanks _____ _____, fill in the ways
in which you have been hurt. Then I'll
fill in the blanks, and we'll send rosters
of hurt to each other, mail them, stock
them for the record, to say: *Giorgio Di Cicco*
has been hurt in this way x many times.
We will stock closets of Sarah's hurt,
Barbara's hurt, my hurt, Bobby's hurt.
This is where the poem peters out . . . oops!—that's
penis mentality, that's patriarchal bullshit,
sexist diction and *these line lengths are*
male oriented.
            Where did he get so much male rage?
From standing out like a man for a bunch of
years, and being called the dirty word.
"When you are 21 you will become a Man."
Christ! Doomed to enslave women ipso
facto, without even the right training for it.
Shouldn't have wasted ten years playing
baseball; should have practised
whipping, should have practised tying up the
girl next door, giving her cigarette burns . . .
oops! Male rage again! MALE RAGE—the words ring out—
worse than RING AROUND THE COLLAR, worse than
    KISSED
THE GIRLS AND MADE THEM CRY, jeesus, male rage
In kindergarten. MALE RAGE. You've got
male rage; I look inside myself and scrounge

for all this male rage. Must be there
somewhere. Must be repressing it. I write poems
faster and faster, therapeutically, to make sure
I get most of the rage out. But someone's
always there to say Male Rage—more Male Rage;
I don't leave the house, working on my male rage.

Things may lighten up. My friends may meet
fine women at a party someday and know
what to say to them, like: "I'm not a Man and
you're not a Woman, but let's have dinner
anyway, let's fuck with our eyes closed and
swap roles for an hour."

I'm tired of being a man.
Of having better opportunities,
better job offers,
too much money.
I'm tired of going to the YMCA and
talking jock in the locker room.
I'm tired of all the poems where
I used the word "whore" inadvertently.
I'm tired of having secretaries type out
all my poems for me.
I'm tired of being a man.
I'm tired of being a sexist.
I'm afraid of male rage.
I'm afraid of *my* male rage,
this growing thing, this buddy, this
shadow, this new self, this stranger.
It's there. It's there! How could it have
happened? I ate the right things, said
yes to my mother, thought the good
thoughts.
        Doc—give it to me straight.
How long do I have before this male rage
takes over completely?
                    The rest of your life.
Take it like a man.

Douglas Goetsch

Douglas Goetsch is author of two poetry collections. He grew up in Northport, Long Island, was educated at Wesleyan University and New York University, and currently teaches English and writing at Stuyvesant High School in New York City. In "Bachelor Song," a single man visits some married friends and feels his own isolation more keenly. There are many songs of lusty bachelorhood; far fewer reveal its long arc of loneliness.

BACHELOR SONG

It's Saturday night and Lisa
is burying her husband
and me in Scrabble, long
words coming out of her
like children—theirs
are upstairs, finally asleep
at 9 o'clock, when Lisa's
speech slurs from exhaustion
and Arthur calls me Honey
by mistake. They wrestle
on the carpet in hysterics,
roll into a kiss.

The window in the guest room
douses the bed with moonlight.
I close my eyes picturing
Susan Sarandon in *Atlantic City*
bathing her chest with lemons.
Last night Nina phoned.
She's decided to stop dating.
She hasn't gotten over
Howard, and her hands
are full with her 5-year-old.
She asked about work, about
my poetry. I said, Listen
I feel fine: you're not dating
and I'm glad I was the man

who helped clear that up
for you. I'll never

get to sleep in this light.
Now I remember, it's the last
night of the new comet.
Hale–Bopp, two guys
who spent their lives looking
at the sky, found it.
They say it won't be back
for 2000 years. I don't
understand how a chunk of ice
holds together for that long,
leaving its comb of light
like a whistled song.

Yusef Komunyakaa

Yusef Komunyakaa was born in Bogalusa, Louisiana, in 1947. He has published numerous
books of poems and has received a variety of prizes, including the Pulitzer Prize. Komun-
yakaa sees an ancient story in the male propensity for violence—it is animal, human, and
mythic. Females—animal and human—try to intervene, but it continues unabated.

HOMO ERECTUS

After pissing around his gut-level
Kingdom, he builds a fire & hugs
A totem against his chest.
Cheetahs pace the horizon
To silence a grassy cosmos
Where carrion birds sing
Darkness back from the hills.
Something in the air, quintessence or rancor,
Makes a langur bash the skull
Of another male's progeny.
The mother tries to fight him off,
But this choreographer for Jacob

& the Angel knows defeat
Arrives in an old slam dance
& applied leverage—the Evening Star
In both eyes, something less than grace.

Gary Soto

Gary Soto was born in Fresno, California, in 1952. An anthologist and prize-winning poet and author, he has published more than a dozen books. He lives in northern California. As a Mexican American caught up in the ironies of being a member of both cultures, Soto raises questions of identity, inclusivity, and exclusivity. He illustrates the power of the dominant culture to sweep us along despite our own preferences.

MEXICANS BEGIN JOGGING

At the factory I worked
In the fleck of rubber, under the press
Of an oven yellow with flame,
Until the border patrol opened
Their vans and my boss waved for us to run.
"Over the fence, Soto," he shouted,
And I shouted that I was an American.
"No time for lies," he said, and passes
A dollar in my palm, hurrying me
Through the back door.

Since I was on his time, I ran
And became the wag to a short tail of Mexicans—
Ran past the amazed crowds that lined
The street and blurred like photographs, in rain.
I ran from that industrial road to the soft
Houses where people paled at the turn of an autumn sky.
What could I do but yell vivas
To baseball, milkshakes, and those sociologists
Who would clock me
As I jog into the next century
On the power of a great, silly grin.

Oceania, Australia, and New Zealand

Les Murray

Les Murray was born in 1938 in Bunyah, New South Wales, Australia, where he continues to live today with his wife Valerie and two youngest children. The author of a dozen books of verse, he is considered Australia's foremost living poet. His poem here exhibits a masculinity inextricably connected to a sense of national character. For historical and cultural reasons, masculinity in Australia is frequently associated with a laconic, ironic, private persona, which nonetheless has a certain linguistic flamboyance and flair.

FOLKLORE

What are the sights of our town!

Well, there is that skeleton they hang
some nights in the bar of the Rest
and everyone laughing in whispers
the barmaid broke down one time, laughing.
The cord goes up through the ceiling
to the undersprings of the big
white bed in the Honeymoon Suite
and when those bones even jiggle
there's cheers (and a donnybrook once)
and when they joggle, there's whooping
and folk stalking out in emotions
and when they dance—hoo, when they dance!
he knows every tune on the honeymoon
flute, does the hollow-hipped fellow.
There are a few, mind, who drink on
straight through it all. Steady drinkers.
Up over the pub there's the sky
full of stars, as I have reflected
outside, while guiding the course of my
thoughts. Some say there's a larger

cord goes up there, but I doubt it
I mean but then I'm no dancer.

Besides that, there's meatworks and mines.

Les Murray

What man has not been concerned with performance? What male has not given at least
some part of his attention to "plumage," " strutting," and looking good in the eyes of the
world, in the eyes of women? In this verbally playful and metaphor-laden poem, Les Mur-
ray also reminds us of the sense of failure hidden in every triumph.

PERFORMANCE

I starred last night, I shone:
I was footwork and firework in one,

a rocket that wriggled up and shot
darkness with a parasol of brilliants
and a peewee descant on a flung bit;
I was busters of glitter-bombs expanding
to mantle and aurora from a crown,
I was fouéttes, falls of blazing paint,
para-flares spot-welding cloudy heaven,
loose gold off fierce toeholds of white,
a finale red-tongued as a haka leap:
that too was a butt of all right!

As usual after any triumph, I was
of course inconsolable.

John A. Scott

John A. Scott was born in 1948 in Sussex, England. A graduate of Monash University in
Melbourne, Australia, he has written scripts for TV and radio and lectured in media stud-
ies. He now teaches in the Creative Arts Department of the University of Wollongong,

New South Wales. In this poem a man loses his heart to a woman briefly seen on the street—or does he have a heart attack? Or does he just drop his pack of cigarettes? Or are all these images conflated to say something else?

MAN IN PETERSHAM

He's dropped his heart!
His heart has fallen to the footpath.
But no one seems surprised and least of all
the office girl whose stockings violin
across this empty road. He's dropped his heart!
It surely must be this and not his cigarettes.
The way he stares so long and makes no effort
to redeem it. And his suit is an immaculate grey,
and his shoes a duco white. And his feet are
frozen in the tiny refrigerators of his shoes.
With all the colours running out, he stares
upon his fallen heart. His mild-blue heart
shattered in its twenty filtered pieces.

Luke Icarus Simon

Luke Icarus Simon, born in Nicosia, Cyprus, in 1963, writes in both Greek and English. He has worked in many different genres: fiction, poetry, drama. He has also written for television. The subject of "Ravine" is politics—national, ethnic, and sexual—and the land mines and pitfalls that must be negotiated when different perspectives collide. Our various needs and desires compel us to create compromises, accommodations—even new cultures.

RAVINE

One of them was a Turk
the other a Greek
a national crime their relationship
in a country where both could be killed

everything started out all right as it does
like always   two men   buddies   mates

but soon enough
The Marbled King
the injustice of Aphrodite's island
Constantinople or Istanbul
religion
disemboweled Smyrna
the fortitude of tradition
who would yield   whose guilt was greater
who would play the man
all these innate riddles
discordant ingredients   a disharmony
like an unsightly irritation   or swelling
on the body

You're so inflexible   one of them shouted
And you're so unbending   said the other
dissimilarity disseminates liberalism

later   at night   in their own greenhouse
self-deprived of rules   of national history
naked devout servants   understanding each other's needs
they map out their own culture

   translated by the poet

Russell Soaba

Russell Soaba is a fictionist and poet from Papua New Guinea. He has a degree in creative writing from Brown University and has taught at the University of Papua New Guinea. Here the poet asks the reader to honor the ways of the father and the ancestors. Nothing new there—but the surprising image that carries the heart of that message is surely a unique and powerful one.

LOOKING THRU THOSE EYEHOLES

Once an artist went overseas
His father died in his absence
and was buried in the village

He followed a rainbow upon his return
and came to a cemetery
he dug in search of reality
till he broke his father's skull
to wear its fore-half as a mask

try it / look thru those eyeholes
see the old painting / view the world
in the way the dead had done.

Dimitris Tsaloumas

Dimitris Tsaloumas was born on the Greek island of Leros in 1921. He has lived in
Melbourne, Australia, since 1952. Since beginning to write in English in the 1980s, he has
published five collections of poetry. In "Epilogue," the poet compares himself—as many
men do—to one kind of animal or another. He takes us through various traits he shares
with other creatures in the biosphere, and only when he moves close to the human does
he lose his perspective.

EPILOGUE

My joys are those of the spare autumn birds
that haunt the trees of sunset cities.

My sadness is in the patient eye of the ox,
the vast lament of the ass in night paddocks.

I claw and peck and bristle at competition
like a pink-stalked gull, and my greed

is infinite, though I loathe my brother the pig.

My lust is the lust of the goat who spies

the bare-breasted tourist on the rock
and shakes his beard with rage and climbs

down the bluff to take a sniff at the brine.
Only my thoughts are human, but I look

for alternatives. They bring me too close
to you, old friends; my perspective suffers.

Men and Women

For a man and a woman. For one plant divided
Into masculine and feminine which longed for each other.
—Czeslaw Milosz

Men have written a great many love poems about women in virtually all languages during all periods of human history. The ancient Greeks and Romans, the medieval troubadours, the Elizabethan sonneteers, the Cavalier poets of seventeenth-century England, the Romantics of the nineteenth century—all have given us a long tradition of "courtship and marriage" poems and celebrations of feminine beauty. The contemporary period is no exception, although relations between men and women have become much more problematic as gender roles in many of the world's cultures have become more fluid. In large part, these changes are a result of the modern women's movement, born in the United States in the late sixties and still spreading throughout the world. In some cultures those roles are changing much more slowly than in others, but the U.S. influence—through movies, television, music, magazines, and so on—has changed awareness if not actual conditions virtually everywhere.

Men seem to be more aware of the consequences of "objectification," the negative aspects of inequality, the long buried female anger that they must now confront. They are also more conscious of economic inequities and other social injustices that women have had to endure. But many contemporary men recognize certain eternal verities about the male-female attraction that feminism hasn't negated, and they seem more ready to speak openly about those truths.

Sensual and sensuous love poems by men once again seem to be flourishing in all parts of the world. The Nigerian Chinua Achebe describes the "Earth / perfumed in dewdrop / fragrance" after a session of lovemaking. He speaks of men's domination of the earth in the daytime, but their surrender to a woman's power in the evening. The Iraqi Abdul Wahab al-Bayati sees a woman as an eternal mystery, as do so many of the male poets in this volume and many men who are not poets. The dominant notes in this section are mystery and desire.

But there is anger too, the anger of betrayal and blame. Chilean Oscar Hahn wishes that his ex-lover dreams "with demons / and white cockroaches." The late Czech poet Vladimir Holan writes of the inability to communicate with a woman. The Argentinian Sergio Kisielewsky describes his soul being kicked around like a soccer ball by a woman and being left with an empty space where his heart used to be.

These are powerful expressions of "the oldest story." For all of our technological progress, cultural sophistication, and sexual liberation, men and women are still falling in love, protecting and nurturing one another, as well as falling out of love, betraying and attempting to dominate and control one another. And there is nothing new under the sun in the sense that men are still writing about it, albeit in ways that reflect the new realities of male and female roles in the world.

Asia

Rafiq Azad

Rafiq Azad is an award-winning Bengali poet who is well known for his antimilitaristic verse. In contrast to the traditional dual stereotypes of woman as Madonna or whore in the West, the archetype of the "Eternal Woman" presented in this poem is seen almost exclusively in terms of familial and domestic attributes. She is a mother, sister, and daughter, all of whom are able to exert a powerful influence on the male psyche.

WOMAN: THE ETERNAL

How shall I address you, my Beloved Woman?
>I can call you "mother,"
>No harm if I call you "sister" either,
>Maybe, you are my daughter.
But I won't call you by any given name today.
>I don't need to.
I'll have you in the fullness of every moment of my life.
>Whatever name satisfies me,
>Whatever name reverberates inside me in every cell,
>I feel I should call you by that very name.

When the outside world strikes me nearly dead,
When I cower in absolute hopelessness,
When I am exhausted and totally beaten,

I feel like calling you "mother" and
Throw myself in your arms.
That is the time when everything is obliterated except
Your likeness to my mother.

You are not my age.
You are so small that from time to time,
Looking at your sweet little face,
I feel like calling you "my baby."
I believe you are the only one who could
Govern me.
I know no one but a daughter could rein in
An unruly father.
I am that restless, parched, unruly father.
I call you, come, my daughter,
Rein in your tormented father.
I am your powerful, domineering father.
But I bow to you today, woman.
My daughter, my little daughter.
Come, restrain me.

Once in a while I see in you,
The face of my only blood sister,
And I feel like calling you "sister."
You, who are standing at the door, unmoving like a picture.
You who have the face of my mother, sister, and daughter.
Come, let me embrace you, the Eternal Woman.

translated by Afia Dil

Sadhu Binning

Sadhu Binning was born in 1947 in India. He emigrated to Canada in 1967, where he now
teaches Punjabi at the University of British Columbia in Vancouver. He is the author of
more than fifteen books of poetry, fiction, plays, and research. In "Revenge," the sight of a
beautiful white woman on the side of the road distracts the driver and evokes wild and
strange thoughts. In what way are the woman's blue eyes responsible for three hundred
years of butchery, for the enslavement and rape of the driver's mother? Does the narrator
see her as a symbol of woman or of whiteness? Or both?

REVENGE

hands on the steering wheel
comfort of driver's seat
power of fast speed—
I'm intoxicated

then the woman
behind the white thumb
on the edge of the road
dances wildly in my head
and thought is choked—
those blue eyes evoke in me
memories
three hundred years
of butchery and robbery

a voice inside shouts
REVENGE!
those blue eyes are responsible
for enslaving and raping your mother
by whatever means
take revenge

the spell of momentary madness
brakes
and a question sharper
than a slave's pain
grows in me—
what kind of thought is this
to turn a meeting
like this into a crime
on the edge of the road

translated by the poet

Yi Cha

Yi Cha, who is of both Han and Kazak background, was born in Sichuan in 1966. He teaches at the Xian Foreign Languages Institute. In this very politically incorrect poem, he thinks of the lives of his lesbian neighbors as a "waste" and speculates about how to "rescue" them. He is startled, however, when they treat him with hostility; when the women talk about men as "dirty" and "garbage," why isn't that politically incorrect as well?

NEIGHBORS

A lesbian couple
lives next door,
protected
by the free air of our country.
They're more honest
and happier
than I, a bachelor scrounging every day for food.
Their wanton laughter from morning till night
makes my life miserable.
In an age when the wolves outnumber the sheep,
what a waste
to let these two girls alone.
I often think about how to rescue them,
but every time I knock on their door
pretending I need to borrow some soy sauce,
they answer in unison: "Meiyou!" "No way!"
One day I listened outside their window.
What I heard really depressed me; they
were talking about men.
The word "dirty" came up,
as did "garbage."

translated by Wang Ping and Richard Sieburth

Faiz Ahmed Faiz

The recipient of several literary awards, notably the Lenin Prize, Faiz Ahmed Faiz was
born in Sialkot, Punjab. He had a varied career as teacher, army officer, journalist, politi-
cal leader, trade unionist, and broadcaster. "Before You Came" demonstrates love's power
to transform us utterly, turning us upside down with its magic and urgency, giving every-
thing in the world a symbolic dimension. But in the end, we must return to earth with a
new appreciation for everyday reality.

BEFORE YOU CAME

Before you came things were just what they were:
the road precisely a road, the horizon fixed,
the limit of what could be seen,
a glass of wine no more than a glass of wine.

With you the world took on the spectrum
radiating from my heart: your eyes gold
as they open to me, slate the colour
that falls each time I lose all hope.

With your advent roses burst into flame:
you were the artist of dried-up leaves, sorceress
who flicked her wrist to change dust into soot.
You lacquered the night black.

As for the sky, the road, the cup of wine:
one was my tear-drenched shirt,
the other an aching nerve,
the third a mirror that never reflected the same thing.

Now you are here again—stay with me.
This time things will fall into place;
the road can be the road,
the sky nothing but the sky;
the glass of wine, as it should be, the glass of wine.

translated by Naomi Lazard

Huan Fu

Huan Fu (b. 1922) is the senior member of the generation of so-called Bamboo Hat poets in Taiwan. He is also a translator of modern Japanese poetry. The maiden described in the prose poem that follows has archetypal qualities. She hovers between mythological and actual being, becoming a "clever but common girl" when she removes the flowers that adorn her sensual parts. But even removing that mythological layer, the woman remains, in the eyes of the male speaker, an enormous force, capable of bringing forth life and thereby reconstructing the universe.

FLOWER

Give three flowers to a maiden: one on her hair, one on her breast, one on her shame. Then, she is very happy to be a woman—a dream she once had. In the dream, she feared bearing horrible fruits. She is afraid of fruits. Deep in her eyes afire with love, she refuses all fruits, which is a pronoun, a substitute of virtue for scandal.

But she does not dwell on the problem of fruit. She can put off a decision, can stop on the moment, before the climactic point. Then she takes off the last flower and becomes, once more, a clever but common girl.

She claims to be a stubborn woman, one who breaks half and half conservatism and liberalism, who falsifies the flower she is. But her speech isn't stubborn, is it? When in others' eyes she wishes to appear a good woman, she will break her silence with longwindedness; when she sees a submissive man moved by her long tongue, she fantasizes the bright eyes of three flowers. She dreams beautiful dreams, with the complete dedication of love.

A flower on her hair. A flower on her breast. A flower on . . . She again removes the last flower, reconstructing once again the entire universe.

translated by Dominic Cheung

Hung Hung

Hung Hung emerged as an important Taiwanese poet in the 1990s. He has authored four volumes of poetry and translated numerous works from English and European languages. Undoubtedly an intriguing story lies just under this poem's surfaces, under its expressed gratitude for the mountains of Hualien, sleep, injustice, love, transgression, and a woman's beauty. The reader is left to imagine just what that story may be.

A HYMN TO HUALIEN

Blessed is the lord for bestowing on us these gifts which we are so unworthy of
    receiving.
The mountains of Hualien. The azure of a summer evening at the stroke of seven.
Deep sleep. The broad sweep of the sea tilting out of kilter on those hairpin
turns we take at 60 miles per hour. Love
and transgression. His injustices.
Your loveliness.

translated by Steve Bradbury

Nadir Hussein

Nadir Hussein (1939–79) was born in Calcutta and educated in London, Paris, Switzerland, and the Philippines. He had a rich and varied career as a journalist, cricket commentator, and broadcaster. He lived in Pakistan, and many of his poems were discovered posthumously. In "A Wedding," an arranged Pakistani marriage arouses lust in the bridegroom but patience in the bride, who transforms herself from bride to erotic mentor in the poem's last stanza.

A WEDDING

A tidal wave over-runs the island,
The young man adjusts his pliant turban,
His deathly pallor reflected in the sea
Of swirling faces round him, his brows lined
With the effort of trying to combine
The present with the future's mystery.

Escorted by a caravan of cars,
A strange and somewhat mournful procession,
He goes to claim his prize. Meanwhile the girl,
Wise beyond words, dressed like a party doll,

Bows her head in silent recognition
Of her destiny. With their unvoiced cares

The two sit side by side, the man, impatient
To drink from the ocean of her body,
The girl, unaware of his lust, too shy
To look him in the face. All is ready,
The deal completed, the glittering show
Over, the hosts relieved and complacent.

What of the two, no longer the centre
Of attraction? Dumb on another stage
Without an audience, the man, overwhelmed
By his manhood, in an uncontrolled rage
Over-reaches himself; the girl, condemned
To knowledge, moistly becomes his mentor.

Takagi Kyozo

Takagi Kyozo died in 1987 at the age of eighty-four. He was born in Aomori City, Japan, in 1903 and graduated from a medical university in Manchuria. His poetry, much of it characterized by wit and humor, is written in the Tsugaru dialect spoken in Aomori Prefecture, in the region facing the Japan Sea. "How to Cook Women" is surely the most politically incorrect poem in this book. Clearly Takagi Kyozo intends its macabre description both metaphorically and humorously—and ultimately with love.

HOW TO COOK WOMEN

To cook women,
First of all, put them on a chopping board
And slice into three parts.
No knife is needed, you may use your bare hands.
Care should be taken to check
Whether those you wish to cook are young or old.
In the case of middle-aged or elderly ones,
The meat can easily be sliced from the bones.
But it is not so easy to cut up the young ones.

They have a lot of small bones.
You have to pick them all out as carefully as possible.
When all the bones are taken out,
Stroke the meat tenderly with your palms
As if making it into rounds.

People say women,
Especially those who are middle-aged or elderly,
Are not edible, even if you boil or bake them.
That, of course, is not true.
The best way to do them is as a *tempura* dish.
So let me tell you how to fry them.
You should use plenty of oil.
There is a certain knack to frying them on the strong heat of passion
So that they turn out crisp, not soggy.
When you serve them on a platter,
Don't forget to sprinkle evenly over them
The leaves of love, chopped small.
Eat before cold.
That's all.

translated by James Kirup and Michio Nakano

Yang Mu

Yang Mu was born in 1940 in Taiwan. He graduated from Tunghai University and received his doctorate in comparative literature at the University of California, Berkeley. The relation of love, landscape, and the seasons in this quiet and beautiful love poem is quintessentially Chinese. The line where nature ends and the man and woman begin is blurred, and the poem itself seems to want to throw itself to the wind.

LET THE WIND RECITE

1.

If only I could write you a summer-poem,
When the reeds
Drastically multiply;
The sun leaps up to the waist
And flows divergently past the two legs;

When a new drum
Starts to crack, if only

I could write you an autumn-poem,
Swinging in a small boat,
Wetting twelve watermarks;
When sadness curls
Like a yellow dragon in the riverbed,
Letting the rushing mountain stream arise
From the wounded eyes splashing, if only

I could write you a winter-poem,
To witness finally the ice, the snow,
And a shrunken lake;
To witness someone's midnight visitation
To you, awake in a bed of hurried dreams—
When you were relocated in a faraway province,
Given a lantern, and asked
To sit with patience,
Without tearful eyes.

2.
If they won't allow you
To mourn or to weave
For springtime;
If they ask you
To sit quietly, to wait,
A thousand years later,
After spring passes,
Your name will remain, summer;
They will return you,
Take away your ring, your dress,
Cut your hair short
And leave you at my tolerant water's brink;
You will belong to me at last.

At last, you will belong to me,
To be bathed, to be given wine,
Peppermint candies, new dresses;
Your hair will grow again

To the length of former days;
Summer will remain your name.

3.
Then I will write you
A spring-poem, when all
Has regenerated—So young and shy
To see one's own maturing shadow
In the water,
I will let your tears fall freely,
Will design new dresses for you,
Will make candles for your first night.

Then you will let me write on my bosom
A spring-poem;
Heartbeats will be the rhythms,
Blood, the rhymes,
Breasts will be the images,
And a mole, the metaphor.
I will lay you down on a warm lake,
And let the wind recite.

translated by Dominic Cheung

Shuntarō Tanikawa

Shuntarō Tanikawa was born in Tokyo in 1931. He has published many books of poetry since his first, *Twenty Billion Light Years of Loneliness*, appeared to wide acclaim in 1952. In "Kiss," he describes a man's reaction to infidelity and how deeply it changes his connection to his woman. The response seems an almost involuntary reflex; even if the man wants to pretend it hasn't happened, he can't.

KISS

She came home smelling of another man,
and I just could not kiss her.
Then taking quilts still warm from the sun
we went to bed together.

It had been such nice weather that day;
still I could not kiss her.
She pressed her breasts firmly to my chest;
still I couldn't do it.
I felt she was a different girl,
as if we had never met.
Still without getting between her legs,
it seemed like a Sunday
     when I used to go fishing alone
and would watch the soft sun of winter
     beside that little pond.
It seemed like the times
     I used to wait to meet someone.
I was frightened—
Still I couldn't do it.
Then sometime I fell asleep.
The night was like a huge prairie
for as long as one could run,
     for as long as one could run.

translated by Harold Wright

The Middle East

Adonis

Ali Ahmad Sa'id was born in Qassabin, Syria, and writes under the name Adonis. He studied philosophy at Damascus University and at St. Joseph University in Beirut, where he obtained his Doctorat d'Etat in 1973. He was imprisoned for six months in 1955 for political activities and membership in the Syrian National Socialist Party. Upon release from prison he settled in Lebanon in 1956, later becoming a Lebanese national. Adonis currently lives in Paris. This cryptic dialogue between a woman and a man suggests the enormous gulf between the two. The man and woman try to know one another, but both end up asking the same unresolved question.

A WOMAN AND A MAN

(Conversation, 1967)

Woman:	Who are you?
Man:	A clown without a home,
	A meteorite, a son of Satan.
	Who are you?
	Have you travelled in my body?
Woman:	Many times.
Man:	What did you see?
Woman:	My death.
Man:	Have you crept in my blood, sat down,
	Undressed, washed and worn my face?
	Seen my sun like a shadow
	And explored my soul?
Woman:	Do you know me now?
Man:	Have you told me all? Are you sure?
Woman:	No.
Man:	You got what you want from me? Still afraid?
Woman:	Yes.
Man:	Do you know me now?
Woman:	Do you know me now?

translated by Abdulla al-Udhari

Yehuda Amichai

Yehuda Amichai (1924–2000), born in Wurzburg, Germany, was Israel's most highly regarded contemporary poet. "An Ideal Woman" considers the consequences of male objectification of women and suggests something of an atonement for centuries of confusing idealism with objectification.

AN IDEAL WOMAN

I know a man who put together an ideal woman
from all his desires: the hair
he took from a woman in the window of a passing bus,
the forehead from a cousin who died young, the hands

from a teacher he had as a kid, the cheeks from a little girl,
his childhood love, the mouth from a woman he noticed
in a phone booth, the thighs
from a young woman lying on the beach,
the alluring gaze from this one, the eyes from that one,
the waistline from a newspaper ad.
From all these he put together
a woman he truly loved. And when he died, they came,
all the women—legs chopped off, eyes plucked out, faces slashed in half,
severed hands, hair ripped out, a gash where a mouth used to be,
and demanded what was theirs, theirs, theirs,
dismembered his body, tore his flesh, and left him
only his long-lost soul.

translated by Chana Bloch and Stephen Mitchell

Abdul Wahab al-Bayati

Abdul Wahab al-Bayati (1926–99) was an Iraqi poet who was a major innovator in his art form. He died in Damascus after returning there from Amman, Jordan, early in 1999. In "Secret of Fire" he reminds us that fire is as essential as water, in the same way that males and females dance and exchange their respective energies. Who can say, in the end, what either essence is? That they are is somehow miracle enough in this mysterious poem.

SECRET OF FIRE

On the last day
I kissed her hands,
Her eyes / her lips.
I said to her: you are now
Ripe like an apple
Half of you: a woman
The other half: impossible to describe.
The words
Escaped me
And I escaped them
Now I pray
Both of us collapsed.
For the childhood of this light face

And for this ripe, burning body
I bring my face closer
To this gushing spring,
Thirsty.
On the last day, I said to her:
You are the fire of the forests
The water of the river
The secret of the fire
Half of you cannot be described
The other half: a priestess in the temple of Ishtar.

translated by Bassam Khalil Frangieh

Sa 'di Yusuf

Sa 'di Yusuf (b. 1943) is an Iraqi poet whose *Collected Works* was published in 1979. Unlike many Arabic poets, whose work has deep philosophical roots, Yusuf writes about the life of his own time and place. Here he idealizes "a woman" as so many men do and evokes the memory of an actual lost love. The narrator struggles to revive both love and idealism, which have been smothered by "the pain of . . . years."

A WOMAN

How should I direct my steps to her now?
In which land might I find her,
on what streets of which city should I ask?
Suppose I were to locate the path to her house,
even imagining it,
would I press the doorbell?
And what would I say?
How would I greet her,
would I stare into her face,
press the glistening wine of her fingers . . .
Would I unload
The pain of my years?
Once
twenty years ago

in the air-conditioned train
I kissed her the whole night long . . .

translated by Lena Jayyusi and Naomi Shihab Nye

Amal Dunqul

In the Egyptian poet Amal Dunqul's "Corner," the perennial themes of sex, love, war, death, and compassion are woven together in a complex masculine and feminine ethos— partly composed of Middle Eastern traditional values, modernism, and an achingly inadequate humanism.

CORNER

He sits in the corner,
writes, as the naked woman
mingles with the nightclub's patrons,
auctions off her beauty.
She asks him how the war is going,
and he answers:
"You needn't worry about the treasures of your body,
our country's enemy
is just like us,
he circumcises males and loves foreign
imports, just like us, he hates pork
and pays for guns and hookers."
She cries.
He sits in the corner
as the naked woman passes.
He invites her to his table.
She can't stay for long, she says:
since morning she's been combing army
hospitals, searching for her brother,
whose unit was encircled
across the Suez (The land
returns, her brother doesn't . . .)
She tells him she has had to earn
the bread in her brother's absence,

how she will wear again her modest clothes
when he gets back.
She shows his picture with his children
on a holiday.
She cries.

translated by Sharif Elmusa and Thomas G. Ezzy

Salman Masalha

The Israeli poet Salman Masalha was born in Galilea in 1953. He is facile in both Arabic and Hebrew and has published work in both languages. Here the speaker imagines that he expedites a woman's freedom each time he is with her, helping to free her from the cage of her life story the society around her has created. Can we read his words without irony?

CAGE

On the palm of her hand the others drew
the lines of a cage, where they imprisoned
her life story. And, son of Arabia that I am,
I hate an imprisoned bird. Each time she
gave me her hand, I erased a line.
And released birds.

translated by Vivian Eden

Nizar Qabbani

Nizar Qabbani (1923–98) was a Syrian poet and diplomat. He was noted for his opposition to the traditional Arabic attitude toward women. In "The Fortune Teller," one of his best-known poems, both Arab nationalism and a distinctive idealization of women are involved in the fortune-teller's prophetic reading of the narrator's future. He is destined to forever pursue a woman he envisions as a filament of smoke and who lives nowhere. The poem's final lines are particularly challenging; how do they relate to Arabic views of womanhood?

THE FORTUNE TELLER

She sat with fear in her eyes
Contemplating the upturned cup
She said "Do not be sad, my son
You are destined to fall in love"
My son, Who sacrifices himself for his beloved,
Is a martyr

———

For long have I studied fortune-telling
But never have I read a cup similar to yours
For long have I studied fortune-telling
But never have I seen sorrows similar to yours
You are predestined to sail forever
Sail-less, on the sea of love
Your life is forever destined
To be a book of tears
And be imprisoned
Between water and fire

———

But despite all its pains,
Despite the sadness
That is with us day and night
Despite the wind
The rainy weather
And the cyclone
It is love, my son
That will be forever the best of fates

———

There is a woman in your life, my son
Her eyes are so beautiful
Glory to God
Her mouth and her laughter
Are full of roses and melodies
And her gypsy and crazy love of life
Travels the world

The woman you love
May be your whole world
But your sky will be rain-filled
Your road blocked, blocked, my son
Your beloved, my son, is sleeping
In a guarded palace
He who approaches her garden wall
Who enters her room
And who proposes to her
Or tries to unite her plaits
Will cause her to be lost, my son . . . lost

———————

You will seek her everywhere, my son
You will ask the waves of the sea about her
You will ask the shores of the seas
You will travel the oceans
And your tears will flow like a river
And at the close of your life
You will find that since your beloved
Has no land, no home, no address
You have been pursuing only a trace of smoke
How difficult it is, my son
To love a woman
Who has neither land, nor home

translated by Issam A. Lakkis, Fred Moramarco, and Al Zolynas

Europe

Radu Andriescu

Radu Andriescu was born in Jassy, Romania, in 1962. "The Apple" expresses a man's fasci-
nation with the creation of life, as well as his sense of separation from that when he's not
with a woman. The mystical dream devolves into an image of a drab and limited actuality.

THE APPLE

The man lays his heavy, square paw on her dress,
on her belly. He feels it
and mumbles happily. He sweats with happiness.
He brings his ear near her belly.
He presses the funnel of his ear against her dress
and listens. He hears. He thinks he's hearing.
He's happy. Dull and happy.
At home, weary with happiness, drunk, dead-tired with happiness,
he falls asleep.
It seems to him that before his eyes a huge globe has arisen.
The globe moves
and he hears a deep, confused noise,
pain mingled with pleasure. It seems to him that
the globe splits like a ripe watermelon. That he can see the long silver
knife and hear the hiss and snap of the rind.
He can also hear a deep and confused noise,
pleasure, pain, pleasure.
It seems to him that the water has broken, the sky gets masked
with a heavy curtain of water and noise.
From behind the curtain, a wondrous forest appears, made from the flesh of the
    globe,
a forest with all that's needed:
a brook, birds, bugs, silence and rustling sounds, winds and
windstorms, leaves small as fingernails,
rabbits, footfalls.
And it seems to him that he's in the forest, seeing and hearing everything.
He's happy.
The globe writhes once more and the plains, the horizons
appear. Nests hidden in the grass, wisps of clouds and
the horizons, unbroken, astounding.
He turns around to see and he's happy. Until he gets a glimpse of the black dot.
It's very tiny,
far away, and that isn't its proper place.
The point moves closer and the horizon, once perfectly round,
looks like an apple now.
The man wakes up, stunned and worn out. He opens the window, takes

a gulp of fresh air. In the street, a dwarf old man
is tramping by, tramping

                                    toward the center of town.

translated by Adam J. Sorkin and the poet

Roberto Carifi

Born in Pistoia, Italy, in 1948, the Italian poet Roberto Carifi lives there still. This untitled poem argues that the things of this world participate in our affairs of the heart, that they feel along with us as we suffer the disappointments of our human relationships.

UNTITLED

Things don't forget;
their memories are too strong.
This window remembers us
back when it was closed, how it protected
our bodies, how it let the air
whisper through, wrap itself around you.
Who knows if it saw the imminent threat,
who knows if the window wept!
And we endure, in things.
They speak, they critique us,
especially when a lamp is lit
and raised by an unknown hand.
Who knows if things weep,
if this chill isn't really their nostalgia.
Do you remember, room, how we waited for her?
And you, worn notebook, window, door,
and you, chair, who hold her form,
or terrace, my suspended likeness,
did you anticipate her return in vain?

translated by Oonagh Stransky

Jose Manuel del Pino

The Spanish poet Manuel del Pino describes his poetry as embodying three themes com-
mon to almost all verse: love, death, and a reflection on the poetic endeavor itself. This
poem reconsiders the story of Samson and Delilah, the archetypal parable of the power of
a woman to render a man helpless. The poet here imagines what Samson might have been
thinking as he brought down the temple after regaining his strength.

DORÉ V

It was Delilah who mercilessly
dealt Samson so great a blow
in cutting off the mane of his strength.
Like a bull drained of blood or a yoked ox,
he pushed the wooden bar, having no hope for color.
His suffering not being able to gaze upon
her perfect face or round breasts
surpassed the pain in his solitary sockets.
And so Samson was a child, a helpless telamon;
like an infirm tiger he became ferocious only
when making the buckets on the squeaky waterwheel turn round.
Humiliated each morning, he was a slave of the treadmill and the days.
Astonishment blinded his mind, he could hardly understand
her betrayal; he, the strong, sweet lover,
destroyed, sentenced to the beam.

On the day of the Lord his pride split open
a thousand heads.
They took him from his cell, bound, displaying
his renewed black locks,
and pushed him toward the ceremony
where, between two cyclopean columns,
his power overtaking him, he remembered times past.
An incessant mocking hit his ears
just as his muscles
heatedly flexed anew,
and the stony trunks gave way beneath his effort.
The screaming was deafening;
a woman stealthily crossed

the bedroom carrying scissors. She was naked,
sated with love. Howling.
His beloved's red hair
covered her defenseless body.

translated by G. J. Racz

Arnljot Eggen

The Norwegian poet Arnljot Eggen (b. 1923) here plays with the idea that none of us is
self-sufficient. We are an aggregate of qualities and influences, an idea that contradicts the
narrow sense of self-reliant individualism that we—especially men—sometimes assume
and cling to.

HE CALLED HER HIS WILLOW

He called her his willow. Every time he wanted to
bend her, he felt the whiplash.

Among the rich the women are provided with chains of precious
metal. Chains of simpler materials it costs less to break.

One plus one doesn't make one. And sometimes not two either.

Dissatisfaction with each other can come from a suspicion that
two is not enough, that there is a larger community.

Two who in hard times aim their fire at each other have not
yet discovered the common enemy.

He who knowingly lets himself be suppressed is also to blame for
his suppression.

No one would be worth loving if we were not more than
ourselves alone.

translated by Nancy Coleman

Kjell Hjern

Kjell Hjern (1916–84) was a native of Gothenburg, Sweden, a life-long freelance writer, art magazine editor, theater and art critic, local historian, and translator and anthologist. In "To My Love," the speaker embraces his lover with all of her inherent faults and porcine characteristics. Has there ever been a more ardently nonsentimental tribute paid to a man's lover?

TO MY LOVE

You have as many defects as a pig has lice and you will rub against me in vain to get rid of them. Your dishonesty is as great as your reputation for honesty, which is also great. I alone know you, my love, and know your measurements and sing your praises in true poetry. Perhaps there are women who are more beautiful than you and who lie less often, but I do not want to exchange you for any of them if I do not have to. Like the pig, you are good throughout, and as long as I am in my right mind, I shall love you with a great and insatiable appetite.

translated by William Jay Smith and Leif Sjöberg

Vladimir Holan

Vladimir Holan was born in Prague in 1905 and died in 1980. "Meeting in a Lift" describes a brief and erotic encounter in an elevator between a man and a woman—does it happen in fact or only in the man's mind? Either way, the poem shines light on a particular form of male erotic fantasy.

MEETING IN A LIFT

We stepped into the lift. The two of us, alone.
We looked at each other and that was all.
Two lives, a moment, fullness, bliss.
At the fifth floor she got out and I went on up
knowing I would never see her again,
that it was a meeting once and for all,
that if I followed her I would be like a dead man in her tracks

and that if she came back to me
it would only be from the other world.

translated by Jarmila and Ian Miher

Vladimir Holan

Poetry lives in the gap between what is said and what is left unsaid. For the late Czech poet
Vladimir Holan, however, what is unsaid is a noncommunication that results in disappoint-
ment and regret.

SHE ASKED YOU

A girl asked you: What is poetry?
You wanted to say to her: You are too, ah yes, you are
and that in fear and wonder,
which prove the miracle,
I'm jealous of your beauty's ripeness,
and because I can't kiss you nor sleep with you,
and because I have nothing and whoever has nothing to give
must sing . . .

But you didn't say it, you were silent
and she didn't hear the song.

translated by Jarmila and Ian Miher

Tasos Leivaditis

Tasos Leivaditis was born in 1922 in Athens. Author of over twenty books of poetry, his
work has been translated into a dozen languages. It's tempting to read this minimalist dia-
logue between a man and a woman as an archetypal exchange between Man and Woman. Is
Leivaditis suggesting that the capacity to "fall asleep" (that is, live an "unawakened life") is
equally shared by both sexes?

ETERNAL DIALOGUE

And the man said: I am hungry.
And the woman placed bread on the table.
And the man ate. And the woman gazed at him constantly.
And the woman said: You are strong but I do not fear you.
And the man said: You are beautiful but I fear you.
And the man pointed to their bed.
And the woman ascended it as if ready for sacrifice.
And the man said: I am thirsty.
And the woman gave him her breast to drink.
And the man touched her. And the woman was repaid.
And the woman leaned her head to his side.
And the man stared into the distance.
And the man said: I would like to be a god.
And the woman said: In a while I shall give birth.
And the woman fell asleep.
And the man fell asleep.

And it dawned a new day.

translated by Minas Savvas

Virgil Mihaiu

Virgil Mihaiu was born in 1951 in Cluj, Romania. He is an essayist and jazz critic as well as a poet. Though "The Ultimate Luxury Woman" can certainly be read ironically, the poem retains its strong flavor of political incorrectness. The speaker fantasizes the perfect woman, objectified with all the erotic trappings of our age, contained and possessed by the male—at least for the duration of the poem.

THE ULTIMATE LUXURY WOMAN

I keep you locked up in a black display cabinet
You're hyperactive
You're woman-as-object
I could calm you down
I could turn you on

You could climb the staircase to
Your private office
With your elongated silhouette
Focused in sharp relief
I'd guide you with
A golden leash
You'd be wearing a touch of makeup
Your décolletage plunging deep down
To the source of fever
A cleavage through all
Your clothes
A laser beam cleaving
Your memory with scenes from
Our common post-adolescence
You—a promise of
The perfect woman's body
Put in its place

translated by Adam J. Sorkin and Liviu Bleoca

Czeslaw Milosz

Czeslaw Milosz was born in the Lithuanian village of Šeteiniai in 1911. A Nobel laureate, he is one of the truly seminal writers of our modern era. He is professor emeritus of Slavic Languages and Literatures at the University of California, Berkeley. From a somewhat lofty perspective, though one full of compassion and understanding, the poet celebrates the coming together of a man and woman, whose love for each other is, after all, an echo of divine love and has the power to transform the "peeling porticoes" of this ordinary world.

AFTER PARADISE

Don't run anymore. Quiet. How softly it rains
On the roofs of the city. How perfect
All things are. Now, for the two of you
Waking up in a royal bed by a garret window.
For a man and a woman. For one plant divided
Into masculine and feminine which longed for each other.
Yes, this is my gift to you. Above ashes
On a bitter, bitter earth. Above the subterranean

Echo of clamorings and vows. So that now at dawn
You must be attentive: the tilt of a head,
A hand with a comb, two faces in a mirror
Are only forever once, even if unremembered,
So that you watch what is, though it fades away,
And are grateful every moment for your being.
Let that little park with greenish marble busts
In the pearl-gray light, under a summer drizzle,
Remain as it was when you opened the gate.
And the street of tall peeling porticoes
Which this love of yours suddenly transformed.

translated by the poet and Robert Hass

Pentti Saarikoski

Pentti Saarikoski (1937–83) was one of Finland's most influential poets, the author of numerous books, and an influential translator of important Western texts into his native language. Here a man describes a woman as a kind of natural force, both his inspiration and his undoing. The paradox is an ambivalence many men feel.

UNTITLED

I lived in a ruin called The Lion
a woman sat on the floor
her breasts were watching me

Woman a region
a place of birds
with lips down below like willowleaves
L'amor che move il sole e l'altre stelle

I wrote a justified apocalypse
an ungodly play
I was dead
Christ dwindled to a fish
and a flashing eye

translated by Herbert Lomas

Marin Sorescu

Marin Sorescu (1936–97) was born in Romania. The author of some ten books, he was well known as a poet, novelist, playwright, and essayist. Here he gives the Don Juan legend a contemporary twist. Women want to get revenge on Don Juan for his excessive womanizing, but he has given up pursuing them; instead of killing him, they are poisoning their husbands and loved ones. Moral: a woman can't put down men generally without impacting those men who are closest to her.

DON JUAN (AFTER HE'D CONSUMED TONS OF LIPSTICK . . .)

After he'd consumed tons of lipstick,
The women,
Cheated of their holiest expectations,
Discovered a means of revenging themselves
On Don Juan.

Each morning,
Before the mirror,
When they've penciled on their eyebrows,
They paint their lips
With rat poison,
They daub rat poison on their hair,
On white shoulders, on eyes, on thoughts,
On breasts,
And they wait.

They show themselves white on balconies,
They search through parks,
But Don Juan, as though forewarned,
Has turned into a bookworm in the library.

He caresses only rare books
And a bevy of paperbacks,
But never anything bound in skin.
Dust on old second-hand volumes

Now seems more refined to him
Than perfume in the boudoir.

So the women go on waiting for him.
Poisoned in all five senses—they wait.
And if Don Juan were to lift his eyes
From his new obsession,
Every day he'd see through the library window
How another loving husband is buried,
Accidentally killed by friendly fire
While kissing his wife
In the line of duty.

translated by Adam J. Sorkin

Mustafa Ziyalan

Mustafa Ziyalan was born in 1959 in Zonguldak, Turkey. He is a graduate of the University of Istanbul in medicine. He currently works as a psychiatrist in New York City. The speaker below sees the archetypal woman embodied in one woman observed briefly on a bus—a mysterious, enigmatic figure of great sensitivity and fragility, one who is too good for the misery of this world.

NIGHT RIDE ON 21

There she sits, cross-legged
like a drop from the full moon
which would burst
if you would touch it with something
other than the tip of your tongue.

The bus will stop when she leaves
and remain like a skull
forgotten in the desert night.

There she is, her ankles
too fragile for these roads

her heart too big
too big for our backstabbing misery.

The breeze which sweeps
the red-hot emptiness, she is
and she leaves.

translated by the poet

Africa

Chinua Achebe

Chinua Achebe was born in 1930 in Ogidi, Nigeria, into an Ibo and Christian family. He
achieved world renown as the author of the seminal African novel and modern world classic
Things Fall Apart. "Love Cycle" is an aubade, a morning poem in which lovers lament the
coming of the new day because it brings their lovemaking to an end. The poem is deeply
gendered: the sun is masculine, earth is feminine, and as the day progresses the man moves
further away from the glow of making love and more deeply into the workaday world, with
its labor and its hostility. But the night promises another cycle of love, which is seen as a
manifestation of feminine power.

LOVE CYCLE

At dawn slowly
the Sun withdraws his
long misty arms of
embrace. Happy lovers

whose exertions leave
no aftertaste nor slush
of love's combustion; Earth
perfumed in dewdrop
fragrance wakes

to whispers of
soft-eyed light . . .

         Later he
will wear out his temper
ploughing the vast acres
of heaven and take it

out on her in burning
darts of anger. Long
accustomed to such caprice
she waits patiently for

evening when thoughts
of another night will
restore his mellowness
and her power
over him.

Kojo Laing

Kojo Laing was born in 1946 in Kumasi, Ghana, and was educated in Ghana and Scotland.
He is a past secretary of the Institute of African Studies at the University of Ghana, Legon,
and longtime head of St. Anthony, a private school founded by his mother. The Ghanaian
poet here creates a speaker, a recently dead husband, who communicates to his less-than-
mournful wife, criticizing her for her failings and acknowledging his own. The funniest no-
tion in this poem is peculiarly male: the speaker imagines he is survived by his erect penis.

I AM THE FRESHLY DEAD HUSBAND

I am the freshly dead husband,
I write my death to a fashionable wife:
Dear Dede with the new-bought guarantees, Dede
with the obsession to push hurriedly some
shared memories into my crowded box, crowded
with the two parts of me that were still alive:
        brain and popylonkwe
            still vibrant above the desolation of my other parts,
                above the rotting of my stylish wrists.
I was not properly dead,
I could hear you chat prettily as I lay in state . . .

and what a state, involving an accident
with a supertobolo girlfriend still alive . . .
With a funeral cloth of the best style, paid
from the breathless anticipation of my retiring benefits.
Boxes and benefits, hearts and betrayal, ginnnnn!
How can you mourn me!
To shed tears you had to borrow
from the sorrow of your father's funeral
held last year, when I couldn't cry.
Together my actions and your inventions pushed
all grief to the children who,
not knowing any better, loved my carefree syncopations.
Dede with the black-brown eyes
whose shades were deeper in the left eye, I
salute your show of courageous grief when
you convinced my mother of the authenticity of your tears!
Bless you, your grief was becoming so successful
that you were, with decorum, fantastically enjoying my death.
I am dead but hungry for guavas . . .
I foolishly imagined the rainbow,
with its inappropriate joy,
torn from a sky that never gave me any sign till I was dead.
Dede, don't let them push my hearse so fast, have
a little posthumous consideration
for my erection of the after-life:
a dead man can't go to God with his popylonkwe at attention.
God forgive your speed
for you want to disgrace me before the ancestors!
Hurrying to bury me . . .
hey wait, the erection still stands . . .
was the horror for my mother, whose
tears, so bewildered, could not quite reach me
in my wooden flagless castle . . . she
was beginning to sense a picnic atmosphere,
demure girls danced in their walk by my grey skin
now spiritual at last, at last.
And I wish my funeral would panic!
Dede, I agree I often betrayed you, usually
just at the point when you were

simultaneously betraying me, I
imprisoned you in my successes and excesses,
I took your gin and doubled it.
As I speak these words,
fresh ants crawl over me with their white eggs, I
noiselessly knock and bite my coffin! For
it is too tight for me to wear, I need a different size!
Dede, help me, I demand air-conditioning, I need
the coolness now that you never gave me! But
your back is turned, you adjust your duku in the mirror.
You look in great fashion by my rotting chin.
Did you really have to try so hard
to stop yourself from laughing, as
you realised that I was dreaming
about being buried next to that girl that I REALLY loved!??
And she did burst out laughing as the last dust covered me . . .
And her laughter said: I was truthful about all my boxed lies.
Yes, but I will write again!
I see the ginnnnn of resurrection glass to glass!

Taban lo Liyong

Taban lo Liyong was born in the Sudan and raised in Uganda. He participated in the Honors Program of Howard University and graduated from the University of Iowa Writers' Workshop. He has taught internationally in Kenya, Papua New Guinea, Australia, Japan, and South Africa. This segment from a longer poem takes an imaginative leap and presents the poet as a woman, sexually unsatisfied, angry with her husband for his deeply unconscious sense of privilege and superiority. Does the male poet recognize himself in the woman's description of how men are?

55

I do not mind the embrace
I do not mind the kiss.
You can in fact now do anything with me.
I am already weak—
    the veil is gone
    the hair has tumbled in disarray

my nipples are turgid
my private part is already wet—
In fact, to leave me in midstream is bad enough.

But, it is afterwards—
when you've squeezed out your last drop
when you're snoring your satisfied head off
when, as Aristotle says, you've purged your emotion
That my hell begins:
my curling up like a centipede
my vulva squeezing and yawning . . .
my refusal to see your face again
my detestation of man for prevailing over me
my self-hatred for having let myself go
my self-hatred for having failed myself yet again . . .
It is afterwards that my torture begins.

Taban lo Liyong

The charm of this poem by the Ugandan poet Taban lo Liyong may derive largely from its flat-footed obviousness.

60

Sisters-in-law are a tribe apart:
Presumptuous, impetuous, erratic, they behave as if they are
also married to you.
Genetically hewn from the same flower and pod as your wife
With features, voice quality, stench or smell, gait or hesitancy
that drew you to their sister
They are, more or less.

Play not with them, at least don't extend the play too far:
The result may be a pregnancy or worse.

South America

Antonio Cisneros

Born in Lima in 1942, Antonio Cisneros is a widely published Peruvian poet. This simple dedicatory poem reaffirms his undying love for his wife, despite any changes in circumstances. In men, this kind of steadfastness is rarely noticed.

DEDICATORY (TO MY WIFE)

I think of a wineglass
and of a book
by Dawson about China
and of a crimson tower.
I love you. And I don't love you
because of the wine,
the book about China,
the crimson tower.
Nor will I stop loving you
if the wine is sour,
the book, boring,
and they bury me
beneath that crimson tower.

translated by Carol A. Klee

Carlos Drummond de Andrade

Carlos Drummond de Andrade (1902–87) was born in a small mining town in Brazil, in the state of Minas Gerais. As a young man Drummond was influenced by modernism and by a growing sense of Brazilian national identity, which gave rise to his uniquely Brazilian aesthetic. He is widely regarded as one of Brazil's great modern writers. In this ballad, he takes a historical excursion through the various roles men have played, especially in relation to women. While the violence and suffering he associates with men does not glorify the past, the literal Hollywood ending he gives the poem makes us question the superficiality of masculinity in the present.

BALLAD OF LOVE THROUGH THE AGES

From the beginning of time,
I liked you, you liked me.
I was Greek, you were Trojan,
Trojan but not Helen.
I sprung from a wooden horse
to kill your brother.
I killed, we quarreled, we died.

I became a Roman soldier,
persecutor of Christians.
At the catacomb door
I met you again.
But when I saw you fall
naked in the Colosseum
and the lion coming toward you,
I made a desperate leap
and the lion ate us both.

Next I was a Moorish pirate,
the scourge of Tripoli.
I set fire to the frigate
where you were hiding from
the fury of my brigantine.
But when I went to grab you
and take you as my slave,
you crossed yourself and drove
a dagger through your heart.
I killed myself as well.

Later on, in happier days,
I was a courtier at Versailles,
clever and debauched.
You dreamed of being a nun . . .
I vaulted over the convent wall

but difficult politics
led us to the guillotine.

These days I'm totally modern:
dancing, jogging, working out.
And I have money in the bank.
And you're a fabulous blonde:
dancing, jogging, working out.
None of it pleases your father.
But after a thousand reversals,
I, one of Paramount's heroes,
give you a hug, a kiss, and we marry.

translated by Mark Strand

Oscar Hahn

Oscar Hahn was born in Chile in 1938. He teaches Hispanic American literature at the University of Iowa. "Good Night Dear" is a bitter, angry invective. The saying goes that "Hell hath no fury like a woman scorned," but this poem suggests that some scorned men can give a woman a run for her money.

GOOD NIGHT DEAR

Good night dear
may you dream with demons
and white cockroaches

and may you see eye-sockets
of death looking at you
from my eyes in flames

and let it not be a dream

translated by James Hoggard

Oscar Hahn

It is unclear whether Oscar Hahn's "Little Phantoms" is a poem of regret or a poem of fierce distancing. Does the speaker mourn a failed relationship or merely assert the fact of his and his lover's childlessness? The poem claims a reality for what never happened, and never will, and that phantom reality reaches into our ordinary world. Fearful, too, is the knock at the door, in a place where door knocks have an ominous history beyond welcomed visits from friends and family.

LITTLE PHANTOMS

Our children my love
are little phantoms

I listen to them laughing in the garden
I hear them playing in the empty room

And if someone knocks at the door
they run to hide under my sheet

the little phantoms

the children we never had
and never will have

translated by James Hoggard

Oscar Hahn

Oscar Hahn is one of Chile's most original poets and a master of understatement. This deceptively simple poem is written in the voice of a man stood up on a date, his expectations for a romantic and intimate evening transformed into feelings of disappointment, abandonment, perhaps even betrayal and despair.

CANDLELIGHT DINNER

I look at the night through the window
I look at the building's parking slots

I see two lights approaching
and they stop beside my car

Anxious I light the candles
and put on your favorite song

But no one knocks at the door
no one knocks at the door
no one knocks at the door

translated by James Hoggard

Sergio Kisielewsky

Sergio Kisielewsky was born in Buenos Aires in 1957 and is one of the founders of the Argentine literary movement called "The Forty." "Cough Drops" portrays both men and women as complicit in one man's betrayal of another. The narrator is betrayed by his friend, his father, and his girlfriend. He needs to learn to get along in the world "without a heart."

COUGH DROPS

Bitch opened the tent fly
and found Mario kissing my girlfriend.
Mario was my friend,
and my girlfriend had ditched me.

The next night
bitch came back to the tent
and saw my father
raping my girlfriend.

Bitch took off with my soul
to a soccer field,

kicked it around like a ball.
It's not yours anymore, she told me.
Get along without a heart.

translated by John Oliver Simon

Marco Martos

Marco Martos was born in Piura, Peru, in 1942. He was codirector of the magazine *Hip-
ocrita Lector*. In "Casti Connubi," a long-term marriage is portrayed as tedious, boring, full
of dully repeated sex, and characterized by a mysterious and minimizing image at the end
of the poem.

CASTI CONNUBI

Every morning, man and wife, seated and washed,
eating their toast, munching of mice,
reading the papers, swatting the flies,
talking about the weather, every morning,
they wait for night, sexual tedium,
to pretend they're asleep, to pretend they're awake,
to tell themselves words out of books about love,
every morning, man and wife,
they go off to work, come back home, eat their lunch,
they go off to work, come back home, go to bed,
fat, shiny, years full of years,
they wait for night, devouring toast,
slaughtering flies, demolishing papers,
annihilating the weather, every morning, fat,
clowns, they wait for night, sexual tedium,
to pretend they're asleep, to pretend they're awake,
to tell themselves words out of books about love,
eating their toast, munching of mice,
every morning, mouse and mouse, mice, mice, mice.

translated by Margaret Greer

Central America and the Caribbean

Lord Kitchener

In this wry bit of calypso, Lord Kitchener (b. 1922) from Trinidad, one of the Carribean's most renowned calypsonians, demonstrates the power of his music to convert the uniniti-ated. The "tourist dame" of the first stanza is acting like a native islander by the end of the poem.

MISS TOURIST

A tourist dame,
I met her the night she came,
She curiously
Asking about my country,
She said, "I heard about bacchanal
And the Trinidad carnival,
So I come to jump in the fun
And I want you tell me how it is done."
    I say, "Doudou come in town Jou'vert* morning;
    Find youself in a band,
    Watch the way how the natives moving;
    Hug up tight with ah man,
    Sing along with the tunes they playing,
    And now and again you shouting
    'Play mas!† Carnival!'
    Miss tourist, that is bacchanal."

The following day
We went to Maracas Bay.
Every step we walk
She start with this Jou'vert talk.
She said, "Kitch, from what I've been told,
Carnival is out of this world.
Just the thought is worrying my brain:

Well, let me hear that lesson again!"
    I say, "Doudou, *etc.*"

Jou'vert morn
You'll swear that is here she born!
We holding hand,
Jumping in a Jou'vert band.
When the rhythm hot up the pace,
She say, "Play mas'" shaking she waist,
"Kitch, will you phone Hotel Normandie
And tell them don't leave no breakfast for me."
    I say, "Doudou, *etc.*"

She turn and say,
"Kitch, I now feel to break away!"
She say, "Come on, man!"
And drag me in front the band!
Mama, when we reach Independence Square,
She kick and she raise she dress in the air,
Bawling, "Becchenel! Becchenel!
I am the Queen of the Kenevel!"

Jou'vert or *Jour ouvert* (pronounced 'joo-vay') is Carnival Monday morning, the start of the main two-day festivities.

†*mas*—carnival (from "masquerade").

Roberto Fernández Retamar

Roberto Fernández Retamar was born in 1930 in Havana and studied in Paris and London. He has published numerous books of poetry and literary studies and has been an editor and director of some of Cuba's important journals and publishing houses. In this romantic, mystical poem, when the narrator sees a man and a woman together on the street, he is thrown into a moment of pure seeing, of recognition of love and—perhaps more importantly—its rarity and preciousness.

A MAN AND A WOMAN

> Who must there be?
> A man and a woman.
> —Tirso

If a man and a woman happen down streets that no one else notices,
Back streets where night is about to fall and the wind is rising,
The landscape beyond, both new and old, more like music than landscape;
If a man and a woman cause trees to spring up at their step,
And walls to burst into flame,
And make heads turn as if surprised by the sudden blast of a trumpet
Or the gaudy colors of a circus parade;
If when a man and a woman approach the neighborhood chatter falls silent,
The sidewalk rocking chairs cease their rocking, corner keychains no longer swing

And tired breath becomes a sigh,
Is it because love so rarely passes by that to see it
Brings wonder, shock, astonishment, nostalgia,
As if one heard a language perhaps once known
Which the tongue scarcely remembers
Except as whispers and the remains of whispers?

translated by Mark Weiss

Jaime Sabines

Jaime Sabines (1926–99) was born in Chiapas, Mexico. Before turning to the serious study of literature, he spent three years as a medical student. He also participated in politics, becoming the federal deputy for the state of Chiapas from 1976 to 1979 and eventually for the federal district in 1988. W. S. Merwin's translation of "I Love You at Ten in the Morning" reveals the painful, inevitable—yet joyful and potentially fulfilling—playing out of the primal male-female relationship with its frightening and exhilarating combination of the known and the mysterious.

I love you at ten in the morning, at eleven, at twelve noon. I love you with my whole soul and my whole body, sometimes, on rainy afternoons. But at two in the afternoon, or at three, when I start to think about the two of us, and you thinking about dinner or the day's work, or the amusements you don't have, I start to hate you with a dull hatred, with half of the hatred that I reserve for myself.

Then I go back to loving you, when we go to bed and I feel that you are made for me, that in some way your knee and your belly are telling me that, that my hands are assuring me of that, and that there is nowhere I can come to or go to that is better than your body. The whole of you comes to meet me and for a moment we both disappear, we put ourselves into the mouth of God, until I tell you that I am hungry or sleepy.

Every day I love you and hate you irreparably. And there are days, besides, there are hours, in which I don't know you, in which you are as strange to me as somebody else's wife. Men worry me, I worry about myself, my troubles bewilder me. Probably there is a long time when I don't think about you at all. So you see. Who could love you less than I do, my love?

translated by W. S. Merwin

North America

Leonard Cohen

Leonard Cohen was born in 1934 in Montreal, Quebec. Cohen was one of the most influential and popular Canadian writers in the 1960s and has won many awards throughout his lifetime, both for his poetry and his song lyrics. "Suzanne," that signature song of the sixties, remains one of the most compelling examples of the romanticization of the feminine. For many males of Cohen's generation and later, Suzanne lives as the embodiment of the ultimately desirable and unattainable woman.

SUZANNE

Suzanne takes you down to
Her place near the river
You can hear the boats go by
You can spend the night beside her
And you know that she's half crazy
But that's why you want to be there
And she feeds you tea and oranges
That come all the way from China
And just when you mean to tell her
That you have no love to give her
Then she gets you on her wavelength
And she lets the river answer
That you've always been her lover
And you want to travel with her
And you want to travel blind
And you know that she will trust you
For you've touched her perfect body with your mind.

And Jesus was a sailor
When he walked upon the water
And he spent a long time watching
From his lonely wooden tower
And when he knew for certain
Only drowning men could see him
He said "All men will be sailors then
Until the sea shall free them"
But he himself was broken
Long before the sky would open
Forsaken, almost human
He sank beneath your wisdom like a stone
And you want to travel with him
And you want to travel blind
And you think maybe you'll trust him
For he's touched your perfect body with his mind.

Now Suzanne takes your hand
And she leads you to the river

She is wearing rags and feathers
From Salvation Army counters
And the sun pours down like honey
On our lady of the harbour
And she shows you where to look
Among the garbage and the flowers
There are heroes in the seaweed
There are children in the morning
They are leaning out for love
And they will lean that way forever
While Suzanne holds the mirror
And you want to travel with her
And you want to travel blind
And you know that you can trust her
For she's touched your perfect body with her mind.

Galway Kinnell

Galway Kinnell was born in 1927 and lives in New Hampshire and New York. His many books of poetry have won virtually all the important literary prizes in the United States. In "The Perch," two lovers walk through the woods in winter. A shot rings out. A deer is probably killed. The narrator is reminded of the senseless violence men commit, but the moment is redeemed in the eye contact between him and his lover, his memory of their making love, and the image of a man and a woman together that elevates life and softens the journey from cradle to grave.

THE PERCH

There is a fork in a branch
of an ancient, enormous maple,
one of a grove of such trees,
where I climb sometimes and sit and look out
over miles of valleys and low hills.
Today on skis I took a friend
to show her the trees. We set out
down the road, turned in at
the lane which a few weeks ago,
when the trees were almost empty

and the November snows had not yet come,
lay thickly covered in bright red
and yellow leaves, crossed the swamp,
passed the cellar hole holding
the remains of the 1850s farmhouse
that had slid down into it by stages
in the thirties and forties, followed
the overgrown logging road
and came to the trees. I climbed up
to the perch, and this time looked
not into the distance but at
the tree itself, its trunk
contorted by the terrible struggle
of that time when it had its hard time.
After the trauma it grows less solid.
It may be some such time now comes upon me.
It would have to do with the unaccomplished,
and with the attempted marriage
of solitude and happiness. Then a rifle
sounded, several times, quite loud,
from across the valley, percussions
of the custom of male mastery
over the earth—the most graceful,
most alert of the animals
being chosen to die. I looked
to see if my friend had heard,
but she was stepping about on her skis,
studying the trees, smiling to herself,
her lips still filled, for all
we had drained them, with hundreds
and thousands of kisses. Just then
she looked up—the way, from low
to high, the god blesses—and the blue
of her eyes shone out of the black
and white of bark and snow, as lovers
who are walking on a freezing day
touch icy cheek to icy cheek,
kiss, then shudder to discover
the heat waiting inside their mouths.

Charles Simic

Charles Simic was born in 1938 in Yugoslavia. A recipient of the Pulitzer Prize for Poetry and MacArthur Foundation Fellowship, he teaches English at the University of New Hampshire. A simple cookout among friends provides the poet the opportunity to observe men's responses to the "secret" conversations their wives have between themselves. The poem's startling last image reminds us that in regard to power between males and females, both sides can make more than adequate claims.

AT THE COOKOUT

The wives of my friends
Have the air
Of having shared a secret.
Their eyes are lowered
But when we ask them
What for
They only glance at each other
And smile,
Which only increases our desire
To know . . .

Something they did
Long ago,
Heedless of the consequences
That left
Such a lingering sweetness?

Is that the explanation
For the way
They rest their chins
In the palms of their hands,
Their eyes closed
In the summer heat?

Come tell us,
Or give us a hint.
Trace a word or just a single letter

In the wine
Spilled on the table.

No reply. Both of them
Lovey-dovey
With the waning sunlight
And the evening breeze
On their faces.

The husbands drinking
And saying nothing,
Dazed and mystified as they are
By their wives' power
To give
And take away happiness,
As if their heads
Were crawling with snakes.

Quincy Troupe

Quincy Troupe was born in 1943 in New York City and grew up in St. Louis. He was professor of creative writing and American literature at the University of California, San Diego, and currently lives in New York. "Change" captures a feeling many men experience but few discuss. When a new child enters the picture, a husband may feel the first pangs of a jealous rivalry with his son for the attentions and affections of his wife.

CHANGE

for Margaret & Porter

use to be eye would be laying there
in margaret's lap, longside her sweet
soft thighs, on sunday mornings, sipping
champagne, sucking on her soft, open lips
drinking in the love from her moist, brown eyes
now, porter's there, giggling, twenty month old
squirming squeals—a tiny, spitting image of me—
his eyes kissing everyone, including me, & me?

well, eye'm sitting here, apart from them
hungry, alone, in my favorite chair
watching television
& watching them, watching me

Al Zolynas

Al Zolynas was born in Austria in 1945 of Lithuanian parents. He has lived in Germany,
Australia, and, since 1960, the United States. He is the author of a number of books of
poetry—and coeditor of this anthology—and teaches at Alliant International University in
San Diego, California.

WHISTLING WOMAN

What new woman is this?
What twenty-first century
phenomen-*a!?*
Bopping along,
her thick-heeled boots
whomp the pavement,
snug pedal pushers,
exposed midriff, silver stud
in her out-y belly button.

What complex and virtuoso
trills and whistle-yodels,
what inter-melodic
jazz riffs and glissandos!

This confident, extroverted
young female striding
the postmodern urban landscape—
she picked the right
new century to whistle
the world's attention
onto herself.

Myth, Archetypes, and Spirituality

He couldn't separate what he'd chosen
from what had chosen him
—Stephen Dunn

In *The Power of Myth,* Joseph Campbell writes, "The images of myth are reflections of the spiritual potentialities of every one of us. Through contemplating these, we evoke their powers in our own lives." Poets seem to sense this intuitively, and knowingly or not, their poems earn them and their readers a measure of power. This power, of course, is not the power of the everyday world, with its ambitions and requirements for livelihood, domestic duties, and its demands for successes of one sort or another. Rather, it's the quiet power of coming to some understanding or acceptance of the mysteries of life.

Some poems function archetypally, trying to catch something of the universal, as in Jamaican poet Evan Jones's poem "Genesis," in which he sees God's creation of human beings as a "flourish to his signature," a capstone creation to the manifest universe. Nonetheless, that sense of incompleteness and yearning so common to human beings is presented in the poem as "the dimensions lost / Transferring from eternity to time." He explains our human dilemma and predicament—the nagging "gap between the intended and the done / The utter sadness of magnificence not quite"—as a necessary condition.

On a related theme, Dennis Scott presents time in the image of an avuncular spider-man who slowly spins his web around us all. To know that we cannot escape time is—at least momentarily through the agency of the poem—to experience the timeless or the eternal. The best myths allow us that: the full acknowledgment of our human frailties and the felt experience of something larger or transcendent.

In their modernity, not all poets are as accepting of older mythological views. In a wry postmodern twist to the archetype of the "return," American poet Stephen Dunn gives us a version of Odysseus most males can relate to: a man who wants it— and will have it—both ways; he will have his adventures, and he will have his faithful Penelope awaiting his homecoming. Or so he thinks. The Indonesian poet Chairil

Anwar expresses the particularly modern love-hate relationship to Divinity that many feel these days: "Afterwards He burned in my breast. / All my strength struggles to extinguish Him." Oswald Mbuyiseni Mtshali from South Africa reminds us that "God is / that crippled beggar / sprawling at the street corner" and that "Hell is / the hate flickering / in your eye." And Peter Reading of England writes of the mysterious and unfathomable workings of fate, how we are all in the hands of what he names a "random Weird" that shapes our days and lives. In a tongue-in-cheek poem, Canadian Howard White evokes images of the tough men of bygone generations, extolling their heroic virtues and strengths while at the same time poking a little fun at their innocence and lack of awareness.

Directly or indirectly, these poems acknowledge the presence of something larger in the lives of men—call it fate, chance, spirit—that propels them onward and compels them to re-create and reflect on its trials and gifts. Between the ideal of manhood and its actuality, there is almost always a substantial gap. These poets are chroniclers of that gap.

Asia

Chairil Anwar

Chairil Anwar (1922–49) was an Indonesian poet who lived wildly and died young, and had a profound influence on Indonesian postcolonial poetry. For some Muslim men, one of the attractions of the faith is the promise of erotic fulfillment in the afterlife. But why postpone pleasure? asks Chairil Anwar; after all, the beautiful women of the real world may be more enticing and reliable.

HEAVEN

Like my mother, and my grandmother too,
plus seven generations before them,
I also seek admission to Heaven
which the Moslem party and the Mohammedan

Union say has rivers of milk
And thousands of houris* all over.

But there's a contemplative voice inside me,
stubbornly mocking: Do you really think
the blue sea will go dry
—and what about the sly temptations waiting in every port?
Anyway, who can say for sure
that there really are houris there
with voices as rich and husky as Nina's, with eyes
that flirt like Yati's!

translated by Burton Raffel

houris—the beautiful nymphs of the Moslem paradise, among the rewards of faithful Moslems.

Chairil Anwar

In this ironic and fierce poem, the speaker sees himself in a supreme struggle with God, who is envisioned traditionally as great male father, the one to oppose and not give into, even if it means the destruction of both.

AT THE MOSQUE

I shouted at Him
Until He came

We met face to face.

Afterwards He burned in my breast.
All my strength struggles to extinguish Him

My body, which won't be driven, is soaked with sweat

This room

Is the arena where we fight

Destroying each other
One hurling insults, the other gone mad.

translated by Burton Raffel

Tsujii Takashi

Tsujii Takashi is the pen name of Tsutsumi Seiji, an influential Japanese businessman and leader. He has won a number of Japan's prestigious poetry awards. Takashi's *Disappearance of the Butterfly* includes several poems about women engaged in various activities—singing, wandering, printing, writing in their journals. Each poem ends with a surprise transformation. The woman in this poem clearly seems archetypal. Yet the poem also suggests that the days of woman as archetype may well be numbered.

WOMAN SINGING

The singing woman moves upstream on the river of night
her voice her oar   she sweeps away time
Twisting her body she shoots her eyes upwards aslant
No stars are to be seen
the sound of the wind has died
The water splashes noise
and around her dress   artificial light clamors
The town's shadows sway
Rows of listening houses
crouch over hearths she left behind
Even if she laments her captivity
she doesn't know what holds her
so remembering young girls in chorus
or the sound of a dog howling at the moon
will not free her
Inevitably   a song sparkles inside her
and raises fireworks into the darkness
The flow of the river is gentle
and hackneyed phrases   newspaper articles
slowly   without rest   drift toward the sea

For whom was the banquet prepared
Only for those who cannot belong
Knowing she is permitted her song
the woman clasps her hands
and once more raises her voice
Like birds of passage that fly into a beacon lamp and fall
the melody hits a wall and scatters flower petals
The broken musical scales flutter lightly
and fly away into the night sky
In the path of dreams where she is left behind
the woman becomes burnt-out ashes

translated by Robert Brady and Susanne Akemi Wegmüller

The Middle East

Admiel Kosman

Admiel Kosman was born in 1957. He is the author of five books of poetry, a newspaper columnist, and professor of Talmud at Bar Ilan University, Israel. The speaker of "Something Hurts" complains to God about a pain in his side. Is it his sexuality? Is it the pure pain of being a man, of being human? Is it, like Adam's rib, the vestige of the primal pain of separation?

SOMETHING HURTS

Something hurts me here, on the side, do You see, my Lord?
Something swells, sticks out, juts
out, like a broken
finger; out of contemplation, my soul grows
a long horn of misery.

Something hurts me here, on the side, do You see, my Lord?
Loneliness spawns an angle, a sharp protrusion; a spasm
like a long snake grows and emerges
from my back toward the streak of light, and curls on my chest

like a tail that must be cut off, hurry, my Lord,
now. Cut it off and throw it away.

Something hurts me here, on the side, do You see, my Lord?
Clothes do not conceal it. My clumsy movements
only make it more ridiculous. Something hurts me. In the streets
outside revelers dance and in the fields,
wondrous spring. Flowers. Women. Something hurts me here, on the side,
my Lord, aren't you listening?

translated by Lisa Katz

Europe

Risto Ahti

Risto Ahti was born in 1943 in Lahti and lives in Tampere, Finland's largest industrial
town. Many men fall under the spell of the face of their beloved, which haunts their inner
lives long after a relationship ends. This face may also be reminiscent of Rumi's "Beloved,"
the face of a divine, eternal love, or, as Zen teachings say, the face you were "before your
parents' birth."

THE BELOVED'S FACE

Because the greatest of these is love,
and because these are the features of love,
they'll never burn, though the frame burns:
never, through misdoing, amnesia, or mortality,
can you slash or foul this face—

its birth in you means utter forgiveness:
wipe out the world, it will remain.

It was born like a diamond
the earth-mother bore. The house will burn
but not burn this: your void life

slips off, but this face
is never effaced.

translated by Herbert Lomas

Peter Armstrong

Peter Armstrong was born in Blaydon on Tyne, England, in 1957. He trained as a psychi-
atric nurse and has worked as a cognitive therapist in Newcastle. In "Sunderland Nights,"
the narrator learns that an old friend of his has become a priest. He reminisces about their
past lives together and speculates how they each have come to deal with the vagaries of life
in their own distinct ways.

SUNDERLAND NIGHTS

for Maurice Pierce, on hearing of his ordination.

Brother,
        word has come, a grey decade after
our questionable mysteries, that you have put on black.
Pray for us, who, rat-arsed in high-ceilinged bars
dribbled metaphysics into our beer
and wanted women.
                        Remember the stations we kept,
neon or the moon glancing off a wet road,
an east wind harassing
the sad provincial streets. God and alcohol:

I see you hunched over your smoke
and drink. "Tonight I knelt in my room
and repented of my sins"; and me
yelling back across the swamped formica table
my crack-brained marriages of Paul and Sartre.

But let that be,
for now you come to mind I see us
stumbling to some outlying town,
aimless circling speech having petered into silence,
a quick-moving stranger gaining ground behind us.

Mircea Cartarescu

Mircea Cartarescu, born in 1956, has published five books of poetry. He has won major literary awards in Romania and France. In an attempt to describe a single day in his life, the narrator of the following poem seems to take in everything, both the suffering of humanity and its joy, the excitement of life and its boredom. In a long, meandering meditation, he engages us in trying to understand just what happiness is and whether it really is possible.

A HAPPY DAY IN MY LIFE

1
a few days ago
somebody told me on the phone about a sure-fire recipe for happiness.
it's kind of old, but not lacking in interest
because human beings don't live too long
and would like at least to be happy.
you put, he said, your hand on the table, take a hammer and strike at your fingers:
each time you miss, you should be bursting with happiness.
but i am not such a cynic
and would like to tell you something sort of different from this recipe,
namely, a happy day in my life.

2
it was sunday, november the 8th.
at 7 in the morning i was standing in the lobby of my apartment building
and the morning was frozen, the ground was crusty with puddles of frost
the sidewalks were clean, a parked *moskvich* flashed a steamy windshield
boulevard stephan the great was still torn up from the construction like it
had been for the past six months, cables the color of raspberry were
being towed, the street cars were forced to run on a single line
and when they approached through the bluish air
you might get surprised by an out of service wagon
like some kind of an unpainted bus shell
with a hanging noose of some sort mounted on its rear platform.
individuals in vinyl jackets hustled down the sidewalks in front of the store
windows
women with round buttocks showcasing through their overcoats and scarves
around their necks
crossed paths with electricians in silver hats

who clambered up towers of yellow iron to screw on ellipsoid light bulbs of milky
   glass
on top of reinforced concrete pillars.
when i pushed past the corner of my apartment block with the home
appliance store that also fixed television sets
looking to my left i couldn't believe my eyes:
the circus alley was filled with frost
and over it floated steam. above the circus dome
the sky was the color of misty saffron.
my breath was the same color, maybe a little rubier
while the brand new apartment block windows were literally screaming with red
reflecting the huge ruby globe,
which lifted into the pale sky towards *bucur obor.*

3
i crossed through the horridly frozen air towards the new deli
and hopped on the 276, reeking of infected plastic and gasoline
and motor oil and brake fluid
and oily tool boxes. i sat
in the middle of a large spare wheel abandoned in the back
on the rubbery floor, and stared out the window.
a few *dacias* followed us at a docile pace, without ambition.
colentina way was chilly, bleak, gloomy, frozen
ghica-tei park was full of shrubs with rusty leaves
and a hound spotted with black and ash bounded through them for all he
could, in desperation, with astounding swiftness
over the dry alleys and the foggy grass.
you were figuring his spine would snap, the way he arched and crouched.
yellow buses shot ahead of us, and from time to time a limousine or some concrete
   mixer . . .

4
the street-car depot sparkled in the distance.
as for myself, no one crowded me
sitting on my wheel with the brass valve.
i was staring at a girl
about 27, wearing a sort of a short greenish leather jacket
hair combed plainly and lots of golden and silvery rings
on her fingers with painted nails.

she was staring at herself in the window, about 20 centimeters from me, heaps of
     make-up
pretty, though with an odd shape to the lower lip.
i jumped off at the PECO station. there was a huge line of compact and sub-
     compact cars
and the long banners, yellow and blue, with PECO written on them,
thwacked in the wind. the road was now rosy
and the water tower crumbled like glass. the plum trees and the weeds
with black oil stains from the turn-about street-cars
were unrecognizable because of the finger deep frost.
the pipe welding factory
and the bulging hill ahead
were so familiar to me
that i stared through them like through glass things.

5
how entrancing the morning was! bakeries
frosty puddles, the antiseptic air
the industrial odor
the industrial sunrise, constructed as though from tiny screws and rosy nuts,
scattered in the air and on the road
the silence and the yellow dogs sprawled on their bellies
in front of the self-service station painted apparently by a madman
kelly-green and candy-pink
finally the sun, the lungs at rest
everything made you feel, if not happy
because it was still freezing
at least disposed to forgive many things the world in which you lived
and give it, say, yet another century of existence.

6
in front of the dirty school, built in the old style,
the chestnuts shook off their leaves like in animated cartoons:
quickly, as though it were snowing.
not a second went by without the whooshing of 5 or 6 leaves dropping from their
     barren branches
large and yellowish, withered at the edges.
on the ground, heaps and heaps.

in the lobby the green metal file cabinet, the fig tree, the post-cards with the
   voronetz monastery, with the red lake
the light globe on the ceiling, the creme-colored phone
everything was precise, cold, comforting.
blowing out steam
i plugged in the radiator with the two rods
and when the wire curling around the rods became incandescent
i placed it on my desk very close to my face
so that i could feel my eyelashes singeing. i pulled out from my briefcase a book
by krishnamurti. our world

7
he says, is not well made.
it's headed toward catastrophe on account of our technical progress
having been accomplished to the detriment of our real progress
the progress of the human being as a whole.
the world is a flop, while humans are unhappy and afraid
not only of death, but of life
of their own selves, of others.
the brain registers good or evil without any ability to discern between them
and an insult or injury suffered by who knows what or when ancestor
is a scar on our brains now.
we can't live like that anymore, he says.
we must understand our wishes and needs
we must change everything
in order to give our species a chance
to emerge out of this misery.

8
i look out the window, the heat's made me drowsy.
i stare at the spiraling plastic of the phone line.
though things are stupidly simple
they attract me, and make me ashamed of the way i live
of the poetry i write
and i am afraid i am not on the right road.
how much sense does it make, the permanent aesthetic effort, endless inventions
the torment to be new with each line?
the better you write the more you are regarded with indifference, the more
you are isolated

and you have nothing besides the self-reflective pleasure of writing
because the ambition to gain entrance to the history of literature is an idiocy
while to create images . . . voronca, in his late period
said, about his own images: i recall
a few of them, but what's the good of it? . . .
i would like to forget
everything i know about poetry and to write another way
with the brain sensible like the skin on a blind man's finger.
you can't change poetry
if you continue with image and metaphor:
you get tired, disgusted of so much lack of communication
the tv, the comb, the window displays, the phone—
they are the much better poets
who, if they can't make a test tube with tentacles
a graveyard in a bathrobe, leafing through a factory on the sofa
they could at least cause the human being

9
to walk on two paws
to be of two sexes
to wear clothes, go to work
to put on nail polish
to eat rum cake
to make love with someone one shouldn't, out of curiosity or boredom
to not know how to have fun
to haunt the bars and the discos and not to have any fun at all
to get married and have children and still not have fun
to buy blue-jeans and still not have fun
to round up after-shave and cassettes and boom-boxes and still not have fun
to lie between the windows of a hearse and still not have fun
to secure a contract to buy a house and still not have fun
to have illuminations and visions, to speak to the archangels
and still not have fun
to feed the cow and still not have fun
to understand lacan, to publish in *revue roumaine*
to get cured of trichinosis
to fall from the fourth floor
and end up with nothing but a sprained shoulder
to get one's paws on one's best friend's lover

to do everything to her and still not have any fun at all
to fall in love, to never surface all night from under the satin sheets
for fear of UFOs
to go fishing and to go see year in and year out at the *cinemateque*
nothing but buñuel, tarkovski, bergman, fellini
to never have to eat canned fish or soup
to know what asparagus tips are
and oysters like juicy little ears, caviar
and J & B
to smoke only cigarettes upwards of pall-mall
and still not have fun
to be the best writer in the whole continent
or at least in romania
to understand the underpinnings of the great political powers
to play competition level bridge
to have no pimples
and in spite of all these still not have fun
not to know how to have fun
not to know how to be happy
and if you are happy
not to know what good happiness is
to not recognize it
to hate it
to go to the butcher's to have it cut out
like a tumor in a shameful zone of the body
like a fibroma splashing inside the brain.
it's possible to end up like this.

10
in fact, i can't say i give too much of a damn
if humans know how to be happy or not.
i only wanted to describe a happy day in my life.
what i wrote above are just happy thoughts in the course of a happy day.
on the field in the school's courtyard
a few children in red sweat suits played soccer. the cleaning lady
set a heap of dead leaves on fire
and two little boys shoved sticks into a polyethylene bag
thrusting it into the tongues of the flames, to get it to curl
to sizzle and to drip here and there

big drops of burning plastic.

at one i went home swimming back through the city the color of tobacco, more
    motley now

than the morning, and sunnier . . .

11

to make a long story short, at lunch i listened to a lot of music

i had recorded a cassette from a pink floyd album, very soothing

you could go to sleep to it, and dream nice dreams:

little blue clouds over factories with barred windows

little pigs and other gentle animals

which are nice to think of

but also a thin strand of blood nearly unseen

from the corner of the wet lips, appetizing, of a fully clothed woman . . .

in the afternoon i went out in the city and saw a movie

simple and with lovely colors, without psychological complications or existential

when i left i was moved, walking by the tobacco shop and the store that fixes
    lighters

in the twilight which backlit the domes of the old buildings, renovated, in the
    center of bucharest

against a mauve luminous background, without any stars.

the cars glided so intelligent, so gentle and wondrous through the coffee colored air

that i nearly started to cry.

in the window display my face reflected a darkish pink.

when bucharest turns to dust, i thought

only ten minutes will pass

when the ramshackle buttresses of this

world collapse.

it will be a tough

ten minutes for them

they will want to collapse on their own.

12

at night, when i turned off the light and closed my eyes

i continued staring at, luminous under my lids

all sorts of trucks and cars, blue and green

cruising down the boulevard.

translated by Julian Semilian and Sanda Agalidi

Carlos Edmundo de Ory

Carlos Edmundo de Ory was born in Cadiz, Spain, in 1923. A major figure in twentieth-century Spanish literature, he has been compared to Allen Ginsberg in his efforts to revitalize tired conventions of Spanish poetry. He currently lives in France. Men are sometimes criticized for being taciturn, for being unable to put their feelings into words. But here the poet finds a palpable poetry for silence, and he makes us "hear" it with a new awareness.

SILENCE

No one's here   I'm alone with the violin of silence
Silence is a murmuring crystal rain
In the silence you can hear the slow steps of a madman
pacing back and forth all alone in a bedroom
I've lost my fingers inside an infinite piano . . .
A phantom piano inside my heart
Silence, silence! I believe silence
is an angel listening to God speak
In silence you can hear autumn leaves falling
You can hear waves and kisses and the magician of time
in his chariot of hours with silk wheels
on a beach humid with laughter and pain
An angel's tongue my heart soaked
in the water of silence with no rhyme nor reason
it wants to sing just like God was singing
Today God's feet trample my green heart

In the rainy afternoon a sexless woman
a woman of air and mist drifts   I go
towards her and she doesn't exist   I only see her eyes
and her mouth and hair   But she doesn't exist
No one's there   I'm alone   My soul is a giant bow
that goes with the violin of silence in a sky of love
I go to the window . . . It's still raining   Still . . .
A bitter woman weeps tonight out of

divine nostalgia for something distant
The rain in the night becomes a blossoming guitar

There is no moon tonight . . . I'll build the moon when I die

translated by Steven J. Stewart

Herbert Gassner

Herbert Gassner was born in 1955 in Zillingtal, Burgenland, now part of Austria. He has been a cultural adviser for the Austro-Yugoslav Society. While fear knows no gender, of course, this poem includes among its list of fears a few male-specific items.

FEAR

fear of the icy moon
fear of the butcher's big knife
fear of the deadly whip
fear of the blood-covered axe
fear of lightning out of a clear blue sky
fear of lost time
fear of exams
fear of falling
fear of not getting it up
fear of a broken condom
or head
like a soap bubble

my forehead is not covered
with sweat
nor water nor blood
but with fear
and I don't know where
this damn fear
comes from
which is again

caught in my throat
like a primordial scream . . .

translated by Herbert Kuhner and Peter Tyran

Primo Levi

Primo Levi was born in Turin in 1919. As a young man, at the time of the persecution of Italian Jews, he joined a band of partisans, was soon captured, and in 1944 was sent to a concentration camp near Auschwitz. The camp was liberated by the Russians in January 1945, and Levi gradually made his way back to Italy where he began to write about his experience. These two poems offer a gender-based interpretation of that eternal biblical couple, Samson and Delilah. Taken together, the poems purport to give the male and female perspectives on this archetypal relationship. Does he have it right?

SAMSON

Son of a sterile mother
I too was announced
By a messenger with an awesome face.
I was a child of the Sun, a sun myself;
I had the Sun's strength
Compressed into my bull's loins.
I, sun and wild beast,
Have killed my enemies in the thousands,
Broken down doors and burst chains,
Ravaged women and set fire to harvests,
Until a Philistine Delilah
Cropped my hair and my stamina,
Extinguished my eyes' light.
There is no struggling against the dark.
My hair grew back
And so did my brute force.
Not the desire to live.

DELILAH

Samson of Tinnata, the rebel,
Mountain-splitting Jew,
Was, in my delicate hands,
Soft as potter's clay.
It was child's play to wrest the secret
Of his much-vaunted strength.
With praise and blandishments
I lulled him to sleep in my lap,
Still full of his foreign seed,
Blinded him, cut off his hair,
Destroying the power of his loins.
My rage and wantonness
Have never found so much peace
As on the day when I saw him in chains—
Not when I felt him penetrate me.
Now let him meet his fate. What do I care?

translated by Ruth Feldman

Harry Martinson

Harry Martinson (1904–78) was born in Jämshög, Sweden. A self-taught inveterate wanderer, he became one of Sweden's most important proletarian writers. In 1974 he was awarded the Nobel Prize for Literature. This poem is a refreshing take on the big saintly ogre of many of our childhoods. Some of us still remember the terror of our first time in beery old Santa Claus's lap.

SANTA CLAUS

Each year when the trees turn white
the hateful old smiler returns,
the nursery's Rasputin. He shakes his cotton-wad beard
and high-booted forces his way into everybody's heart.

translated by William Jay Smith and Leif Sjöberg

Semezdin Mehmedinovic

Semezdin Mehmedinovic was born in 1960 in Kiseijak, Bosnia-Herzegovina. He has a degree in comparative literature from Sarajevo University and has been an influential editor and poet. In 1995 he left Sarajevo and now lives near Washington, D.C., where he works for Voice of America. In the midst of war and human suffering, maintaining faith in divinity is a difficult test—not for the speaker's mother, though, who reminds the poet of his own calling and the primacy it gives to the power of imagination.

AN ESSAY

This evening stroll deserves a poem:
the aeroplane's wink above the suburbs
as it sinks toward a bluish dark;
the sparking wires above the trolleybus.
A woman has lost an earring on the street,
and as she turns back now to look for it
I suddenly feel pity: for her,
for the boy squinting at his reflection
in his bicycle-bell;
for the old man on the bridge, who whispers
the river is run dry. How can this happen
here, of all places, where we're so humane?
Even, in the end, a sorrow
for the scattering of freckles on my mother's face
as we walk along, with her trying to convince me
that where I think of him
or imagine him to be, there God exists.

translated by Kathleen Jamie and Antonela Glavinic

Peter Reading

Peter Reading was born in 1946 in Liverpool and lives in Shropshire. A winner of multiple poetry prizes—including the Dylan Thomas Award—he has published over twenty poetry books. Men are ruled, the poet tells us, "by a random Weird." The sense of accident that pervades our destiny is the subject of this ambitiously titled poem. Reading creates a line reminiscent of Anglo-Saxon verse with its alliterative beats separated by caesurae, reminding us how long and deep the English literary tradition is, and how the topic of man's fate is older than English writing itself.

FATES OF MEN

Many children are fathered,   fondled by parents,
fostered, sent forth;   but Fate is impartial:

maybe a man dies   mauled in his youth
by wandering wolves,   the wily heath-dwellers
for some folk, famine   finishes all things;
hurricanes hurl   much hardship on one man;
ash-spears may bloody him;   the battle field fell him;
one may go blundering,   blindness afflicting him;
another is lamed,   his leg's bones sundered
so that he moans,   menaced by Fate's lot;
one, forced to wander,   wearies of foreigners—
few men befriend him,   fearing his strangeness;
justice demands   the gibbet for one man,
then ravens visit him,   his viscera feed them;
the fierceness of fire   finishes many;
one man at his mead,   mouthing imprudently,
falls in a brawl,   a bright blade quietens him;
one, of a surfeit   supped at the beer-benches,
ends life in misery,   mindless, a self-slayer;
one man is fortunate,   finds joy early,
the company of kinsmen   comforts his dotage.

Thus men are ruled   by a random Weird:

one is regaled   with riches and youthfulness
one, a warrior,   on the war-field is honoured;
one at the gaming-board   gains a great fortune;
a scholar is wealthy   in wisdom and intellect;
one is gifted   in the goldsmith's art,
adorns the corslet   of a king who gratefully
rewards him richly   with realms of his own;
one brews liquor   to lighten men's burden—
is hailed as a hero   and highly respected;
one procures patronage   plundering the word-hoard,
his skill in singing   is sought-after, paid for;
one become famed   as a falconer taming

the wild hawk's spirit,   he speaks to it, feeds it,
its foot in a jess,   it gently succumbs . . .

Divers are the destinies   dealt out by Fate to us.

Mihai Ursachi

Mihai Ursachi was born in 1941 in Iasi, Romania. Currently he teaches at the university in Iasi and also works as secretary of the Writers' Association. As his translator Adam Sorkin says, this poem exhibits an "odd relation to gender: poet as prophet, as god-wrestler, as major historical persona." Here the speaker is Emperor Caesar himself, the giver of the Julian calendar to the West, speaking of topics high and low, the last words he has to say before his fateful death.

A MONOLOGUE

I am the one who determined that the year must number 365 days and be divided into 12 months, one of them being given the name of my *gens*, Julia.

Last night I suffered nightmares once again, among which a particular dream from my youth tortured me even worse than my persistent backache.

If I had allowed, the days, the months and the weeks would still be reckoned according to the calendars of Romulus and Numa Pompilius. Thus I would never know how many years I had lived, nor when the Ides of March is to fall.

And this constant companion, my inexplicable infirmity. No one must notice it, neither Calpurnia nor the slaves, not to mention the Senate . . .

The month dedicated to Mars has always been favorable to me, as well as Mars himself. Maybe the recurrence of that long and horrible nightmare, much more interminable and intense than before, during my adolescence, could be a good augury.

Then, in my adolescence, the Chaldeans told me, and later the priests of Rome confirmed, that my dream of violently possessing Aurelia, my mother, signified that, by dint of arms, I would possess this world, the matriarch of everything.

What a joke the gods played on my son-in-law, Pompeius Magnus! (He was, I believe, only two years older than I.) Ha! Rather than believe in the gods, much better you should be related to them.

And baldness continues to progress, just when all my vital functions, in fact, are becoming more and more painful. Again this morning I did not do my exercises, but instead I tarried in the bath much longer than usual. My hair grows gray everywhere I don't need it, and it falls all the time from where I should wish to have it.

In the bath, after massages, and after I ordered them to depilate my neck and my calves, I contemplated my body in the mirrored room. I contemplated it minutely, as a matter of fact precisely, as I have made my habit since adolescence. Contemplating my body, I could not refrain from calling to mind the Venus Genitrix, the source of my *gens*.

And truly the soothsayers were right in how they interpreted the dream with Aurelia. If the world bear the name Cleopatra, I possessed the world every way in which something can be possessed. But neither this woman—nor any woman, nor the world, nor eternity likewise—can be possessed at all. Indeed, they possess you.

Today promises to be another ordinary day.

Yet once more to the Roman people and the Senate: to you I brought Africa, Asia, and Gaul! Tenants should pay their rent, debtors, their debts. And the interest should be forgiven. Comrades in arms! (And I shall promulgate a new Julia law.)

And finally, the soldiers and gold. It's simple: the soldiers want gold, and gold you can only obtain *manu militari*. Here is the snake that bites its own tail, which they showed me in the temple of the goddess Isis. Are the Egyptians barbarians? No Roman woman can compare to her, the descendent of Ptolemy. I gazed upon the face of the Sphinx, but I was not impressed.

Her voice sounds better than Cicero's. Her decency is far superior to that of Cato, who is a lush. True decency manifests itself in the bed.

Calpurnia's nightmare. (Poor woman!) So what, what if the peak of your house shall not stand? In the province of Judea, some misfits have been prophesying this very thing for a long time. In any case, Jerusalem should not have been destroyed.

And the horrible fire in Alexandria, during which, had I not been exercising regularly by swimming, I could very well have drowned in the Nile. Curiously, no crocodile attacked me in the course of my obligatory swimming party. I hear that some libraries burned, too. But books are always being written. I myself am writing still another one at the moment.

Well, in regard to the veil of that goddess, it seems that not even a thousand legions would be able to raise it from her face. Even I, who descend in a direct line from *vaginum Veneris*, am unable to raise the veil.

And ultimately that tiny tribe in the province of Judea could well be right. They proclaim the end of the world all the time, no less than from the beginning of the world. Nothing ends and nothing begins, not today, not yesterday, not tomorrow. What further wars should I wage? The title, *Dictator perpetuus*, humiliates me. So does the title *Imperator*. One cannot live with them.

But I must take care, I have arrived at a subject which, exactly like debts, I persist in postponing or avoiding. Being the master of the world, I am bankrupt.

Not even the interest on the interest shall I ever be able to pay, were I to live to be 150 years old. Naturally, I cannot accept the word *Rex* added to my name. I am not a king: I am Caesar.

Vida Nedici?* Who was Vida Nedici?

You are seeking a pretext. (The "textualists" write boring texts.) A text is a trifle next to the fifty-six years that I have lived. The "text" about the Gallic Wars was written at the time of the Gallic Wars. Caesar directed the campaign, which took no fewer than nine years.

On the other hand, it is a certainty that this world resists reducing itself to Gaul, Africa, and Asia. I could conquer India as the consequence of a lengthy war of attrition, which would distinguish me from Alexander. What good would India do me, for in Rome the Civil War, the true civil war, has barely begun to brandish arms?

And even were I to be the winner in this war, I would remain the vanquished. Octavius must bear the humiliating burden, which will be his supreme triumph. What sign might still portend against me, after my crossing that miserable little stream? All the signs are favorable to me.

Of course, sooner or later, technological progress will lead to migrations to other worlds, beyond even the sphere of the universe. I have not tired, but no differently from actors in the theater, I must heed the curtain's fall.

Against Chronos, there exists no possibility of winning a war. And if you cannot win a war, you should not go to war. Yet, this very day, I am going to win the most terrible war, against none other than Chronos. I shall need to renounce even the pleasures of Venus.
Caesar, where are your legions?

The price for the biggest pearl in the world, which I gave as a gift to Servilia, the mother of Marcus Brutus, I shall pay this very day. This time neither military force nor strategy or diplomacy will prove of use to me. Just as in the arms of Venus, I must be alone. And never has a woman remained unsatisfied by Caesar.

Nonetheless, I believe that Servilia gave me as a gift the most profound of pleasures, for she gave me Tertia, her virgin daughter. And it is she who, by means of the hand of the very issue who sprang from beneath my own toga, will grant me absolution of every debt.

This petty planet has come to bore me. Her boundaries constrain me. The planet which bears the name of my old ancestral mother calls me to her. Her molecules hold out their arms and beckon to me.

I have only ten minutes left.

And how could I forget the soldier Martius in the tent, who fucked me. And the golden and perfumed bed of the King of Bithynia . . .
O Stella Martis.

It's time for me to go forth and take no notice of anything. The distance is nothing. My last testament has been made. I even know the place from which they will come. Grammarian, don't intrude upon me. Look . . . Here they are

translated by Adam J. Sorkin and the poet

*Vida Nedici was a torturer during the early Stalinist years in Romania, notorious for her specialty of beating male prisoners on the genitals, and probably also a spy; later, in the mid-fifties, she became an officer in Serbia under Tito.

Africa

Oswald Mbuyiseni Mtshali

Oswald Mbuyiseni Mtshali was born in 1940 in Natal, South Africa. He writes in both Zulu and English. He has been a dispatch rider in Johannesburg and the headmaster of a school in Soweto. His second book of poems, *Fire Flames,* was banned by the apartheid government in 1981. He currently teaches in New York City. In the following poem, the poet's dead mother gives him a few important lessons in metaphysics and religion in a dream. She reminds him that heaven and hell exist in this world rather than some removed supernatural sphere.

A VOICE FROM THE DEAD

I heard it
in my sleep
calling me soft.

It was
my mother
speaking from her grave.

My son!
there is no heaven
above the clouds.

WHAT!

Yes, Heaven is in your heart.
God is no picture
With a snow-white beard.

WHAT!

Yes, God is

that crippled beggar
sprawling at the street corner.

There is no hell burning
with sulphur and brimstone.

WHAT!

Yes, Hell is
the hate flickering
in your eye.

Al-Munsif al-Wahaybi

Al-Munsif al-Wahaybi was born in Qairwan, Tunisia, in 1929. He studied Islamic philos-
ophy and literature at the University of Tunis and has taught in both Tunis and Libya. His
poem "The Desert" has the feel of a creation myth and shows how masculine and feminine
life forces are embodied in the culture of desert peoples.

THE DESERT

In the beginning the desert
was the ashes of a woman
inhabited by a storm.
Hidden secrets echoed,
and the silent poet
lay down on its grasses alone
or sat between its light
and shade, looking for something
that had disappeared
in its endless, rust-colored mirrors.

At the beginning, the language of the desert
was grass blooming against the wall of wind,
tall palms swaying in the season of seeding
and cinders carried by air
to the blue welcome of warm sand.

She was our first fountain, our mother,
who held us, then gave us away
to the age of waiting cities.

translated by Sakna Khadra Jayyusi and Naomi Shihab Nye

South America

Juan Carlos Galeano

Juan Carlos Galeano was born in the Amazon region of Colombia in 1958 and moved to the United States in 1983. He teaches Latin American poetry at Florida State University. In "Tree," a resonant and suggestive poem, the poet describes the relationship between man and his environment. Is the tone here playful? Or deadly serious?

TREE

to Frederick De Armas

A man in love with a tree goes to live with him awhile before getting married.

"Now you no longer need to look for sunshine, water, or food," his friends say.

Every night the man combs the tree's hair and then
they sit down to tea with their friends, the planets and the closest stars.

Life and the environmental magazines tell their love story to the entire world.

But one day the man gets tired of seeing the same faces of the sun, the moon, and the stars.

Relatives, environmentalists, and their best friends, the stars, come and ask him why he doesn't want to live with the tree anymore.

The man tells them that he is thinking of marrying a river, a cloud, or something
more versatile.

translated by Delia Poey

Central America and the Caribbean

Jorge Esquinca

Jorge Esquinca was born in Mexico in 1957. He is the author of five books of poetry and has
received two National Prizes for Poetry. He lives in Guadalajara. The wolf in this fable is
surely a metaphorical wolf. Does it represent the thought of death, which stalks the hunter;
the act of writing, which haunts the writer; or the desire for fame or success, which hunts
down many good men? Whatever it is, it keeps the poet up all night, and it inspires a poem
from him in the bargain.

FABLE OF THE HUNTER

to José Emilio Pacheco

A man begins to think about a wolf.
At first this wolf is only an unmoving silhouette:
a dark gray bulk crouched in darkness,
a panting snout.

Days later the thought of the wolf returns.
It seizes his memory with four powerful paws.
The man then aims a faint lantern
and locates the lurking figure of this thought-wolf.
In this sudden clarity two yellow pupils awaken,
two rows of razor-sharp teeth, glistening.
From the center of the lighted circle a large gray wolf watches him,
with the fixed gaze of an animal facing danger.
Every muscle subjected to a precise tension.

The hair on its back erect, electric.
Its lips moist, its claws extended.

The night surprises the man leaning over his work-table.
Defiantly, the thought of the wolf marauds him.

Determined, the man grasps a pencil:
he has resolved to hunt the wolf.
Hours pass and the blank pages are filled with ferocious drawings:
in its every move his hand slides with an inexplicable agility, almost feline.
His strokes become more than spontaneous: instinctive.

Soon his wolf is a single line.
A visible leap between life and death.
Then the man pauses: he has understood.

He scarcely trembles when he hears the long howl from the back of the garden.
He rises from the table and walks out into the dawn.
He doesn't even notice that the last stars are already disappearing.

translated by Robert L. Jones

Evan Jones

Evan Jones was born in Jamaica in 1927. He was educated in the United States and at Oxford University. He has lived in England since 1956, writing full-time, primarily for films and television. "Genesis" is his own spin on the creation story. The god in the poem is male—whether intentional or simply a patriarchal carryover, we cannot be sure—but he feels an all too human sense of incompleteness and lack of perfection, which he imposes on the animal he made "in his own image."

GENESIS

He was a young god
So he worked with furious abandon
Strewing his precious suns around
In largely useless galaxies

Grandiose in his use of mountains, water, sky,
But not merely bombastic
For the detail of the microscopic was ingenious
Beyond the imagination of his predecessors
And the uses, particularly, of form and colour . . .

But he wasn't sure
Not quite sure, even when he had finished,
Especially then,

That he had solved such questions as
The relation of stability to change . . .

Cycles of birth and death were a masterpiece
But they weren't, not quite . . .

Yet, oh, the thing was beautiful
Turning and glittering and many-coloured
Infinite in all directions in space and time
And yet completely self-complete . . .

But he wasn't sure

So, as a sort of flourish to his signature
An underline for curtain
He made an animal in his own image
Except of course, for the dimensions lost
Transferring from eternity to time
Gave it the last perception of his mind
The sense of incompleteness

The gap between the intended and the done
The utter sadness of magnificence not quite

He gave it that
And asked of it perfection.

Dennis Scott

Dennis Scott was born in 1939 in Jamaica. A prizewinning poet, he is also a director, play-wright, actor, and dancer. He has been associate professor of directing at Yale University. Here the poet, writing in "nation language," objectifies time as a cunning uncle, the ulti-mate trickster figure, destroyer of female beauty, a spider who spins his web around all of us, leaving us in tears.

UNCLE TIME

Uncle Time is a ole, ole man . . .
All year long im wash im foot in de sea,
long, lazy years on de wet san'
an shake de coconut tree dem
quiet-like wid im sea-win' laughter,
scrapin away de lan'. . .
Uncle Time is a spider-man, cunnin an cool,
im tell yu: watch de hill an yu si mi.
Huhn! Fe yu yiye no quick enough fe si
how im move like mongoose; man, yu tink im fool?
Me Uncle Time smile black as sorrow;
im voice is sof as bamboo leaf
but Laard, me Uncle cruel.
When im play in de street
wid yu woman—watch im! By tomorrow
she dry as cane-fire, bitter as cassava;
an when im teach yu son, long after
yu walk wid stranger, an yu bread is grief.
Watch how im spin web roun yu house, an creep
inside; an when im touch yu, weep . . .

206

North America

Michael Blumenthal

Michael Blumenthal is the author of five books of poetry, most recently *Dusty Angel,* which won the 1999 Isabella Gardner Award for Poetry. He lives in Austin, Texas. Blumenthal here considers how much our lives are shaped by forces beyond our control and gives this question mythic dimensions by connecting our mundane experiences with those of classical legend. He speculates that there might be an Oedipus in all men, moving inexorably toward a fated destiny.

THE FORCES

Who, having lived more than a moment,
hasn't contended with them? You go out,
dreaming a mastery of your own life, bending the brush
as you walk, kicking the leaves. Just yesterday,
in a numinous moment, you were king
of your own book, a blank slate that could strut
and choose, a walking freedom with legs
that could say, *I am this,* and—poof!—
you were it. But, today, you're your old self
again, deep in the grooves of your past lives
like a skier come late to a mountain who,
frictionless, almost, and full of himself for no reason,
glides down the path of all who preceded him.
Sure, you've grieved and mourned, you've lain down
on numerous couches, and, still, the childhood wishes,
with their minute, occasional lisps forward,
are waiting to greet you. Who hasn't come
to the place of the three highways and, thinking
himself a free man, taken the road toward Delphi
merely to wind up with his head in the lap
of his own mother? Who hasn't swashbuckled his way
into a freedom at once so terrifying and familiar
he thinks he's arrived at some island exotica

only to stagger up over a hill and see there,
before him, the old door, the mansard roof,
the white tiles, of that strangely familiar place
he has no choice but to call: *home.* Who among us
wouldn't gladly be the chooser, if only choice
weren't a vast road looping over and over
to arrive at the same place? So why not
make peace with it? Every mother is enterable,
and every father dead on some highway to Thebes
or some truck-stop heading toward Kansas or Manhattan.
So ski down the hill, friend, enjoy the fresh air,
the illusory high, the dark fact that something
chooses us over and over until we're chosen for real.

Stephen Dobyns

Stephen Dobyns is a poet and novelist who teaches in the M.F.A. program at Warren Wilson College. He has authored eight volumes of poetry, eighteen novels, and a book of essays. This intriguing poem proposes the education of a character named Heart, perhaps an attempt to personify male emotional experience. Certainly men need emotional education, but often that can't be learned from books, no matter what Heart and his professors think.

WHY FOOL AROUND?

How smart is smart? thinks Heart. Is smart
what's in the brain or the size of the container?
What do I know about what I do not know?
Such thoughts soon send Heart back to school.
Metaphysics, biophysics, economics, and history—
Heart takes them all. His back develops a crick
from lugging fifty books. He stays in the library
till it shuts down at night. The purpose of life,
says a prof, is to expand your horizons. Another says
it's to shrink existence to manageable proportions.
In astronomy, Heart studies spots through a telescope.
In biology, he sees the same spots with a microscope.
Heart absorbs so much that his brain aches. No
ski weekends for him, no joining the bridge club.

Ideas are nuts to be cracked open, Heart thinks.
History's the story of snatch and grab, says a prof.
The record of mankind, says another, is a striving
for the light. But Heart is beginning to catch on:
If knowledge is noise to which meaning is given,
then the words used to label sundry facts are like
horns honking before a collision: more forewarning
than explanation. Then what meaning, asks Heart,
can be given to meaning? Life's a pearl, says a prof.
It's a grizzly bear, says another. Heart's conclusion
is that to define the world decreases its dimensions
while to name a thing creates a sense of possession.
Heart admires their intention but why fool around?
He picks up a pebble and states: The world is like
this rock. He puts it in his pocket for safe keeping.
Having settled at last the nature of learning, Heart
goes fishing. He leans back against an oak. The sun
toasts his feet. Heart feels the pebble in his pocket.
Its touch is like the comfort of money in the bank.
There are big ones to be caught, big ones to be eaten.
In morning light, trout swim within the tree's shadow.
Smart or stupid they circle the hook: their education.

Stephen Dunn

Stephen Dunn was born in 1939 in Forest Hills, New York. He has published twelve books
of poetry and has been awarded numerous grants and prizes, including the Pulitzer Prize in
2000 for his collection *Different Hours*. He is a professor of creative writing at Stockton
State College in New Jersey. Dunn lets us in on a secret—that, like Odysseus, many hus-
bands are wanderers at heart. Though they are happy to return to hearth and home, they
never quite lose their desire for adventure.

ODYSSEUS'S SECRET

At first he thought only of home, and Penelope.
But after a few years, like anyone on his own,
he couldn't separate what he'd chosen
from what had chosen him. Calypso,

the Lotus-eaters, Circe;
a man could forget where he lived.
He had a gift for getting in and out of trouble,
a prodigious, human gift. To survive Cyclops
and withstand the Sirens' song—
just those words *survive, withstand,*
in his mind became a music
he moved to and lived by.
How could *govern,* even *love,* compete?
They belonged to a different part of a man,
the untested part, which never had transcended dread,
or the liar part, which always spoke like a citizen.
The larger the man, though,
the more he needed to be reminded
he was a man. Lightning, high winds;
for every excess a punishment.
Penelope *was* dear to him,
full of character and fine in bed.
But by the middle years this other life
had become his life. That was Odysseus's secret,
kept even from himself. When he talked about return
he thought he meant what he said.
Twenty years to get home?
A man finds his shipwrecks,
tells himself the necessary stories.
Whatever gods are—our own fearful voices
or intimations from the unseen order
of things, the gods finally released him,
cleared the way.
Odysseus boarded that Phaeacian ship, suddenly tired
of the road's dangerous enchantments,
and sailed through storm and wild sea
as if his beloved were all that ever mattered.

Fred Moramarco

Fred Moramarco was born in Brooklyn, New York, in 1938. He is editor of *Poetry International,* published at San Diego State University where he has taught for more than thirty years. He is also coeditor of this anthology. In our particularly heroless times, it's sad to see one more archetypal hero, The Man of Steel himself, reduced to his all too human identity.

CLARK KENT, NAKED

They found him in a phone booth, huddled,
frail as a fetus, shivering in the cold.
The problem, he said, was that when he began
to take off his clothes for the usual transformation,
the blue and red suit with the yellow *S*
emblazoned across the front just wasn't there.
He couldn't believe it, he said, and kept disrobing
when he was assaulted by a transient who took the pile of clothes.
He insisted that no one tell Lois as they led him away
covered by a wool blanket, babbling incoherently
to the air in front of him, remembering how things used to be.

Marco Morelli

Marco Morelli was born in 1975 and grew up on Long Island, New York. After volunteering in Nicaragua, he began translating poems he had collected there and eventually published a book, *Ruben's Orphans: An Anthology of Contemporary Nicaraguan Poetry.* Presently he lives in Boulder, Colorado, where he works for Ken Wilber's Integral Institute. In this direct, openhearted poem, a young man reveals what a human being can be when all the dross of our defenses is stripped away.

A VOLUNTEER'S FAIRY TALE

Once upon a time, a young man
versed in ideas, but inexperienced,
traveled to Nicaragua as a Volunteer—
seeking Revolution, Poetry, and Life.
A philosophy student in college,

his mind crammed with Nietzsche, Hegel, and Kant,
he wanted mud on his hands
and faces of real blood to encounter.
A poster on the wall in the lecture hall
said: "Volunteer, Live and Learn!"
and his heart was transfixed like an instant
of lightning.

Later that day,
he borrowed a book from the library:
photos of war, death, poverty . . .
and faces of love.
And in the epilogue of the book,
a revolutionary who was also a poet
wrote, "Nicaragua is a land of poets. . . .
in the *barrios,* in the *campo,* in *las pulperías,*
Nicaragua is a land of struggle and poetry;
and the struggle is poetic and the poetry embodies
that same struggle."
Thus a romance was born.

That young man
went to Nicaragua with a team
of volunteers he'd never known
and who let him be crazy sometimes,
and together they dug ditches, carried bricks,
mixed cement, got sweaty, sick, exhausted,
awoke with the roosters, joked with the workers,
slept under stars bright as children's eyes,
built a clinic of health and hope, . . .
learned to think of the people they met
as friends, and struggled with themselves
and one another to create a little beauty
or find that voice
that had always been calling.

That man went searching
in cities and schools and dirt-floored shacks
and hells where humans like any others
eat garbage for words that could open

the heart in people's minds.
And he met others like himself with eyes torn open.
Mouths bleeding. Hands broken, but tending the Fire nonetheless.
He stepped across the imaginary threshold of worlds
in the night of humanity and discovered:
that the Revolution was over,
that Poetry doesn't exist,
and that Life IS Death.

And the young man came home
weary but glad for the experience
and for the words still speaking to him
in his mother's tongue.
And he found an abyss to rest in,
and he slept through the winter. . . .
In a thousand dreams and nightmares
he encountered the same faces
phantasmagorically appearing and dissolving
in the nothingness of time.
And one morning he awoke
to see the face of Dawn shining in a thousand bodies:
Working, smiling, trembling behind masks,
some bitter and fearful, others pure with love. . . .
And he realized at once
that all the faces—were his own.

That man
will return to Nicaragua,
with the silence of a heart
in his hands and speak the words born in him
from the voices of a dream,
and perhaps he'll write a book
or travel to some other land
or speak the language of ghosts forever.
But the faces will remain
transfixed in a flash of time
where they glimpse their own eyes
in each other's, shine open,
and disappear.

Howard White

Howard White was born in Abbotsford, British Columbia, in 1945. A former heavy-equipment operator and construction company owner, he is the author of a half dozen books and is also the owner of Harbour Publishing in British Columbia. Among his awards are the Canadian Historical Association's Career Award for Regional History and the Stephen Leacock Medal for Humour. This poem has fun with the romantic notion that there was a time when men were tough, resourceful, uncomplaining—all the old macho values. But a certain ambivalence comes through. Are we supposed to miss the good old days when men were "really" men?

THE MEN THERE WERE THEN

It sounds like something that's been
said before too many times,
but I want you to know
I mean it, now, when I say
there are no men around today
like the men there were then.
You see those enormous tree stumps
with the notches in, and you don't think.
Those were big trees.
There are no trees like that today.
We think today what we do with machines
is hard work, but our trees are tiny,
and they did it all by hand.
They did it all standing on springy, narrow
boards, stuck twelve feet up above the ground,
sometimes canyons below them,
swinging their axes into that big wood.
To move along they'd give a hop with one toe
held under the springboard, to swing it.
Then they'd stick the axe in the wood
and stoop to reach their saws. I never
heard of one who fell.
But one time one man when he
turned to reach for his saw,
he brushed that razor sharp axe,
and it slit his middle
right along the belt line for about eight inches.

It didn't bleed so much, but
his intestines came looping down like bunting.
When we came with the stretcher this man
was under the cut crouched on his knees
delicately holding up these gut loops,
one by one splashing sawdust off 'em
with water from his water bag.
There are no men like that
around today.

Oceania, Australia, and New Zealand

Peter Skrzynecki

Peter Skrzynecki was born in 1945 in Germany. He is of Polish-Ukrainian heritage. He has published thirteen books of poetry and prose and won several literary prizes. He teaches at the University of Western Sydney, Macarthur. Skrzynecki considers the moment of grace that sometimes comes after great suffering, after the body has been weakened, the spirit seemingly crushed—a moment of transcendence, peace, and acceptance, a gift from the universe itself.

BUDDHA, BIRDBATH, HANGING PLANT

Three things stopped him in his stride
when he stepped out
into the garden—three things
under the great peppercorn
that he planted years ago:
the statue of a Buddha,
a birdbath and a plant in a basket
hanging from one of the peppercorn's branches.

The Buddha pointed to the earth,
to the "here and now."
The birdbath, filled with water,

reflected the tree above it.
The plant, a flowering hoya,
hung over the Buddha and birdbath like a crown.

His time of sorrow
vanished—as if pain and fear
had been nothing more than vapours
trailing through his imagination.
Somewhere, from out of an ancient past,
he heard a voice, "The centre of the universe
is a bellylaugh."
The Buddha smiled; the water
in the birdbath rippled;
the hoya stirred
in a circular motion.

He stepped back, startled—
as if someone had pushed him.
Then he saw the great tree itself.

Politics, War, Revolution

I will not keep the truth from my song.
I will not bar the voice undressed by the bees
from entering the gourd of my bow-harp.
I will not wash the blood off the image . . .
—Frank Chipasula

Some people think of poetry as an elitist art, interesting only for aesthetic reasons. The poets whose words appear in this section are clearly of a different mind. They see poetry as a testimony to the times in which they live and as a force that can shape perceptions of political realities. Most of them would agree with the French existentialist Jean Paul Sartre, who said words are bullets. These poets are revolutionaries, men of action, who believe their words can change the world.

The Ghanaian poet Kofi Anyidoho, for example, provides us with a view of the Gulf War from a Third World country, where it is not celebrated as a triumph of right and a victory for freedom. Anyidoho, using both American names for the war simultaneously, forces us to consider its actual effect on a real person: "And out there in the Gulf / A widowed mother's only son / Bleeds to Death in Desert Storms." The Malawian Frank Chipasula insists that he will not avoid the truth in his song and wants his "volatile verbs" to burn through the lies of political propaganda and shine light on the actualities of injustice in his own country and the world.

While politics, war, and revolution are no longer strictly male preoccupations (one wonders if this is progress), clearly men have been long absorbed by power struggles and the violent confrontation between conflicting ways of seeing the world. One of the insights gained from looking at these poems is the ability to view conflict from various and contrasting perspectives. These underscore the unfortunately universal nature of struggle, confrontation, and the power of might to make right.

This universality is most strikingly revealed in the Israeli and Palestinian poems collected here side by side. The Palestinian Mahmud Darwish asks his mother to give birth to him again so that he can know what land he belongs to. And though he sees himself as a stranger in his native land, he remains true to himself through defeat, occupation, and humiliation. The Israeli Admiel Kosman hears both Hebrew and Arabic spoken over cell phones and uses that image to convey the shared fate of these Semitic people, both sacrificing their youth to the continuing strife. Salman Masalha, who has published work both in Hebrew and in Arabic, sees himself as a man without a country but views this condition as a positive state, enhancing his freedom to be human. The Israeli Rami Saari says he won't write a political poem, but in the process of developing a poem around that idea, he questions whether that is really possible in the cauldron that is the Middle East; while the late Palestinian poet Tawfiq Zayyad makes no attempt to camouflage his politics as he expresses the anger of a whole generation of Palestinian men.

From around the world, these men's voices are the voices of protest, anger, anguish, and sometimes despair. They insist that we not avert our eyes from the pain, suffering, poverty, injustice, and economic and social inequality we see everywhere. They tell us the function of poetry is to awaken our dormant consciences—to illuminate the darkness of lies and misinformation that we find ourselves lost in, especially in a public relations, media-saturated world. Political poetry, they insist, is more necessary than ever.

Asia

Kriapur

Kriapur (Kristanto Agus Purnomo) was born in Solo, Central Java, in 1959 and died in a traffic accident in 1987. His poem "Men on Fire" begins from the knowledge that when hunger, poverty, and injustice are severe enough, men turn to violent revolution. Kriapur treats this ancient progression matter-of-factly but powerfully through a series of simple but compelling images.

MEN ON FIRE

Leaving their villages, men on fire
head for cities spattered with blood,
to destroy property, houses,
the wind and time

white leaves
written on the trees, rain
written across the cities,
men wandering in a haze of ideas,
hurling rocks from their villages,
hurling fire

men on fire walking
toward the cities
on battered clogs,
heading for the arena
where hungry men fight,
their blood burning
their wounds alight

translated by Harry Aveling

Shin Kyong-Nim

Korean poet Shin Kyong-Nim (b. 1935) has played a leading role in the world of socially in-
volved poetry in Korea. He has served as president of the Association of Writers for Na-
tional Literature and of the Federated Union of Korean Nationalist Artists. He reminds us
of the time after war when, presumably, old enemies can step back and see the bigger pic-
ture beyond their own limited partisan passions.

YOLLIM KUT SONG

Sung by spirits wandering along the Armistice Line

Your bones have crumbled and turned into stones,
your limbs have been crushed and turned into water

and risen up now as vast mountains, deep rivers,
risen up in this country's heart.

Your flesh has rotted and turned into soil,
your blood has turned into compost enriching the soil
and blossomed now, all kinds of red and yellow flowers
have blossomed at mountain foot, along river banks.

How many thousand nights have we spent returning,
how many thousand days lamenting, wandering
on death's tawny path with its ninety-nine crests,
you with the pain I gave you, I tormented with pain by you?

Now is the time we meet, brethren together, embrace and weep,
when I strike my tongue against your shattered skull
and you apply your lips to my broken shoulders,
as we wail laments with open hearts.

We mourn the time when we were stupid, and crazy.
We set out in quest of those who slashed us to bits,
divided us, alienated us from one another.
As we cast aside the gun that shot, the knife that stabbed,

as we wipe away the sordid dust soiling our bodies,
wash the hearts defiled by our enemies;
now as we silence our laments and wash away the
dirt and stains that adhere to our flesh;

look: these brothers that once shot and stabbed one another,
now lament as they gently caress each other's sore wounds.
They weep, lightly embracing rotten crumbling limbs.
Vast mountains, deep rivers weep in accord.

All the red and yellow flowers are weeping too.
The reeds that cover the meadows weep.
But now as we set out along the path
in quest of our foes, they are weeping with glaring eyes.

translated by Brother Anthony

U Sam Oeur

Cambodian U Sam Oeur (b. 1936) lived through the atrocities committed by the Pol Pot regime in the 1970s. In this harrowing poem, a new father mourns the loss of twin girls murdered at their birth during this horrific time. Oeur expresses his poetic philosophy as follows: "As a poet, I wish to express the oppressed feelings of the silent world (the world which cannot speak for itself) and a cry of anguish for the plight of my people and my country, balanced by an unflagging faith in our imminent return to freedom and stability. I would like to be a good ambassador of the silent world."

THE LOSS OF MY TWINS

Deep one night in October, '76
when the moon had fully waxed,
it was cold to the bone;
that's when my wife's labor pains began.

I searched for a bed, but that was wishful thinking;
I felt so helpless. Two midwives materialized—
one squatted above her abdomen and pushed,
the other reached up into my wife's womb and ripped the babies out.

What a lowing my wife put up
when she gave birth to the first twin.
"Very pretty, just as I'd wished, but those fiends
choked them and wrapped them in black plastic.

Two pretty girls . . .
Buddho! I couldn't do a thing to save them!"
murmured my mother.
"Here, Ta!" the midwives handed me the bundles.

Cringing as if I'd entered Hell,
I took the babies in my arms
and carried them to the banks of the Mekong River.
Staring at the moon, I howled:

"O, babies, you never had the chance to ripen into life—
only your souls look down at me now.

Dad hasn't seen you alive at all, girls . . .
forgive me, daughters; I have to leave you here.

Even though I'll bury your bodies here,
may your souls guide me and watch over your mother.
Lead us across this wilderness
and light our way to the Triple Gem."

translated by Ken McCullough

Edwin Thumboo

Edwin Thumboo was born in 1933. He is professor emeritus at the National University of Singapore. As an influential poet, anthologist, editor, and scholar, he has been given numerous awards for his own work and for his tireless advocacy of Southeast Asian writing. "The Exile" records what happens to a man who is constitutionally unsuited for politics but gets caught up in the issues of his time anyway. Perhaps because of his naïveté and lack of attention, he ends up being betrayed by the more sophisticated operatives around him who are better at making quick adjustments when they're needed.

THE EXILE

He was not made for politics,
For change of principles,
Unhappy days, major sacrifice.
Even a bit part in a tragedy
Seemed most unlikely.
There was in him a cool Confucian smile.
Some suitable history would have been
A place in the Family Bank,
Consolidated by a careful match,
A notable gain in family wealth,
A strengthening of the Clan.
An ordinary life, ordinary longevity.

Of these things his father sadly dreams.

He was not made for politics.
But those days were China-wrought,

Uncertain of loyalties, full of the search
For a soul, a pride
Out of ancestral agony, gunboat policy,
The nation's breaking up,
The disaster of the Kuomintang.
So the new people took him in
To cells, discussions, exciting oratory,
Gave him a cause.

Work quietly, multiply the cells,
Prepare for the bloom of a hundred flowers.

The flowers came, fast withereth too.

Made conspicuous by principles
And the discipline of the group,
He thought to stand his ground, defy the law.
Re-actionaries he said.
And so he stood in the dock.
Many documents were read. Those who planned
The demonstration, allotted tasks
Had run to fight another day—they had important work,
Could not be spared, were needed to arrange
More demonstrations.
Impersonally, the verdict was
Exile to the motherland,
A new reality.

He stood pale, not brave, not made for politics.

The Middle East

Mahmud Darwish

Mahmud Darwish was born in Al-Birwah near Akka in 1941. He has been a Palestinian po-
litical activist nearly all his life. In this heartfelt poem he expresses the exiled grief of a man
without a country. The narrator longs to be born again so he can know what people and
land he belongs to.

GIVE BIRTH TO ME AGAIN THAT I MAY KNOW

Give birth to me again. Give birth to me again that I may know
    in which land I will die, in which land I will come to life again.
Greetings to you as you light the morning fire, greetings to you, greetings to you.
    Isn't it time for me to give you some presents, to return to you?
Is your hair still longer than our years, longer than the trees of clouds
    stretching the sky to you so they can live?
Give birth to me again so I can drink the country's milk from you and
    remain a little boy in your arms, remain a little boy
Forever. I have seen many things, mother, I have seen. Give birth to
    me again so you can hold me in your hands.
When you feel love for me, do you still sing and cry about nothing?
    Mother! I have lost my hands
On the waist of a woman of a mirage. I embrace sand, I embrace a
    shadow. Can I come back to you/to myself?
Your mother has a mother, the fig tree in the garden has clouds.
    Don't leave me alone, a fugitive. I want your hands
To carry my heart. I long for the bread of your voice, mother!
    I long for everything. I long for myself . . . I long for you.

translated by Abdulla al-Udhari

Mahmud Darwish

Here is a keening lament and prayer to the father—divine and temporal. One of the most lauded Palestinian poets navigates through the anguishing complex of emotions surrounding the centuries-old issues of land, sovereignty, and identity. The "son" describes to the "father" their mutual paralysis in the face of forces larger than themselves.

ON A CANAANITE STONE IN THE DEAD SEA

The sea opens no door before me . . .
I say my poem
is a rock flying at my father
like a partridge. Father,
have you heard what has happened to me?
The sea closes no door before me.
No mirror I can shatter makes a path
of slivers before me
or a path of foam. Does anyone
weep for anyone, that I
may carry his flute and reveal
the secrets of my own wreckage?
I am of the shepherds of salt
in al-Aghwar. A bird plucks
at my language, building a nest in my tents
from the scattered azure.
Is there still a country
that flowed out of me
so I can look at it as I wish,
so it can look at me
at the west coast of myself on the stone of eternity?
This absence of yours is all trees
looking at you from yourself
and from this smoke of mine.
Jericho sleeps under her ancient palm tree.
I find no one to rock her cradle.
Their caravans grow quiet, so sleep.
I looked for a root for my name
but I am split apart
by a magic wand. Do my dreams reveal

my victims or my visions?
All the prophets are my family.
Yet heaven is still far from its land
and I am far from my words.
No wind lifts me above the past here.
No wind tears a wave from the salt of this sea.
There are no white flags for the dead to wave
to surrender, no voices for the living
to exchange declarations of peace . . .
The sea carries my silver shadow at dawn
and shepherds me to my first words,
to the breast of the first woman.
It lives dead in the pagan's dance
around his space and dies alive
by the pairing of poem and sword.
At the crossroads of Egypt, Asia
and the North, stranger, halt your horse
under our palm trees. On Syrian roads,
foreigners exchange war helmets
bristling with basil
sown from doves that alight
from the houses; and the sea died
of monotony in the undying testaments.
I am myself if only you yourself
were there as yourself. I am the stranger
to the desert palm tree from the time I was born
into this crowded mass. And I am myself.
A war rages against me. A war rages
within me . . . Stranger, hang your weapons
above our palm tree so I may plant
my wheat in the sacred soil of Canaan . . .
Take wine from my jars. Take a page
from my gods' book. Take a portion
of my meal and gazelle from the traps
of our shepherds' songs.
Take the Canaanite woman's prayers
at the feast of her grapes. Take our customs
of irrigation. Take our architecture.
Lay a single brick and build up

a tower for doves, to be one of us,
if that's what you desire. Be a neighbor
to our wheat. Take the stars
of our alphabet from us, stranger.
Write heaven's message with me
to mankind's fear of nature and men.
Leave Jericho under her palm tree
but do not steal my dream, the milk
of my woman's breast, the food
of ants in cracks of marble!
Have you come . . . then murdered . . . then inherited
in order to increase the salt of this sea?
I am myself growing greener
with the passing of years on the oak's trunk.
This is me and I am myself. This is my
place in my place, and now I see you in the past
the way you came, yet you don't see me.
I illuminate for my present
its tomorrow. Time sometimes separates me
from my place, and my place separates me from my time.
All the prophets are my family.
Yet heaven is still far from its land
and I am still far from my words.
And the sea descends below sea level
so my bones float over water like trees.
My absence is all trees. The shadow
of my door is a moon.
My mother is a Canaanite and this sea
is a constant bridge to the Day of Judgment.
Father, how many times must I die
on the bed of the legendary woman
Anat chose for me, so a fire
will ignite in the clouds? How many
times must I die in my old mint garden
every time your high northern wind
envelops the mint and scatters letters like doves?
This is my absence, a master
who reads his laws upon Lot's descendants
and sees no pardon for Sodom

but myself. This is my absence,
a master who reads his laws
and mocks my visions. Of what use
is the mirror to the mirror?

A bond of familiarity lies
between us, but you will not arise
from history, nor erase the sea steam
from you. And the sea, this sea,
smaller than its myth, smaller than
your hands, is a crystalline isthmus.
Its beginning is like its end.
There is no sense here for your absurd entry
in a legend that grinds armies into ruin
just so another army may march through,
writing its own story, carving its
own name into a mountain. A third will come
to chronicle the story of an unfaithful wife
and a fourth comes to erase the names
of our forebears. Each army has a poet
and a historian, each a violin for the dancers,
cynical from first to last. Hopelessly, I seek
my absence, more innocent than the donkeys
of the prophets that tread the foothills
carrying heaven to mankind . . .
And the sea, this sea, lies
within my grasp. I will walk
across it, will mint its silver, will grind
its salt in my hands. This sea is not occupied
by anyone. Cyrus, Pharaoh, Caesar, Negus
and the others came to write their names, with my hand,
on its tablets. So I write: The land is in my name
and the name of the land is the gods that share
my place on the seat of stone. I have
not gone, have not returned with slippery time.
And I am myself despite my defeat.
I have seen the coming days gilding my first trees.
I saw my mother's spring. Father, I have seen
her needle stitching two birds, one for her shawl

and one for the shawl of my sister, and a butterfly
unscalded by a butterfly for our sake. I have
seen a body for my name. I am the male dove
moaning in the female dove. I have seen
our house furnished in greenery and I saw
an entry door and an exit door
and a door that was both.
Has Noah passed from that place to that place
to say about the world, "It has
two different doors," but the horse flies with me
and the horse flies with me higher still and I fall
like a wave that erodes the foothills.
Father, I am myself despite my defeat.
I saw my days in front of me and I have seen
among my documents a moon
overlooking the palm trees.
And I saw an abyss. I saw war after war.
That tribe became extinct and that tribe
told the present Hulagu, "We're yours."
I say, "We're not a slave nation,
and I send my respects to Ibn Khaidun."
I am myself despite being smashed on the metallic air.
I have been handed over by the new Crusader war
to the god of vengeance and the Mongol
lurking behind the Imam's mask.
And to the salt women in a legend
etched into my bones. I am myself,
if only you were my father, but I am
a stranger to the palm trees of the desert
from the time I was born into this crowded mass.
And I am myself. The sea opens
no door before me. I say my poem
is a rock flying at my father
like a partridge. Father,
have you heard what has happened to me?
The sea closes no door before me.
No mirror I can shatter makes a path
of its slivers before me . . .
And all the prophets are my family,

but heaven is still far from its land
and I am far from my words.

translated by Muna Asali van Engen

Admiel Kosman

The Israeli poet Admiel Kosman (b. 1957), a religious intellectual, is professor of Talmud at
Bar Ilan University. He is the author of five books of poetry and a newspaper columnist. In
"Games" the conflict between old enemies is represented in images of mobile phones and
competing languages. Despite state-of-the-art technology, our communication often re-
mains primitive. Death remains the great equalizer here at the "end of games"; the com-
petitors all come down the hill in body bags.

GAMES

I have a mobile phone in my mouth,
he also has one, a military one,
like mine, but with a different mouthpiece.
We are playing games with the language bag,
Hebrew and Arabic,
we are punching the language bag
with little smacks of hatred,
the Hebrew bag,
and the Arabic bag,
landing little blows
in order to see
if the mouthpiece
will suddenly break into bits;
we are shaking the language bag,
making experiments,
torturing cats a little,
and why? Just
in order to see
if the language will finally learn something
from a few kicks, a few blows;
how many blows can the language live with?
Is it a Hebrew cat, or an Arabic one?
It doesn't matter, we are learning to kick,

to beat the mobile phone very hard.
How many blows can it take?
Whether it is Arabic or Hebrew
doesn't matter.
We are playing games,
making experiments, in order to see
whether it is made of steel or plain metal.
It doesn't matter, we shoot a bit too
in the games.
Because I have a mobile phone,
he has one also, and the two of us play.
Both of our mouthpieces are broken now,
Hebrew and Arabic;
it doesn't matter what we break,
perhaps the mouthpiece is different,
but broken to bits,
perhaps it's a similar mouthpiece,
just a little different, built differently.
A Hebrew or an Arabic mouthpiece, to whom does it matter
what it says,
and which way it turns?
The main thing is that the mouthpiece is afraid.
Here at the end of games,
we will break the circles open,
and then we will
all descend the hills
in bags,
the officers and the soldiers too.

translated by Lisa Katz

Salman Masalha

Salman Masalha was born in Galilea in 1953. He is facile in both Arabic and Hebrew and has published work in both languages. He is currently studying pre-Islamic Arab poetry at the Hebrew University. The poet as free spirit, as anarchist, has been a perennial romantic theme among male poets especially. In the context of the Mideast's pernicious and ongoing problems, the cry for individual liberty—free from any state's pressure or concern—is that much more plaintive.

ON ARTISTIC FREEDOM IN THE NATIONALIST ERA

Because I am not a state, I have
no secure borders or an army
guarding its soldiers' lives
night and day. And there is no
colored line drawn by a dusty general
in the margins of his victory. As I am
not a legislative council, a dubious
parliament, wrongly called a house
of representatives. As I am not a son
of the chosen people, nor am I
an Arab *mukhtar*. No one will falsely
accuse me of being, supposedly,
a fatherless anarchist who spits
into the well around which the people
feast on their holidays. Rejoicing
at their patriarchs' tombs.
Because I am not a fatalist or a member
of an underground that builds churches,
mosques, and synagogues in the hearts
of children. Who will no doubt die for
the sake of the Holy Name in Heaven.
Because I am no excavation contractor
or earth merchant, not a sculptor
of tombstones polishing memorials
for the greater glory of the dead.
Because I have no government, with
or without a head, and there is no
chairman sitting on my head. I can,
under such extenuating circumstances,
sometimes allow myself to be human,
a bit free.

translated by Vivian Eden

Rami Saari

Rami Saari was born in 1963 in Finland and now lives in Israel. He has published four books of poetry in Hebrew. He also translates and publishes poetry from Finnish, Turkish, Spanish, and Greek. He teaches at the Hebrew University. The speaker in this ironically titled poem bemoans the old tradition of winning land through war and conflict. But though he claims this won't be a political poem, in the final analysis, is that really true?

THE ONLY DEMOCRACY (IN THE MIDDLE EAST)

This won't be a political poem, brothers;
I'm fed up
with Cowboys and Indians,
and Cops and Robbers.
Are these really the young men
who were supposed to play before us,[1]
stroking Palestinian forces with mortar fire?
And my darling son[2] with a club and rubber bullets?

What can I say? The movie is fascinating
even if most of us have minor parts;
we still hope
to win, like men, a big win:
eating, gorging, consuming everything
like live fire, like man in God's image,
like idolaters ardently worshipping
a biblical whore, a temple prostitute, a furrow of earth, a city of fools;
the Wild West
settles in ancestral graves
here in the East.

translated by Lisa Katz

1. 2 Samuel 2:14 [author's note]   2. Jeremiah 31:20 [author's note]

Tawfiq Zayyad

Tawfiq Zayyad (1932–94) was one of a group of highly influential Palestinian poets. He published several collections of poetry and was once elected mayor of Nazareth. He captures the anger and determination of Palestinian men in this intense poem, which vows to pass on that anger and determination to another generation. Beneath that rage, however, is the speaker's deep connection to the Palestinian landscape, culture, and people. This kind of attachment may help explain why the situation in the Middle East is so intractable, so far.

HERE WE WILL STAY

In Lidda, in Ramla, in the Galilee,
we shall remain
like a wall upon your chest,
and in your throat
like a shard of glass,
a cactus thorn,
and in your eyes
a sandstorm.

We shall remain
a wall upon your chest,
clean dishes in your bars,
serve drinks in your restaurants,
sweep the floors of your kitchens
to snatch a bite for our children
from your blue fangs.

Here we shall stay,
sing our songs,
take to the angry streets,
fill prisons with dignity.

In Lidda, in Ramla, in the Galilee,
we shall remain,
guard the shade of the fig
and olive trees,

ferment rebellion in our children
as yeast in the dough.

translated by Sharif Elmusa and Charles Doria

Europe

Toma Longinoviç

Toma Longinoviç is a graduate of the Iowa Writers' Workshop. He writes and publishes
both in English and Serbo-Croatian. Here a speaker from a war-torn part of the world con-
fronts human suffering in its seemingly endless permutations. The poem's different jour-
neys, times, places—perhaps voices as well—are linked by pain and suffering, and the
search for transcendence and peace, all connected by a vision of a world both beautiful and
heartbreaking.

GLORIOUS RUINS

I.

    Travels. The jet takes off. Eyes are closed, breathing deep. *Om mani padme hum.*
Om mani padme hum. If we fall now, let my soul travel straight to the clear white
light. One hand touches the other. Smoothness of the skin, even as it ages. The
ignition key is turned on. The metal shell of the bus shakes as gasoline fumes hit
the nostrils. *Rapido, rapido,* the driver yells as the old Mayan woman in a white
dress climbs the stairs. There is no bodily odor, although we are all sweating. This
jungle is dry. Obsidian black hair falls on the plastic seat cover. The whistle blows.
The train begins to move. The peasant with a wooden leg takes out a piece of
crusty dark bread and half of a roasted piglet's head. I am a little boy sitting across
the aisle from him. I am scared. The woman in the seat opposite me crosses her
legs. Her stocking is running. Garlic, slivovitz, and rotten teeth. The anchor is
lifted, the ropes are pulled in. Although we are sailing across the river, the other
side cannot be seen. Cold *pampero* blows over Rio de la Plata as I listen to the
conversation of the people behind me. I am a little girl sitting in my Daddy's lap.
Some people have been disappeared. Many people. A Bosnian child with a shaved
head waves from the front page of *Pagina 12.* Bodies in time, bodies in motion.
Light is left behind them, to be forgotten by those who are not responsible.

2.

Deaths. Six bullets to the head in an Atlantic City motel for twenty-five dollars.
Booze, sleeping pills, and carbon monoxide in a suburban Middleton apartment
for a broken heart. A brain hemorrhage in a Spanish medieval seminary for old age
and knowledge. Everything that has a beginning must also have an end. Reconcile
yourself with this, and when you walk only walk. A fall from the pear tree, a broken
hip, and then lungs gradually filling up with liquid despite an unshaken trust in the
righteous cause of the Communist Party. Cirrhosis of liver and gradual blood
poisoning despite two and a half million DM in a bank and an unshaken trust in
the superiority of white capitalism. A point-blank shot to the back of the head, fall
into an open pit, lime and acid to dissolve the remains, despite an unshaken trust in
the ethnic purity of Croatia. Don't fear when the moment comes, says the book. It
is easy to say, but very hard to be. And then not to be.

3.

Meals. *Moravski vrabec* in the cellar of the "Vltava" restaurant in Belgrade. Beer
is not Pilsner, but a prosaic BIP. Salad of pickled green tomatoes and a side of
boiled noodles. Cigarette smoke fills the basement, girls are laughing and showing
their small teeth. Waiter is rude, it is still socialism. The mind is dull after such a
meal, senses not quite awake. Dead food. Tacos with pickled *nopal* cactus, sliced
pork, and melted cheese in the marketplace eatery on Isla Mujeres. The sun is not
quite as deadly in January as it is in July. Fried bananas with annato seed and a
squeeze of lime juice for dessert. Beer is Negra Modelo, or Corona, or Superior.
One's body feels a need for immersion, for the touch of the turquoise sea. Clouds
often appear on the horizon. That has nothing to do with my mood. I am a
menopausal executive secretary from Memphis, spreading sunscreen over my
hardening nipples. Pressed calf's head on the banks of the Rhine River, with
sauerkraut and roasted potatoes. Beer is Koelnch, the master of beers, no doubt.
Patrons are rich and happy, breeze is gentle, almost medieval. The castles on the
high banks remind us of the history that is repeating itself. We are breathing the
effects of racial cleanup. Abominations that pass through our bowels, on their way
to the water. Chef Boyardee has little to offer today. I am a newborn in the
mountains of Guatemala. There's no milk in my mother's nipple. A suck on the
cotton bag full of coffee grounds, a bite of corn tortilla, and some polluted water.

4.

Masters. Old boys with massive college rings directing traffic in Tuzla. Soldiers
with long beards singing tales of defeat to the ones they will soon slaughter.
Producers making reality happen by the simple pointing of the cameras. They are

hiding their power. I appear to be the product of life given to be squandered in hopeless rumination. The girl with a dragon tattoo on her shoulders knows the meaning of pain. I come and feel guilty. There are also pigs who do not wish to be born in order to be eaten. The old woman with two sacks in her hands does not understand how to be for the other. I am the officer who ordered the execution. They fear the glint of my eye, the omniscient gaze that can be pointed at them any moment. Our master is invisible, hiding in the silence of electronic impulses. The desire to know the future sends us to our knees when we hear the swish of the master's cloak. Obedience will be rewarded with life, disobedience punished by death. Starving them will draw less attention than bombing them from the air. Inherent existence is the root of misery. A little pain goes a long way. Everyone forgot to remind the master to bring the whip to the station this morning.

5.

Fears. The arrival of bread was delayed by shelling. Will there be enough language for mourning? Future will remain. Some will pray and tremble. Desire will never be free. Waking up with a new mole on the surface of your skin. A look in the mirror gives us a false but approximate picture. Singing until your voice cracks and old men begin to weep. Children's innocent smiles, unaware of violence and losses. All those who died. Mother's hands smashing your face. Unable to master transition, she believes that reality can be mastered. Life's small lessons are often found on the other side of words. The ground will be fertilized with the remains of our future. Perhaps melting winter ice with the heat of inexhaustible bodies making love until they fall into the frigid lake will contribute to our understanding of the moment. Holding a girl warms your heart. Who will relieve your pain?

Semezdin Mehmedinovic

Semezdin Mehmedinovic was born in 1960 in Kiseijak, Bosnia-Herzegovina. He has a degree in comparative literature from Sarajevo University and has been an influential editor as well as poet. In 1995 he left Sarajevo and now lives near Washington, D.C., where he works for Voice of America. Through this father-son dialogue, Mehmedinovic captures something of the poignancy of war's aftermath. The war dead seem to be trapped in their bombed-out houses as ghosts. They want to leave, but the doors are no longer there.

THE ONLY DREAM

The bicycle's upturned. Father
hooking back the chain, keeps his head bowed.
Many people are hanging about the garden.

—Dad, are these the dead?
Don't be scared, son,
you can play with them.

Under my foot, ants hide, bigger than brambles
and the swing, with no one on,
swoops toward the sky, then falls back.

They're wearing yellow macs, and looking
for a way out of the garden.
They glance at me, over their shoulders.

Then one of them approaches the wall,
takes in his hand a door-knob
where there isn't one, there's no door there.

But twenty years ago,
father, remember,
how there used to be?

translated by Kathleen Jamie and Antonela Glavinic

Ucha Sakhltkhutsishvili

Ucha Sakhltkhutsishvili was born in Tbilisi, Georgian Republic, in 1946. He is a graduate
of Tbilisi State University and works at the Academy of Sciences of the Georgian Republic.
His poem "Soldiers" celebrates the ways in which life struggles for its foothold in an inhospitable world—and sometimes even flourishes.

SOLDIERS

Crossing the mountains
the young soldiers
carry heavy weapons
on their shoulders.
Suddenly one of them cries:
"Hey, guys, here's an edelweiss!"
They pause at that spot a bit
then pass; the flower stays—and the path
curving a little around it.

translated by the poet and Al Zolynas

Izet Sarajlic

Balkan poet Izet Sarajlic was born in 1930 in Doboj. He has lived in Sarajevo since 1945. A
journalist and editor, he is the author of some dozen books and was one of the most popular
writers of the former Yugoslavia. Here he imagines what it might have been like to die in a
variety of foreign countries where he has traveled. He wants to die on his own native soil
and imagines everyone is glad to see he's returned home.

UNTITLED

If I had died that Friday in Paris
who would have sent a telegram that I'm no more
when it would have taken three days
to convince the police that I existed at all.

If that Saturday I had died in Warsaw,
a beautiful lady would have lost her job,
a beautiful lady from the Polish Writers Union
in whose care my soul was entrusted.

If I had died that Sunday in Leningrad,
it would have been even worse.
The white night would have worn a black band on its sleeve.

Now tell me, what kind of white night would that be with a black band on its
   sleeve?

If that Tuesday I had died in Berlin,
Neues Deutschland would announce that a Yugoslav
writer of the middle generation
suddenly died of a heart attack, while I—and this is not just idle talk—
I need to croak on my native soil.

You see how good it is that I didn't die, and that I'm once again among you?
You can whistle, you can applaud.
You see how good it is that I didn't die,
and that I'm once again among you all.

   translated by Charles Simic

Aleksey Shelvakh

Aleksey Shelvakh is a poet of the "new" Russia, and his poetry is drenched in sarcasm and
irony. "Veterans" considers the absurd priorities of a country where heritage and vodka are
more important than having food on the table.

VETERANS

Only barbarians forget about their fallen;
in our land, babes grieve in their mothers' arms.
Only barbarians water down their vodka
when they toast the Fatherland's peaceful aims.

Do you have an honor roll? I crumple up the names
of the Second Infantry in my smart conversation.
For ten long years I slugged it out, another job,
then choked in a wooden horse just before we won.

The living live well enough. Are you blind to what's good?
We've got clothing and shoes. Nothing's wrong with this flat.

Once a month comes a pittance, and with all due respect,
what's your point when you nastily ask what we eat?

That did it. Enough—I said good-bye.
Prying, gossiping neighbors know what they're up to.
You might as well know, where daffodils break through
we fry them for food to go along with cold vodka.

translated by J. Kates

Africa

Kofi Anyidoho

Kofi Anyidoho, the distinguished Ghanaian poet, teaches at the University of Ghana,
Legon. He received his Ph.D. from the University of Texas, Austin. Here is a view of the
Persian Gulf War from Africa. The narrator clearly identifies with the victims of American
technological violence such as the widowed mother's only son, who is bleeding to death in
the desert.

DESERT STORM

for Naana & for Obiba

i.
So where does one begin?
On what note must we
strike this long distance call
to those things we should have done
things we should be doing with our lives?

Simply then to say sorry,
sorrow for the long silence
beyond the market-place of iron-birds.
You were flying in

from the land of hostile winds &
I was flying away into new snowstorms.

And here I am today,
still holding on
to fragments of resolutions made once so many times
in those heady days of dreams:
The Hope The Promise Somehow
no matter how far afield
the HoneyBee may fly
he must swim the FireFloods
back to his MotherHive
where they say the honey flows in slow driblets,
the QueenBee's labours
forever lost to wayward
dreams of MoonChildren.

ii.
Just returned from Old London.
Yes I've been to London
I've been to London not
to look at the Queen but
bear witness in the troubling case
of Power Marginality & Oral
Literature in Africa
held at faraway courts
of Oriental & African Studies.

So I flew into Old London
in that night of the Death/Line
for Saddam &
for his warrior angels of the apocalypse.
The heavens broke loose next day,
you remember?
and all we do now
is listen even in our sleep
to the screaming hysteria

of war tales told in the relentless relay
of Uncle Sam's Braggart Boys.

It is the age of Old Generals
all dressed in shiny medals
issuing hourly briefs
from cozy conference rooms.
And out there in the Gulf
A widowed mother's only son
Bleeds to Death in Desert Storms.

And all the President's Men
say it is the greatest thing to do:
To call for war and watch The War
from the safe distance
of a whitehouse fortified
against the raging tide of blood
against the lurking danger of the ArmBush.

iii.
And after glorious Booms
of the StarWars Show
the ruthless logic of war
inevitably they say—
back into sad old times
where war is not cannot be
a game of kids played on video screens
by infantmen but a meal of death
cooked in blood and served redhot
at flashpoint of gun and smoke
and the choked breath.

And when it is all over
we shall once more inherit
a generation of cracked souls
for whom we must erect new
monuments and compose new

anthems of praise and the eternal hope of life
beyond the recurring stupidity of war heroes.

JANUARY 31, 1991

Breyten Breytenbach

Breyten Breytenbach was born in 1939 in South Africa. From the 1960s to the late 1990s he lived in exile, eventually returning to his native land, where he now teaches at the University of Cape Town. As an active participant in ending apartheid, Breytenbach points out some important intersections, particularly the inseparability of the inner and outer domains, the private and the public. The pain of exile, the commitment to justice and fairness, the willingness and courage to stand for transformation all make this poem a kind of *cri de coeur* from one of the "fathers" of the new South Africa.

EAVESDROPPER

for Stephen L.

you ask me how it is living in exile, friend—
what can I say?
that I'm too young for bitter protest
and too old for wisdom or acceptance
of my Destiny?
that I'm only one of many,
the maladjusted,
the hosts of expatriates, deserters,
citizens of the guts of darkness,
one of the "Frenchmen with a speech defect"
or even that here I feel at home?

yes, but that I now also know the rooms of loneliness,
the desecration of dreams, the remains of memories,
a violin's thin wailing
where eyes look far and always further,
ears listen quietly inward
—that I too like a beggar
pray for the alms of "news from home,"

for the mercy of "do you remember,"
for the compassion of "one of these days"

but I do not remember,
songs have faded,
faces say nothing,
dreams have been dreamt

and as if you're searching for love in a woman's seaweed hair
you forget yourself in a shuffling nameless mass
of early ageing revolutionaries
of poets without language and blind painters,
of letters without tidings like seas without tides
of those who choke of the childishness of longing,
of those who call up spirits from the incense,
conjure up landscapes on their tongues,
throwing up the knowledge of self
—must I too give a deeper meaning?
that all of us are only exiles from Death
soon to be allowed to "go home"?

no, for now I begin, groping with hands rotted off
to understand those who were here before us
and all I ask of you
in the name of what you want to know
be good to those who come after us

translated by Ernst van Heerden

Frank Chipasula

Born in Malawi in 1949, the Zambian poet Frank Chipasula studied at both Chancellor College, Zambia, and the University of Zambia. Chipasula currently teaches at the University of Nebraska, Omaha. Perhaps because he lives in exile, he insists on absolute truth in his poetry in the face of tyranny and oppression. This is a manifesto for "the poetry of witness" that watches the injustices of the world closely and exposes them in daylight.

My poetry is exacting a confession
from me: I will not keep the truth from my song.
I will not bar the voice undressed by the bees
from entering the gourd of my bow-harp.
I will not wash the blood off the image;
I will let it flow from the gullet
Slit by the assassin's dagger through
The run-on line until it rages in the verbs of terror;
And I will distil life into the horrible adjectives.
I will not clean the poem to impress the tyrant;
I will not bend my verses into the bow of a praise song.
I will put the symbols of murder hidden in high offices
In the centre of my crude lines of accusations.
I will undress our land and expose her wounds.
I will pierce the silence around our land with sharp metaphors,
And I will point the light of my poems into the dark
Nooks where our people are pounded to pulp.
I will not coat my words in lumps of sugar
But serve them to our people with the bitter quinine.
I will not keep the truth from my heartstringed guitar;
I will thread the voice from the broken lips
Through my volatile verbs that burn the lies.
I will ask only that the poem watch the world closely;
I will ask only that the image put a lamp on the dark
Ceiling in the dark sky of my land and light the dirt.
Today my poetry has exacted a confession from me.

Lupenga Mphande

Lupenga Mphande was born in Malawi. Educated in Malawi, England, and the United States, he is currently an associate professor in the Department of African American and African Studies and coordinator of the African Languages Program at Ohio State University. With simple bravery and resigned strength, the speaker in this poem accepts his lot in life: to oppose and resist an unjust regime—for the children's sake and for the ancestors' as well.

I WAS SENT FOR

I was sent for,
As happens in the country. That morning,
I lit the mine shaft for the last time
And proceeded in haste on the long journey home:
Miles by air, miles by land, Welkom to Mzimba.
I traveled through gentle land peopled with white thorns,
On a day that looked endless.
As I approached my village kraal in rainless heat
A pair of wagtails rose to a roof, whistling in flight,
Bobbing and darting; in the sadness of their whistles
I heard my wife's voice telling of "reprisals"
Mounted against our people, our charred countryside,
Our hungry children. She had written,
"The government thinks we are the enemy!"
I remembered our ancestors in rock paintings,
Forever trapped in the searing granite.
I looked at the trees and thought, "A curse on informers!
For our children's sake we must fight."
I have been sent for. It has happened before in our country.

Tanure Ojaide

Tanure Ojaide was born in the Delta region of Nigeria in 1948. A widely published poet, he has won a variety of poetry awards, including the Commonwealth Poetry Prize for the Africa Region and the Association of Nigerian Authors' Poetry Prize. He is currently a professor of African American and African Studies at the University of North Carolina, Charlotte. In a tone of quiet irony barely masking a sense of total outrage, the exiled Nigerian poet describes the repressive and violent regime of one of his nation's leaders, whose thousands of executions all but turned the republic into a "boneyard."

STATE EXECUTIVE

> Wherever we dug for safety, we dug into corpses.
> —Donald Hall, *The One Day*

"Wherever we dug for safety, we dug into corpses."
Whatever we hid in our guts, he found and wiped out.
Wherever we fled, he sent his lightning envoy to strike us.
We could not shrug off this vicious head from our lives.

Shreds of intellectuals hang from branches of baobabs,
bones dissolve into the lagoon to assault us with bad breath.
We have dug up arms from distant farms
and wondered if the whole republic were a boneyard.

All the evaporated faces found solace in the soil,
all the spear-tongued critics fed roaming hyenas.
Every year raises the chief's fund of machetes;
winds smother wails and rain washes the topsoil.

From the beginning Ogiso chose cost-effective means
to exterminate the bugs that would ruin his rule;
he found beggar hands to implement blood without stain.
He enlisted assassins from churches and mosques.

For him the long arm of state reaches everywhere
and he circles the land with pointed steel.
The executive wields foreign-forged axes and rifles,
the human-hooded snake steals in to bite dissonant tongues.

Thousands of executions prove his inaugural boast
of peace as an array of still bodies,
a cemetery with a busy stock exchange,
a bloodpool chlorinated for a bath.

His rule a great safari of poachers,
a vast ward of diseased consultants,

and a free market of dismembered bodies.
Ogres parade the streets in smart uniform.

Every day lingers with his infinite arm,
everywhere throws up freshly savaged flesh,
everyone yawns from the blood-laden air.
"Wherever we dug for safety, we dug into corpses."

Jorge Rebelo

Jorge Rebelo was born in 1940 in Mozambique. He was the editor of *The Mozambique Revolution,* and much of his poetry concerns itself with the struggle for independence in his country. "Poem of a Militant" reflects a tradition as ancient as human history: the young male sees it as his duty to protect his group, to struggle for freedom, and to help stem the flood of his mother's tears.

POEM OF A MILITANT

Mother
I have an iron gun
I your son
he whom you saw one day
beneath his chains

(And you wept then
as if my chains tied
and wounded
your hands and feet)
free now your son is all ready
your son has an iron gun

My gun will break all chains
open all prisons
kill all tyrants
give back the land to our people

Mother it's lovely to struggle for liberty
there is a message of justice

in every bullet I fire
and ancient dreams are awakened

In the combat, on the battle front
your image so close invades me
I am fighting for you too, Mother.
So that tears bathe your eyes no more.

Central America and the Caribbean

Ricardo Castillo

Ricardo Castillo (b. 1954) lives in Guadalajara, Mexico, where he leads workshops in creative writing. What begins as a playfully naughty poem about an indelicate subject turns into a fierce revolutionary statement. A bodily function takes on its metaphorical significance of contempt for those who measure life in terms of material comfort, and it becomes a symbol for the equality of all humanity.

ODE TO THE URGE

Urination is the major accomplishment of engineering
at least insofar as drainage is concerned.
Furthermore, to urinate is a pleasure.
What's there to say? One takes a leak
saluting love and friends,
one spills himself long into the throat of the world
to remind himself we're warm inside, and to stay tuned up.
All this is important
now that the world's emitting disaster signals,
intoxicated hiccups.
Because it's necessary, for pure love of life, to urinate
on the silver service,
on the seats of sports cars,
in swimming pools with underwater lights,
worth easily 15 or 16 times more than their owners.

To urinate until our throats ache,
right down to the last drops of blood.
To urinate on those who see life as a waltz,
to scream at them, Long live the Cumbia, señores,
Everybody up to shake his ass,
until we shake off this mystery we are
and the fucked-up love of suffering it.
And long live the Jarabe Zapateado, too,
because reality is in the back and to the right,
where you don't go wearing a tux.
(Nobody's yet gotten rid of TB by beating his chest.)
I'm pissing down from the manger of life,
I just want to be the greatest pisser in history,
Oh Mama, for the love of God, the greatest pisser in history

translated by Robert L. Jones

Fabio Morabito

Fabio Morabito was born in 1955 of Italian parentage in Alexandria, Egypt. After a child-hood in Italy, he moved with his family to Mexico. He has won a number of literary prizes. He writes in Spanish and lives in Mexico City. Instead of the traditional male conqueror of Nature and empire builder, in Fabio Morabito we have a newer voice, one that seems to honor a growing "green" perspective, where man is still the builder of course but one who tries to respect Nature, to take into account where a house "will do least harm."

MASTER OF AN EXPANSE

I will look this land over
slowly, cover it all with my eyes
and my feet
before I set up the first wall,
a virgin panorama
dense and full
of dangers.
I want to remember all this
when it is hidden by the house,
for, I don't want to confuse myself

with the house,
I won't forget
this land
or how I am
now
master of an expanse
of everything I have.
Better to have no house
than be inside one as a blind man.
I will remain here
slow,
native and poor,
see the land as it is,
imagining nothing,
not a wall, not a brick,
listen to it all
until I know
where a house will
do least harm,
where it is best to place
the first stone.

translated by E. Bell

Luis Rogelio Nogueras

The Cuban poet Luis Rogelio Nogueras (1944–85) was born in Havana. He published eight poetry collections and three novels, several of which won prizes in Cuba. Nogueras writes about the relationship between politics and love. Not until a man loves can he truly take on a political consciousness. His love relationship feeds him the strength to step outside himself into the larger world of "strikes and battles."

A POEM

In the vortex of class warfare
he wrote a love poem

Faced with the hunger for justice

he wrote a love poem

Surrounded by death and torture
he wrote a love poem

Amidst blood and bullets
he wrote a love poem

A poem for no one
for a nonexistent love

And now,
loved to the depth of his shadow
by this girl who kisses his wounds
now
that in the chill of night she covers him
with her naked body
he arms himself with pen and paper
and careful not to disturb his lover's dream
he leaves the bed
to write a political poem
a poem shaken by the fury of strikes and battles.

translated by Mark Weiss

Sex and Sexuality

One generation after
another, the blood rose and fell
that lifts us together.
—Jon Stallworthy

The word *sexuality* should probably be written in the plural for this section because men's sexuality is as diverse as men are. But whether the poems here are from heterosexual or homosexual men (we encountered no explicitly bisexual poems, though they surely exist), they share a certain urgency about sex and desire that is explicitly male and that women surely know a lot about. Sometimes that urgency is tender, sometimes desperate, sometimes playful, sometimes deadly serious, but it is almost always, well, *urgent*.

Some of the poets writing here have lived through a "sexual revolution," and poems about male sexuality are probably more candid today (at least published poems) than they were a century ago. Of course, a long tradition of bawdy lyrics predates any sexual revolution and the poems we've published here. But these contemporary male poems about sexuality strike us not as bawdy but as revelatory. That is, they are unusually frank and unapologetic about the primacy of sexual experience for many men. The Hungarian Péter Zihaly even wittily connects his own sexual history with the history of dicators in our time and slyly implies that a man's sexual urgency is a dictator of its own. Michael Hulse reminds us how uninteresting everything else seems when one is about to embark upon a sexual adventure.

Many of the poems about sexuality are celebrations of the female body. New Zealander David Eggleton traces the contours of a woman's flesh as if they comprised a Braille text; the Bengali Sunil Gangopadhyay finds the female form a much greater work of art than even his own poetry and is willing to sacrifice his artistry to it; the Argentinean Ricardo Feierstein takes an architectural view of the body as "a supple organism where every part / works with another and another and another" and which seems designed with sex at its center. Some men linger on particular bodily parts or functions: the Hungarian Zbigniew Herbert waxes eloquent about the "rosy ear" of his lover, while the Australian Clive James asks for the sweat of one of his female idols.

Homosexual feelings, attitudes, and relationships are expressed in poems by Jonathan Fisher, who tells us the "lust story" of an unreciprocated male love affair; by the Russian Aleksander Shatalov, who pays homage to one of his predecessors who wrote about homosexuality when it was regarded as a serious crime in Russia; and by Lucas Icarus Simon, who chronicles the fleeting moments of a love affair between two men. The Cuban American Orlando Ricardo Menes shows us a darker side of male sexuality—older men who prey upon younger ones.

But by far the majority of poems in this section are celebrations. The writers included here offer few apologies for the necessity of their sexual desires and for making those desires a subject for their poetry. They accept the fact that, as the late Allen Ginsberg put it, "this form of life needs sex."

Asia

Rofel G. Brion

Rofel G. Brion is a Filipino poet and former Fulbright scholar. He is currently the chair of the Department of Interdisciplinary Studies at Ateneo de Manila University. His "Love Song" reminds us that a man's fascination with women's breasts can probably be traced to childhood and the nurturing that those breasts may have provided. The speaker in this poem is unnerved by a woman who talks about exposing her breasts publicly in order to feed her child.

LOVE SONG

One long and humid afternoon
As we discussed everything and nothing
Over tall glasses of iced tea,
You bit into your biscuit and said
That, once, in a crowded jeepney,
Your daughter wailed of hunger
So you bared your breast

To feed her.
When you began to explain

How ordinary people in ordinary jeepneys
Remain cool and composed
At the sight of bare breasts
As long as they are a mother's
Wanting to feed her child,
I bit the rim of my glass
As I tried to decide
Whether I wished I were
A stranger in that jeepney
Or the father of your child.

Sunil Gangopadhyay

Born in 1934 in Faridpur, now Bangladesh, Sunil Gangopadhyay is a leading Bengali poet and novelist and lives in Calcutta, India. His sensuous poem "Blindfold" incorporates a number of themes: the male propensity to seek "salvation" through the agency of the female's body, the desire to transcend earthbound limitations through the erotic, a celebration of a male poet's love of a particular woman, and the power of beauty, the power of art, the power of the body.

BLINDFOLD

Arundhati, my all,
open your mouth, push your tongue
down my throat, let our kisses resound
through the universe, through hell, Arundhati,
become a light, make light,   light,
                              Arundhati, light—
Not the flashlight of eyes, but a light in the heart,
Arundhati, won't you be the lighthouse of my life?

Your legs on my chest and fluorescent thighs bring to mind
                              the beauty of fishes
on temple walls—such beauty, why? As if beauty were food

for those born blind, or a red flag to the bull, immersed
in water a prayer to the sun, like love blindfolded.
Arundhati, my life, my all, take my eyes, my breast, my lips,
take your pick,
spoil, break, throw to the winds, Arundhati, fling away.

If you will give me love, Arundhati, I shall stab poetry in the back
and walk away to an avowed death on your pyre, yes that's best,
            fling then one eye into water—
I had so wanted to go to heaven—where else would I find the shade of
breasts to hide my face in—not in the woods of this earth, not in sketches,
                              in the ecstasy of the flesh
Exposed faces are too busy, too riddled with arteries, as though
they move in revenge; they run from one end to another,
                         into space, into disaster.
I too come back from unloving, Arundhati, to drink of the tears of your eyes.
Seeing terrible fires break out on earth, in heaven, on College Street, I too
Whiplash art, pound, break, destroy it, with a kick send it to hell.
Your body is art, my body is art, Arundhati,   yours, mine.

translated by Nandini Gupta

Hung Hung

> The Taiwanese poet Hung Hung has authored four volumes of poetry and translated numerous works from English and European languages. The narrator here juxtaposes the memory of a remarkable session of lovemaking with the image of a tooth lost in childhood. What's the connection? Some things are irreplaceable. Oh, sure, a new tooth will grow in, and other sex will seem to be as grand, but . . .

HELAS!

My earlobe in your mouth, my lips and tongue on your breasts, my palms pressed against your armpits, my penis in some deep and unplumbed place inside you. And, something I had never seen before, myself, as seen from behind, receding in the tableau of your eyes.

These things can never be retrieved, and I've forgotten most of them in any case. I exist in some other body, carried toward some unfamiliar place. I still possess the mirror you left behind, the scent of your flesh, the grain of your voice, the way you look when you stand on tiptoe to reach the wash—how long will these things follow me down the years?

As the sun hangs upside down outside the window, on the winding road I suddenly glimpse a tooth I lost in childhood, glistening in a certain corner of the city.

translated by Steve Bradbury

George Oommen

George Oommen is a poet from India. He works for *The Times of India* and lives in Mumbai. The speaker's "private sorrow" is his own impotence, a topic rarely commented on publicly by men in any culture. His desire is for women to look beyond this "curse of nature" and recognize his manhood in other ways.

A PRIVATE SORROW

Her looks were inviting;
some unquenched thirst was written on her face
to drag the whole sea in
and to submerge in the flood,

And I—
I was all smiles.

You may say that the soul is more important
than the body
for the will comes from within.
My soul was even ready for polygamy.

You know—
What went wrong is neither body nor soul;
it's just a curse of nature.

Woman can be passive in copulation,
may be a gift or curse for them,
but man—

man has to pierce,
pierce and pierce to quench the mutual thirst.

By now you know what went wrong, I
couldn't rise to the occasion.

How much I'd have liked
to become the sea,
to quench her thirst.
But that's a different story.

And if hopes are given wings,
dear women,
you will see the sea raging,
in my looks and walk.

Vikram Seth

Vikram Seth was born in 1952 in Calcutta. Educated at Oxford, Seth was also a creative
writing fellow at Stanford. He is a widely published poet and novelist and a recipient of the
Commonwealth Poetry Prize of Asia. Men's fabled and stereotypically casual attitudes
toward sex find clever expression in his poem "Unclaimed." Just beneath the urbane tone,
though, lies a profound sadness.

UNCLAIMED

To make love with a stranger is the best.
There is no riddle and there is no test.—

To lie and love, not aching to make sense
Of this night in the mesh of reference.

To touch, unclaimed by fear of imminent day,
And understand, as only strangers may.

To feel the beat of foreign heart to heart

Preferring neither to prolong nor part.

To rest within the unknown arms and know
That this is all there is; that this is so.

Europe

Alain Bosquet

Alain Bosquet (1919–98) was born in Odessa, Russia. He enlisted in the U.S. Army and taught for a few years in the United States before settling in France, where he was literary editor of *Le Monde* for many years. In this very French dialogue combining sex and intellectuality, Bosquet reinforces the perception that men always have one thing on their minds, that whatever they discuss with women, sex usually lurks just below the surface.

THE LOVERS

I said: "Your Christian name?"
She said: "Whatever you like."
I said: "Carole, for instance."
She said: "All right, for the time being."
I said: "You are alone?"
She said: "But with you."
I said: "Shall we make love?"
She said: "Your desire has every right to be fulfilled."
I said: "Who are the men you see?"
She said: "Croupiers, industrialists, swimming instructors."
I said: "Your preferences?"
She said: "Those who are sad, but not too sad."
I said: "Shall we eat?"
She said: "Oysters are good for starters."
I said: "You read occasionally?"
She said: "Yes, Sartre, Camus, Thomas Mann."
I said: "You have nice breasts."
She said: "I like them too."

I said: "You are almost divine."
She said: "How right you are."
I said: "My gift to you . . ."
She said: "I don't always have to be paid."
We made love
on Monday, Tuesday, Sunday,
We discussed Flaubert,
then Tolstoy,
I said: "You have unforgettable knees."
She said: "Only knees?"
We grew tired of each other
on the same day, at the same time,
which is rare and commendable.

translated by William Jay Smith

Tonino Guerra

Born in 1920, screenwriter and poet Tonino Guerra has collaborated with many of Italy's most important filmmakers including Federico Fellini and Michelangelo Antonioni. He has written more than fifteen volumes of poetry and fiction, mostly in the dialect of his native Santarcangelo di Romagna in the province of Forli. The straightforwardness of "Canto Twenty-Four" may not seem politically correct. The word *cunt* uttered by a man usually has obscene connotations, but here Guerra turns it into virtually everything and sees it clearly for what it is: the source of all human life.

CANTO TWENTY-FOUR

The cunt is a spiderweb
a funnel of silk
the heart of all flowers;
the cunt is a door
going who knows where
or a wall
you have to knock down.

There are happy cunts
cunts that are totally crazy

cunts that are wide or tight
worthless cunts
chatterboxes that stutter,
and those that yawn
and don't say a word
even if you kill them.

The cunt is a mountain
white with sugar,
a forest entered by wolves,
it's a carriage that pulls the horses;
the cunt is an empty whale
filled with black air and fireflies;
it's the prick's pocket,
its nightcap
an oven that burns everything.

The cunt when it's time
is the face of God,
his mouth.
Everything in the world comes out from the cunt
the trees, the clouds, the sea
and men come out one at a time
from every race.
It's from the cunt that even the cunt comes out.
Praise the cunt.

translated by Adria Bernardi

Zbigniew Herbert

The Polish poet Zbigniew Herbert (1924–98) had degrees in both economics and philosophy. During World War II he was a member of the Polish Resistance. He was awarded the Nicholaus Lenau Prize in 1965 and the Jerusalem Literature Prize in 1991. In the following poem, a woman's ear, "a comic petal of skin," newly rediscovered by her lover, deepens the mystery of life, love, and the erotic.

ROSY EAR

I thought
but I know her so well
we have been living together so many years

I know
her bird-like head
white arms
and belly

until one time
on a winter evening
she sat down beside me
and in the lamplight
falling from behind us
I saw a rosy ear

a comic petal of skin
a conch with living blood
inside it

I didn't say anything then—
it would be good to write
a poem about a rosy ear
but not so that people would say
what a subject he chose
he's trying to be eccentric

so that nobody even would smile
so that they would understand that I proclaim
a mystery

I didn't say anything then
but that night when we were in bed together
delicately I essayed
the exotic taste
of a rosy ear

   translated by Czeslaw Milosz

Michael Hulse

Michael Hulse, the son of an English father from the Five Towns and a German mother from near Trier in the Mosel Valley, was born in 1955 and grew up in Stoke-on-Trent, England. The speaker in his poem "Concentrating" is clearly distracted by a woman—as men notoriously are—but at a very inopportune time.

CONCENTRATING

Standing at the
window watching

three Italian
women rowing,

rocking and tipping and
bobbing, I hear

their laughter find
its natural level

like water. Stay.
Take a look.

Don't you agree,
the flyaway girl

in the cherry cloche
looks like Zelda Fitzgerald?

I'd wave to her
but both my hands

are occupied
unbuttoning your blouse.

Alan Jenkins

Alan Jenkins is deputy editor of the *Times Literary Supplement* in London. He has pub-
lished four collections of poetry. A man's encounter with a prostitute is not often the stuff of
poetry, but Jenkins finds common ground between the narrator's streetwalker neighbor and
himself. They both have secrets; they both fear "the same sad, comical fear of being
caught." But is their unique camaraderie undercut by the last brutal line?

STREET LIFE

I come home at all hours; all hours she receives
her callers, her gentlemen friends, upstairs.
In the street, a car draws up, she breaks into a foolish little run.
I know her. Even in the rawest weather, she wears
no tights or stockings, leaves three buttons of her blouse undone.
Seeing me, calling, she comes over. We are alike, we share
the same sad, comical fear of being caught
together on our corner, of our long views falling
short, of being caught, of being caught.
Flirting with me, she fiddles with her hair, her shoes,
makes something up when I ask her how she got the bruise
that cascades down her cheek, the purples, reds and blues
of a fruit tart; the colours, almost, of my glans the night
I paid her twenty quid and pushed it up her, hard and tight.

Brendan Kennelly

Brendan Kennelly was born in County Kerry in 1936. He is the author of more than a
dozen books of poetry. The act of swimming is seen here as an act of love; woman is seen as
a force in nature—as support, replenishment, acceptance, and a source of strength. Per-
haps this is a bit old fashioned, but a larger view might generously allow for an erotic rela-
tionship with nature and a "natural" relationship with women.

266

THE SWIMMER

For him the Shannon opens
Like a woman.
He has stepped over the stones

And cut the water
With his body
But this river does not bleed for

Any man. How easily
He mounts the waves, riding them
As though they

Whispered subtle invitations to his skin,
Conspiring with the sun
To offer him

A white, wet rhythm. The deep beneath
Gives full support
To the marriage of wave and heart,

The waves he breaks turn back to stare
At the repeated ceremony
And the hills of Clare

Witness the fluent weddings
The flawless congregation
The choiring foam that sings

To limbs which must, once more,
Rising and falling in the sun,
Return to shore.

Again he walks upon the stones,

A new music in his heart,
A river in his bones

Flowing forever through his head
Private as a grave
Or as the bridal bed.

Kemal Kurt

Kemal Kurt (1947–2002) was born in Turkey. A journalist and photographer, he lived for many years in Berlin. In this odd poem of male arousal, the poet seems caught between pure eroticism and lust and the desire to calm down the woman he loves.

GYN-ASTICS

down there
where my feelings for you
come to a head
i feel the strength
of my love
and the flow
of your warmth

the temporary result
of my feelings
is that i desire you
the sight of you
strokes my eyes
your body has
established itself
in my head
and damned me
to speechlessness

I want to
caress
your worn out body

with my soft voice
and calm you

Sleep!

translated by Marilya Veteto-Conrad

Henri Michaux

Henri Michaux (1899–1984) was born in Namur, Belgium. A painter as well as a poet, he traveled widely in Africa and Asia and also supported himself in Paris as a teacher and secretary. What man has not fantasized some version of the complete sexual freedom described by Michaux in the following poem? Through a tongue-in-cheek blend of surrealism, common sense, and outrageous male egotism, the poet arrives at the ultimate reductive male version of the "good life": good sex and good work.

SIMPLICITY

What has been particularly lacking in my life up to now is simplicity. Little by little I am beginning to change.

For instance, I always go out with my bed now and when a woman pleases me, I take her and go to bed with her immediately.

If her ears are ugly and large, or her nose, I remove them along with her clothes and put them under the bed, for her to take back when she leaves; I keep only what I like.

If her underthings would improve by being changed, I change them immediately. This is my gift. But if I see a better-looking woman go by, I apologize to the first and make her disappear at once.

People who know me claim that I am incapable of doing what I have just described, that I haven't enough spunk. I once thought so myself, but that was because I was not then doing everything *just as I pleased.*

Now I always have excellent afternoons. (Mornings I work.)

translated by Richard Ellman

Aleksandr Shatalov

Aleksandr Shatalov was born in 1957 in Russia. He has published four collections of poetry and is the founder of the independent publishing house, Glagol. He lives in Moscow. In this celebration of the male body, which is reminiscent of Walt Whitman and acknowledges Russia's most prominent gay poet, homoerotic love is commingled with images of water and a river.

UNTITLED

I love bathing in the river; you see
your own body through water,
gold light reflects the surface, and
when you dive in and open your eyes
down there, everything is so green, so
green, and you see the little fish rushing
by . . . And it is not true that the body
is sinful, that beauty is sinful . . .
—Mikhail Kuzmin, *Wings**

I don't know how to swim . . .
—Nikolai Sapunov, last words†

the age of aquarius mineral water taking a bath
in the river that smells of dampness the body's contours distorted
fragility of extremities
                    and suddenly transpired well proportioned body
the rainbow of splashes near hands
                                as if a butterfly passed by the eyes
or weeds rushing up from the bottom
towards light again toward quick and strong male body
the greenness of backwater reminds of a place for seduction
chilly and young there is no limit to perfection
see contours the outlines breaking i have to make do
with little such as the hits of a whip
on muscular shoulders the lips tingle a rushing
movement so fast the throat chokes on old
vomit the instinct of self-preservation
but in the morning the icy water will burn me again

and movements of the heavy male body at night
rhythmical just like blood's explosions in the heart

translated by Vitaly Chernetsky

*Mikhail Kuzmin (1872–1936) was Russia's most prominent gay poet and prose writer; *Wings*
(1906), his first novel, is a manifesto calling for the social acceptance of homosexuality.
†Nikolai Sapunov (1880–1912), a painter, was one of Kuzmin's lovers; he drowned in a boating
accident.

Jon Stallworthy

Jon Stallworthy was born to New Zealand parents in London in 1935. He is a professor of
English at Oxford and a Fellow of the British Academy and of the Royal Society of Litera-
ture. In "The Source" he describes entering a woman's body, the source of all human life, as
a transcendent experience, where he connects with previous and future generations. No
wonder male sexuality is so filled with longing.

THE SOURCE

The dead living in their memories
are, I am persuaded, the source
of all that we call instinct.

Taking me into your body
you take me out of my own,
releasing an energy,
a spirit not mine alone

but theirs locked in my cells.
One generation after
another, the blood rose and fell
that lifts us together.

Such ancient, undiminished
longings—my longing! Such

tenderness, such famished
desires! My fathers in search

of fulfillment storm through
my body, releasing now
loved women locked in you
and hungering to be found.

Péter Zilahy

Hungarian poet Péter Zilahy was born in 1970 in Budapest. He is chief editor of Jak Books.
The speaker chronicles his sexual coming-of-age in this wry prose poem, linking his sexual
experiences to the rise and fall of communist dictators, thereby raising questions about the
connections between politics and sex. Perhaps, at bottom, the same impulses drive them
both.

DICTATORS

My bumpy road to sexual maturity was paved with the death of communist
    dictators.
My first sexual experience coincided with the death of Mao Zedong. I was bitten
    by
a girl called Diana in nursery school. My voice broke when Tito died, and I first
    came
when Brezhnev went. For three days there was nothing but classical music on the
    radio,
which I thought was overdoing it; some schools even closed. Then for a long time,
nothing. As an experiment, I took a girl to the movies, but the film was too good,
    and
I got cramps in my hand. Events accelerated in high school. It was only a couple
of months between the first kiss and the first frantic fumbling. Following
    Andropov,
Chernenko also checked out. A couple more weeks, and it was Enver's turn, but I'd
rather not go into that. I first found out about the G spot when Ceausescu was
executed. Kim Il Sung cast new light on my broadening horizons; luckily, the
    charges
were dropped. Fidel . . .

translated by Judith Sonnabend

Africa

Bahadur Tejani

Kenyan poet Bahadur Tejani was born near Mt. Kilimanjaro. He was educated at the Universities of Makerere and Cambridge. He teaches at the University of Nairobi. Tejani feels that the men and women of his culture have in some sense become "untouchable" to each other. Is this a gap between the sexes? Does it have to do with the lack of displays of public affection? The speaker wants men and women to have the spontaneous animal sexuality that he sees in two playing dogs.

LINES FOR A HINDI POET

Walking in the children's park
the poet said to me,
look: those dogs
playing at love

and these men
and their women
camera like
with photographic eyes
drinking deep at
founts of canine spontaneity.

"Verily," said the poet to me
"the brown man should learn
love from these dogs.
See how unafraid they are
how free."

I saw the bitch
offer her belly
but when he came
to smell her
she bounded like

a naughty child
and nipped him
with a quick-kissing mouth
and ran
so he should run after her.

And stood at bay
defying him with the innocent passion
of a pure woman
with love in her eyes
necking gracefully when he came,
with an arched back
and free limbs
he rising and stooping
with her
in mock tension
of love-hostility.

I wanted to tear the sky
or rend the earth with my nails
shrieks to the wild wind
so a cataclysmic call would come.

Lord! Lord!
Let the brown blood
rediscover the animal
in itself,
and have free limbs
and laughing eyes of
love-play.
Lord, make these men
and their women
feel
that each to other
is not an untouchable.

South America

Ricardo Feierstein

Ricardo Feierstein—poet, novelist, and architect—was born in Buenos Aires in 1942.
Hailed as one of the most significant authors of the new generation of Jewish Argentinean
writers, he has published three books of poetry, a book of short stories, a book of essays,
and four novels. Here Feierstein creates a strangely compelling appreciation of the global
sexuality of the human body, its geography, its perfection of interrelated parts, its inherent
capacity to provide us with pleasure and perhaps even transcendence.

SEX

You can sense, after a slow apprenticeship,
the perfume of mystery, of jungle and rivulet,
the greenish fragrance of secret areas
lips coarse as coiled rawhide
and hives slowly rocking back and forth
like honey-grenades on the point of explosion
the unsettled eyes of a woodland animal
the vertigo of immersion in a sea of foam
feeling yourself a fish, a sword, a shark, a fin.

Then they begin to value
the line that runs rapidly down from the neck
to hang at the point of the chin,
the tiny ear, squatting below the brow
the curving helix outlining the shoulders,
a hollow behind a knee,
a shy bump at the wrist,
the sharply angled slope of an erratic ankle,
that no-man's land between the scapulae.

I mean, if you don't already understand,
how the whole body grows limber like a stem
a supple organism where every part

works with another and another and another
where the shoulder and arm lead one way to the throat
or articulate the forearm, hand
and fingers ending in measured nails
a balanced costume of skin and bones
that is always perfect, and sometimes more.

translated by J. Kates and Stephen A. Sadow

North America

Orlando Ricardo Menes

Orlando Ricardo Menes, a poet of Cuban, Peruvian, and U.S. heritage, currently teaches in the creative writing program at Notre Dame University. The rape of a young boy by an older man is the painful subject of this poem. Told from the point of view of the victim remembering the incident as an adult, the story presents us with the distressing details and underscores the long-lasting effects of the trauma.

SODOMY

Greasy and grimy at day's end, the plumbers sat
on broken toilets drinking Miller High Lifes,
smoking twenty-five cent cigars rolled on some exile's sweaty thigh.
A married man with two girls, Pepón threw me
kisses saying *¡Qué rico estás!* How tasty you look!

I was barely thirteen, my voice like a girl's,
no pubic hairs. They laughed, belched. Lips red, swollen—
tabaco macho sears flesh, makes eyes cry—a fat man
roared, *¡Coño, métele tu hierro al mariquita!*
Shit, man, stick your iron rod into that sissy boy.

Pepón made thrusting movements; eyes gleamed,
belly jiggled, sweat smelled of rotten papaya.
I shivered, feet soaked, mouth dry, penis shrunk

to a cashew. Spit shooting sunbathing lizards,
cigar stump like beef jerky, the fat man clapped, stamped,

Dale rabo encendido pa' que pueda gozar.
Give'm your tail on fire to play with.
Pepón pulled out a huge *rabo* through the hole
in his pants, charged like a bull. I ran for the gate,
guard dogs running in circles, pulling at their chains.

Pepón tripped on cast iron, face scraping gravel,
metal shavings; *los plomeros* hurled beer bottles
and shouted *Comiste tierra bugarrón.** You ate dirt. . . .
Days later, as I was threading galvanized steel
on the Ridgid machine, Pepón came up behind me,

squeezing my buttocks, pushing his finger inside.
Suaves como la masa, he whispered. Soft like dough.
I peed in my pants. Pepón touched himself,
making licking noises with his blackish tongue.
Kicking his foot, I spun out of Pepón's grip,

my shirt ripped. Hid behind a parapet of tubs
until the lights went out—weeping, drumming hard
with my fist, saliva soothing scratches.
Muerto de vergüenza, dead with shame, I told no one;
mamá raised me to be macho,

mejor que sea un hijo asesino
que maricón, she'd warn. Better that a son
be a murderer than a faggot.
Ten years later I still could not sleep with buttocks
exposed. Pepón would reappear in nightmares,

breaking through a window, stuffing my mouth
with steel wool as he pumped me from the rear.
I'd wake sweating and screaming,

my hand covering the anus, legs squeezed tight,
sphincter contracted, eyes watching for broken glass.

Bugarrón—in Cuban slang, a man who has sex with effeminate men or boys but does not consider
himself a homosexual

Len Roberts

Len Roberts was born in Cohoes, New York, in 1947. He has published nine collections of
poetry and is a professor of English at Northampton Community College, Bethlehem,
Pennsylvania. Here he describes a dying man telling his friends about "the greatest gift a
woman can give," while bringing up his mother's love-hate relationship with him. The
poem expresses a series of complex erotic interactions.

THE PROBLEM

After he told us that being blown
is the greatest gift a woman can give
he downed another whiskey and coke,
whispered his mother had both hated
and loved him, that was the problem,
the rest of us nodding our heads
as the dark came down and the fireflies
    started their old dance,
our friend dying faster each instant,
slumped in the lawn chair with errant
cells that multiplied into *slender tentacles*,
or so his wife whispered, once he'd passed out,
leaning toward our faces in the charcoal grill glow
as though she were our mother, and we, her children,
    had to know,
waving her arms, while I—forgive me,—
couldn't take my eyes off her lips,
couldn't stop thinking how they felt on his dick,
wondering if she swallowed all his cum
or pulled that old trick, letting it spurt
while she held him tight against her cheek.

Oceania, Australia, and New Zealand

David Eggleton

David Eggleton lives in Dunedin, New Zealand. He began his career as a performance poet in the early 1980s, strongly influenced by the writers of America's beat generation. "Bouquet of Dead Flowers" is the poem of a man hypnotized by the erotic charge of a woman's body, but both the title and the poem's ending remind the reader that such rapture is too often fleeting.

BOUQUET OF DEAD FLOWERS

Her body was braille, was scent bottles uncorked,
was the music score her breath hummed;
and beyond us the sun was the giggling Buddha,
robed in saffron, licking his finger
to tear months from the calendar.
The days withdrew from us like acupuncture needles
each morning when we woke up,
and slipped from the bedding seeking the promise
of orange juice you could lick from the moment.
We sailed through seas of incense smoke together,
tranced by the gorgeous melodies of Indian-thighed summer,
by the gardens of wild poppies which grew all around us,
in the deserted volcanic quarries of the holiday season.
It seemed then that stereo speakers, always vibrating
Their bongo heartbeat, busy bees in the calyx of a flower,
drumming its way through stormy passion.
Spiky juju crystals of the silence between us
were needed to calm that billowing passion,
and the dances we went to at night
only stirred it up, as the whole world duckwalked
with us, or were dirty dogs shaking down,
the brand-new leaves in that summer-of-love tree
fluttering on the breeze of yesterday's sound.

Jonathan Fisher

Jonathan Fisher lives in Christchurch, New Zealand. He is at work on his first collection of poems. In "Six Part Lust Story," Fisher describes a gay man's attraction to a straight man as well as an older man's attraction to a younger man. In doing so he tells the tale of many similar relationships.

SIX PART LUST STORY

1
Steve's very beautiful—
with dirt blond hair
blue eyes, thick brown
eyebrows, a small flattened
nose, pouting lips

features that become more
perfect the longer
you gaze at him

2
He's short & thin, some
would call him weedy
he always wears torn light
blue jeans that frame his nice
compact bum

he sometimes resembles
a disheveled street urchin
in need of a safe haven

I always want to put my arms
around his tight body &
protect him from the horrors
of the world we all inhabit
in the way that nobody can

3

I'm ten years older than he is
this worries me—
when I was his age I always hated
grovelly older men always trying
to pick me up in bars
or as another writer said to me
as we sat outside a café in Auckland
sunshine ogling at some youths
in mock-disconsolence:
"I've become what I've always despised!"

4

He makes music
takes too many drugs
wears his girlfriend's
"Hey Sister" boxers,
when they're together,
lets me hug him when
I'm drunk & is followed
around by a group of other
lusting gay men

5

I don't think a relationship
would work with him
he's all over the place
& not after my last relationship
with a musician
(& let's use that word
in the *broadest* possible sense)
I guess it's just about sex

6
& whenever I run into him
on the street

I imagine tearing off his clothes
kissing him on the lips

& slowly working my way
down

I want to fuck him again
& again & again

but you know what
straight boys are like. . . .

Clive James

Clive James was born in Sydney in 1939. He was educated at the University of Sydney, where he was literary editor of *Honi Soit* and wrote for various university magazines. In this mock-heroic paean to female beauty, James uses the hyperbole of love poetry to express his admiration for a female tennis player. Is he just another man guilty of objectifying women? Can men ever admire women for their skills alone without considering their erotic appeal?

BRING ME THE SWEAT OF GABRIELA SABATINI

Bring me the sweat of Gabriela Sabatini
For I know it tastes as pure as Malvern water,
Though laced with bright bubbles like the aqua minerale
That melted the kidney stones of Michelangelo
As sunlight the snow in spring.

Bring me the sweat of Gabriela Sabatini
In a green Lycergus cup with a sprig of mint,
But add no sugar—
The bitterness is what I want.

If I craved sweetness I would be asking you to bring me
The tears of Annabel Croft.

I never asked for the wrist-bands of Maria Bueno,
Though their periodic transit of her glowing forehead
Was like watching a bear's tongue lap nectar.
I never asked for the blouse of Francoise Durr,
Who refused point-blank to improve her souffle serve
For fear of overdeveloping her upper arm—
Which indeed remained delicate as a fawn's femur,
As a fern's frond under which cool shadows gather
So that the dew lingers.

Bring me the sweat of Gabriela Sabatini
And give me credit for having never before now
Cried out with longing.
Though for all the years since TV acquired colour
To watch Wimbledon for even a single day
Has left me shaking with grief like an ex-smoker
Locked overnight in a cigar factory,
Not once have I let loose as now I do
The parched howl of deprivation.
The croak of need.

Did I ever demand, as I might well have done,
The socks of Tracy Austin?
Did you ever hear me call for the cast-off Pumas
Of Hana Mandlikova?
Think what might have been distilled from these things,
And what a small request it would have seemed—
It would not, after all, have been like asking
For something so intimate as to arouse suspicion
Of mental derangement.
I would not have been calling for Carling Bassett's knickers
Or the tingling, Teddy Tinling B-cup brassiere
Of Andrea Temesvari.

Yet I denied myself.
I have denied myself too long.

If I had been Pat Cash at that great moment
Of triumph, I would have handed back the trophy
Saying take that thing away
And don't let me see it again until
It spills what makes this lawn burst into flower:
Bring me the sweat of Gabriela Sabatini.

In the beginning there was Gorgeous Gussie Moran
And even when there was just her it was tough enough,
But by now the top hundred boasts at least a dozen knock-outs
Who make it difficult to keep one's tongue
From lolling like a broken roller blind.
Out of deference to Billie-Jean I did my best
To control my male chauvinist urges—
An objectivity made easier to achieve
When Betty Stove came clumping out to play
On a pair of what appeared to be bionic legs
Borrowed from Six Million Dollar Man.

I won't go so far as to say I harbour
Similar reservations about Steffi Graf—
I merely note that her thigh muscles when tense
Look interchangeable with those of Boris Becker—
Yet all are agreed that there can be no doubt
About Martina Navratilova:
Since she lent her body to Charles Atlas
The definition of the veins on her right forearm
Looks like the Mississippi river system
Photographed from a satellite,
And though she may unleash a charming smile
When crouching to dance at the ball with Ivan Lendl,
I have always found to admire her yet remain detached
Has been no problem.

But when the rain stops long enough for the true beauties
To come out swinging under the outshone sun,
The spectacle is hard for a man to take,
And in the case of this supernally graceful dish—
Likened to a panther by slavering sports reporters

Who pitiably fail to realise that any panther
With a top-spin forehand line drive like hers
Would be managed personally by Mark McCormack—
I'm obliged to admit defeat.

So let me drink deep from the bitter cup.
Take it to her between any two points of a tie-break
That she may shake above it her thick black hair,
A nocturne from which droplets as they fall
Rash like shooting stars—
And as their lustre becomes liqueur
Let the full calyx be repeatedly carried to me.
Until I tell you to stop
Bring me the sweat of Gabriela Sabatini.

Luke Icarus Simon

Luke Icarus Simon has completed two novels. Born in Nicosia, Cyprus, in 1963, Simon
lives in Sydney, Australia. He writes in both Greek and English. In "Measuring Apollo,"
two male lovers are seen from the perspective of one of them, the insecure one who com-
pares himself unfavorably to his partner. The speaker tries to hold together what seems to
be an unequal, tenuous relationship, as if by paying attention to details of measurement and
difference, he can succeed.

MEASURING APOLLO

We're together again
Two and a half inches separate us
Segregate us in height from each other
In bed the distance is just that
Down there
The same difference

Power walking on the beach at Apollo Bay
A winter mist   Is this heaven?
He's two and a half feet in front

His limbs are elongated   sinewy
I remain swarthy   stumpy

I want to speak
Call out in competition with the swirls of surf
Hey, this is it! This is as good as it gets, buddy!
It doesn't get any better than this.
I've learned though to shut the fuck up

The disquiet inside me feels like surprised ecstasy
As I walk steady towards his back   towards
Remembering his arm around me   three A.M.
The two and a half inches of space that divide us
As we drive around the majestic coast in a slick Cabrio

As we prepare dinner   narcissists   near each other
Two and a half inches   our breaths caress   as he asks
Do you ever think of mermaids? That someone beyond the horizon?
Those inches metamorphose into an uncrossable strait
Our song will always remain the same

Until life turns over the last unfriendly card
The laughing clown in colour   sadistic
Then six feet will replace those inches
Measured time and time again
Between us

APOLLO BAY   FEBRUARY 16, 1999

translated by the poet

Poets and Poetry,
Artists and Art

I chose silence, the turning of verses, the battle with words;
did he do better, my brave Lord, when he chose swords?
—Theo Dorgan

Although many men write poetry, most cultures do not regard poetry writing—or the creation of art generally—as an appropriate male profession. Western cultures in particular equate the writing of poetry with a kind of ineffectuality, perhaps best typified by W. H. Auden's famous lines, "Poetry makes nothing happen." Men are supposed to make things happen, get things done, and in many places if a young man tells his parents that he wants to be a poet, he's in for a stern lecture on how he intends to go about making a living.

That said, there is nonetheless a long tradition of men writing poetry in cultures as diverse as ancient Greece, Latin America, Asia, North America, and Africa—in other words, virtually throughout the world. But many men are self-conscious about the poetic vocation, which is reflected in many of the poems in this section.

This "self"-consciousness is buffered by a connection to the tradition in whatever language or culture in which the poet writes. There are many poems of homage here, and the tributes often cross cultures, as when the Nicaraguan Hector Avellán offers a declaration of love to the American pop icon Kurt Cobain, whose suicide traumatized a generation, or the Norwegian Jan Eric Vold acknowledges the art of the Japanese master Hokusai, or the late Kashmiri American Agha Shahid Ali recognizes the great Israeli poet Yehuda Amachai in a very traditional Arabic form, the *ghazal*.

Some poets try to take poetry a little less seriously. The Russian Evgeny Bunimovich insists that he's *not* a poet and that that's precisely what makes him interesting, while Simon Thompson parodies the romanticism of his fellow Canadian Leonard Cohen, whose song "Suzanne" was one of the great anthems of the 1960s.

Many of these poems remind us that poetry is essentially a metaphoric art. Poets are always showing us how one thing is like something else. Writing poetry is here compared to a woman sorting lentils (the Armenian Turkish poet Zahrad), bees producing honey (the Polish poet Adam Ziemianin), and man creating weapons (the Iranian Ahmad Shamlu). For many men, in many parts of the world, poetry still seems a calling, a vocation. Although poets rarely earn much money, they are regarded in some societies outside of the West with great esteem. Many face the essential question raised in the title of a poem by the Nepalese poet Bishwabimohan Shreshtha: "Should I Earn My Daily Bread, / or Should I Write a Poem?" For those committed to a life of poetry, the question is merely rhetorical.

Asia

Cecil Rajendra

Cecil Rajendra is a lawyer and poet who was born in Penang, Malaysia, and now practices law there. In "Prince of the Dance" he contrasts artists with bureaucrats, noticing in the process how little use the world seems to have for men who define their masculinity in other than traditional ways. He celebrates the gift of a dancer friend, whose art, like his own, gets little social support.

PRINCE OF THE DANCE

for Ramli Ibrahim

There is nothing so necessary to man as the dance. Without dancing a man can do nothing. All the disasters of men, all the fatal misfortunes of which history is full, the blunders of politicians . . . all this comes only from not knowing how to dance.
—Moliere

Your dance is age-
less; it transcends
race/religion/language. . . .

Small wonder, those po-
faced bureaucrats

in bush jackets
could never abide you.

Everytime you leap! soar
across the floor
affirming the universal
verities of art. . . .
your grace & freedom
shames those matchbox-
minds whose movements
seldom extend beyond a gauche waddle.

I rejoice in your talents
dance on, Ramli, dance on. . . .

The Middle East

Ahmad Shamlu

Ahmad Shamlu (1925–2000) was born in Tehran, Iran. His work reminds us that in modern times one of the functions of the poet is to cry out against injustice, to raise a voice in behalf of the inarticulate and long-suffering masses. He spent time living in exile in Princeton, New Jersey, and in England. He was the author of numerous books of poetry and an active translator from French into Persian.

POETRY THAT IS LIFE

The theme of yesterday's poet
was not of life.
In the avid sky of his imagination, he
would not converse with other than wine and mistress.

Night and day drowned in dreams
caught in the snare of a beloved's funny tresses,
while others

with one hand feeling wine-cup and the other a lass's hair
let loose intoxicated cries on God's earth!

. . .

Poetry's theme
today
is a different matter . . .

Today poetry is the weapon of the masses,
for poets
themselves are branches from the forest of the masses,
not jasmines or hyacinths of someone's hot house . . .

translated anonymously, adapted by the editors

Bishwabimohan Shreshtha

Bishwabimohan Shreshtha was born in 1956 in eastern Nepal. He is one of the leading
poets of Nepal and has been awarded the Moti prize for poetry. A man's identity is often
yoked to his work, more specifically to his ability to engage in meaningful work that allows
him to support a family. Shreshtha painfully reminds us what happens when conditions
prevent a man from finding that work. The situation is further complicated when the man
is an artist or poet. How is he to manage his time and energy for that, too?

SHOULD I EARN MY DAILY BREAD,
OR SHOULD I WRITE A POEM?

At home my aged mother
watches for her son
on every festive day,
wondering if he will come
to help her make ends meet;
Each night in her lodgings,
my wife watches the door,
hoping that her husband will bring
something sweet and fine;

My daughter wears torn pajamas
and runs round telling tales

to neighbors, strangers, friends:
this winter father will bring her
a fine new suit of clothes;

My son, sent home from school,
plays all day in the dust
with crowds of local children;
he hopes father will send him
back to school this term;

The little one's asleep now,
teasing milkless breasts,
his nakedness forevermore
mocks my very manhood;

Speak not of brothers and sisters:
for them no work could be found,
for them no spouse was chosen;

How much longer can I go on
in my tattered coat and patched-up jacket,
holding together heaven and hell?
Tell me, oh respected friend,
with such an evening in my arms,
should I earn my daily bread,
or should I write a poem?

Forget the radio, papers, speeches,
speak not of slogans, marches, placards,
and if some time remains
do not push me into darkness
with affectionate intent.
It is hunger I endure,
a greater Everest by far
than any ideal or doctrine.

The drying softness of life,
learning's gentle kindness:
only these can defeat hunger.
It is done: do not make me hesitate

by relating the Buddha's story;
if your dreams delay me,
if your temptations beguile me,
if I do not work these fingers to the bone,
if I neglect to sell my sweat,
my parents, my wife, my children,
will all grow hungry and die;
I am tired, a beaten warrior,
at war with the stomach's demands.

How much longer can I go on
in my tattered coat and patched-up jacket,
holding together heaven and hell?
Tell me, oh respected friend,
with such an evening in my arms,
should I earn my daily bread,
or should I write a poem?

I always bear upon my head
an Annapurna of need,
I always carry on my back
a Kanchenjunga of crisis,
how long can I fight this battle,
lifting a Machapuchare of costs
up onto my shoulders?

I believe that life should mean
flowing onward, a boon from God,
so do not mock my prayer.
Please try not to let me hear
of the horrors of the Falklands
of massacres in Vietnam,
Afghanistan,
they are salt in my wounds.
Life is iron, I know you must
bite down hard upon it.
Life's a desolate shore, I know
you must water it with sweat,

but with what simile, what metaphor,
can I adorn and embellish this life?

How much longer can I go on
in my tattered coat and patched-up jacket,
holding together heaven and hell?
Tell me, oh respected friend,
with such an evening in my arms,
should I earn my daily bread,
or should I write a poem?

translated by Michael James Hutt

Europe

Evgeny Bunimovich

Evgeny Bunimovich (b. 1954) is a poet, essayist, secondary school mathematics teacher, author of mathematics textbooks, newspaper columnist, and a deputy in the Moscow city duma. In the course of telling us he is not a poet, Bunimovich writes a funny poem. The poem is a response to one of his poetic ancestors, Vladimir Mayakovsky, who in his autobiography writes, "I'm a poet. That's why I'm interesting." Perhaps Bunimovich intends to deflate poetry's pretensions.

EXCUSE AND EXPLANATION

I'm not a poet
is there really such a thing as a living poet

I'm a school teacher
I teach math
computer science
as well as ethics and the psychology of family life

on top of this I return home each day

to my wife

as a romantically inclined pilot once said
love is not when two people look at one another
but when they both look in the same direction

this is about us

for ten years now my wife and I
have been looking in the same direction

at the television

for eight years now our son looks that way too

I'm not a poet
is there a hole in the watertight round-the-clock alibi
set forth above

the combination of misunderstanding and happenstance
that leads now and then to the appearance of my poems
in the periodical press
compels me to confess

I write poetry when it becomes unavoidable
while I monitor in-class exams
in spite of all the public school reforms
individual pupils continue to cheat

to prevent this

I'm forced to sit with my neck craned
wide-eyed and vigilant
unblinking gaze fastened on a space just above the floor

this pose leads inevitably

to the composition of verse

anyone who's interested can verify this

my poems are short
because in-class exams rarely last longer than 45 minutes

I'm not a poet

and perhaps
that's why I'm interesting

translated by Patrick Henry

Theo Dorgan

Theo Dorgan, a contemporary Irish poet, is a former director of Poetry Ireland. He has published many books of poetry and is also well known as a critic. Dorgan ruminates about a difficult choice many men face—whether or not to leave behind the worldly success of heroism or "productive" accomplishments for a life of writing poetry. Most contemporary cultures regard poetry as something of an elitist and negligible pastime, suited for women, perhaps, but not for grown men.

THE CHOICE

I watched Odysseus go on board the flagship
and moved to follow but something took hold of me.
I turned my back on the business of campaigning,
all of a sudden sick of captaincy, of ceaseless voyaging;
I turned for the sunlit uplands, my olives and vine farms,
the quiet of purple evenings, and never once looked back.
I might have died at sea, worn out by empty longing,
smashed in the neck with a bronze axe or drowned—
and for what? To have grown old in someone's story,
shade of a warrior with no issue in family or the earth?

I chose silence, the turning of verses, the battle with words;
did he do better, my brave Lord, when he chose swords?

Jan Erik Vold

Jan Erik Vold was born in Oslo in 1939. In this poem Vold tells us that art—whatever its form—grows and matures for those who persist. And ripeness in creation is the reward of that persistence.

HOKUSAI THE OLD MASTER, WHO PAINTED A WAVE LIKE NOBODY EVER PAINTED A WAVE BEFORE HIM

Hokusai
lived
close to 90. When he was 75
years of age, he said

of his pictures: I started drawing
objects when I was
6. What I accomplished
before 50 is of no

merit. When I was 70
I still hadn't
produced
anything good. At the age of 73

I reached an understanding
of the basic
shapes of animals
and plants. When I'm 80, my understanding

will be deeper, and when I'm 90
I shall
know the secrets
of my art

to the core—so when I'm 100
I shall come up with

praiseworthy
pictures. Not to mention

the years
after that.
The main thing now
is to keep going.

translated by the author

Zahrad

The Armenian Turkish poet Zahrad (b. 1924) chronicles the details of an ordinary woman's
life, which could be summed up as endless and repetitive food preparation—perhaps not so
different from the poet's work of endless word assemblage.

THE WOMAN CLEANING LENTILS

A lentil, a lentil, a lentil, a stone.
A lentil, a lentil, a lentil, a stone.
A green one, a black one, a green one, a black. A stone.
A lentil, a lentil, a stone, a lentil, a lentil, a word.
Suddenly a word. A lentil.
A lentil, a word, a word next to another word. A sentence.
A word, a word, a word, a nonsense speech.
Then an old song.
Then an old dream.
A life, another life, a hard life. A lentil. A life.
An easy life. A hard life. Why easy? Why hard?
Lives next to each other. A life. A word. A lentil.
A green one, a black one, a green one, a black one, pain.
A green song, a green lentil, a black one, a stone.
A lentil, a stone, a stone, a lentil.

translated by Diana Der Hovanessian and Marzbed Margossian

Adam Ziemianin

Adam Ziemianin was born in Muszyno, Poland, in 1948. He studied Polish philology at Jagielonian University. He has published several books of poetry, and many of his poems are sung by musical groups. Currently he works as a journalist in Cracow. In the unusual and subtle metaphor at the center of this poem, a man's heart attack is compared to an attack of bees, their production of honey, his production of poems. Who in the end will eat the honey and read the poems?

HEART ATTACK

The sky above Garden St.
is paved with my bees
—you understand me—
they work so hard
you would have to see it
for yourself

Sometimes one of them
flies heavy with cherry
how could you not have
heart for it

I used to live very quietly,
not like in the city,
every free moment
I gave to beekeeping

Even though heaven
is not there
—you understand me—
the sun glistened like honey
but my eyes filled with darkness
and pain so sharp
as if all the bees
entered my rib cage

It is good
they found me still alive

there will be plenty of honey
but who is going to collect it?

     translated by Aniela Gregorek and Jerzy Gregorek

South America

Nicholás Maré

Nicholás Maré (1968–93) was the pen name of Roderigo Suárez, who was born in Santiago, Chile. Here he wrestles with the old paradoxes of silence and sound, meaning and non-meaning, emptiness and plenitude—a man's attempt to both say the "unsayable" and acknowledge his inadequacy in the face of a love he would like to more fully experience, but as yet has not.

YOU CAN SAY THAT THE BIRD AS THE SAYING GOES

says that it says nothing,
you can, Martinez.

Yet I cannot even do that.

I say less than the birds;
I cannot even say what I do not say.

This is all a lie.
I only write in this way
as a certification of emptiness,
this something like a radio
dedicated to programs of silence,
a receptacle made to enclose nothings,
in order to formalize absences,
in order that those same absences
ratify that there is at least something,
there is something in the white leaves

that neither you, Martinez, nor I Suárez
have sufficiently loved.

translated by Gilbert Wesley Purdy

Central America and the Caribbean

Hector Avellán

Hector Avellán, a young Nicaraguan poet, pays tribute to a pop icon, Kurt Cobain, whose suicide traumatized Generation X-ers all over the world. At least on the level of pop culture, today, borders seem to be virtually nonexistent.

DECLARATION OF LOVE TO KURT COBAIN

The night of March 20, 1994,
at your country house in Seattle,
you heard the buzz of the refrigerator
and discerned voices calling.

You went to them
like to a lover's tryst
with yourself,
and you were punctual.

The pistol saw you
like one blind man sees another
within himself.

You put the chill of its lips
to the thirst of yours.

You pulled the trigger,
like flicking on a lamp,

and a bullet like a bird
soared the sky of your mouth.

You hit the floor with the weight of your emptiness.

Total and joyous solitude.

Next the glass, the pistol and the cigarette
were taken by FBI agents
wearing gloves on their hands,
and deposited like corpses into plastic bags.

To search for fingerprints,
but the only ones there were yours.

The news spread
and eyes like tears
fell on you,
like a concert.

And among thousands of letters
you didn't read,
mine was left not giving voice to your eyes.

I could have made you happy,
walking hand in hand
down the Washington streets,
without hearing the men on corners make
faggot comments.

But you were in another dimension,
and I saw you
like Humphrey Bogart
saw Ingrid Bergman
take off in the airplane.

You fled to your house in Seattle
so cameras

wouldn't bite you with their light,
nor journalists.

You went too far.

Now you sleep upside-down,
like a bat.
You didn't read my letter.
My declaration of love
to a rock star.
The letter where I asked:

Have you kissed the mouth of a gun?

translated by Marco Morelli

North America

Agha Shahid Ali

Agha Shahid Ali (1949–2001) was born in New Delhi and thought of himself as a Kashmiri
American. Before his untimely death in 2001, he taught poetry at the University of Utah.
"Hyphenated Americans" often face a conflict between a desire to maintain one's ethnic
heritage and the need to write in the argot of contemporary life. Agha Shahid Ali embodied
that conflict in many of his poems, which he began writing in English at age ten. Here he
uses the *ghazal,* a traditional Arabic form, both to celebrate his native language and to
lament its passing from his life. In the poem's penultimate stanza, he addresses the recently
deceased Israeli poet Yehuda Amichai regarding their common connection to the reality of
life in the Middle East.

GHAZAL

The only language of loss left in the world is Arabic—
These words were said to me in a language not Arabic.

Ancestors, you've left me a plot in the family graveyard—

Why must I look, in your eyes, for prayers in Arabic?

Majnoon, his clothes ripped, still weeps for Laila.
O, this is the madness of the desert, his crazy Arabic.

Who listens to Ishmael? Even now he cries out:
Abraham, throw away your knives, recite a psalm in Arabic.

From exile Mahmoud Darwish writes to the world:
You'll all pass between the fleeting words of Arabic.

The sky is stunned, it's become a ceiling of stone.
I tell you it must weep. So kneel, pray for rain in Arabic.

At an exhibition of miniatures, such delicate calligraphy:
Kashmiri paisleys tied into the golden hair of Arabic!

The Koran prophesied a fire of men and stones.
Well, it's all now come true, as it was said in the Arabic.

When Lorca died, they left the balconies open and saw:
His *qasidas* braided, on the horizon, into knots of Arabic.

Memory is no longer confused, it has a homeland—
Says Shammas: Territorialize each confusion in a graceful Arabic.

Where there were homes in Deir Yassein, you'll see dense forests—
That village was razed. There's no sign of Arabic.

I too, O Amichai, saw the dresses of beautiful women,
And everything else, just like you, in Death, Hebrew, and Arabic.

They ask me to tell them what *Shahid* means—
Listen: it means "The Belovéd" in Persian, "witness" in Arabic.

Virgil Suarez

Virgil Suarez was born in Havana, Cuba, in 1962. He has lived in the United States since 1974 and has published six collections of poetry, two novels, and two poetry anthologies. He teaches creative writing at Florida State University. Suarez's poem acknowledges the fact that men have always sought validation and encouragement from their elders. An imagined García Lorca appears in the poem, and his presence serves to give the poet at least some assurance that he is a participant in something larger, even though that assurance is tinged with sadness.

DUENDE

In the torrential downpours, Lorca arrives one night at our house.
A particularly tempestuous night, not only with the weather
outside but with my father, inside. My father, young then in Havana,

Lorca's age when the great poet was shot, is being driven to drink
and madness by his dissident government views, and Lorca
glides in from the porch shadows, not a drop of rain on him,

not his face, nor his delicate hands. He leaves no mud prints as he walks
into our living room and sits on our worn chintz
sofa. "What news have you of my father?" my father asks the poet.

Lorca looks around, then lights a *cigarillo;* the incandescence of the match's flame lights
up his eyes. He exhales, then says: "He died thrown
from his horse." "True," my father says and runs into another room.

I approach slowly, driven by the smell of brilliantine in the poet's
combed hair. "Tell me about the *duende, Señor* Lorca." He smiles
and aims a puff of smoke at me—it makes my eyes water.

"You think you have it, *Niño?*" he asks. "I don't know," I say. I need the trembling
of this moment, then silence. . . . "If you ever leave
this forsaken country," he adds, "you will neither sing nor play music.

But the *duende* will haunt you, like this memory of me, sitting here. Twenty-five
years

from today, you will live in Tallahassee, Florida,
and it too will be raining. I will knock on your door. You will let me in,

and I will come and sit on your couch. You will ask me what news have I of your
father, and I will say: 'He is where you last left him, on a hospital bed, dead of a
massive coronary.' You will say 'how useless.' I will say:

'*Aprende,* the guitars are weeping. Hear them?'" We will sit in silence and listen to
the rain pour down on the earth. Poet in crinoline,
you come from remote regions of sorrow and return to the labyrinth:

love, crystal, stone, you vanish down the rivers of the earth to the sea.

Simon Thompson

Simon Thompson grew up in British Columbia. He graduated from Carleton University
with a degree in journalism and English. He has worked as a technical writer and a literary
editor and now teaches writing and literature at Northwest Community College in Terrace.
In the long tradition of "talking back" poems, the speaker imagines he is conversing with
the subject of a famous song of the sixties, "Suzanne" by Leonard Cohen (see page 168),
offering her advice, urging her once and for all to forget about him.

ALL APOLOGIES TO L. COHEN

So I said to her,
"Suzanne, you've got to be at least half crazy
to live down by the river,
what with the glue factory and all.
Didn't you invest those royalty cheques
like I told you to?"
Jesus, she could have been living in Mount Royal by now.

To tell you the truth,
she isn't much of a beauty anymore;
dry gray hair, greenish skin and a nasty cough.
I guess a steady diet of tea and oranges would do that to anyone.
And to make matters worse,

she stared at me the whole time I was down there.
God! I never should have told her about that wavelength thing.
Of course she asked if I had seen Len around,
but how could I tell her he lives on top of a mountain
with some sweet naif he calls his bodhisattva?
So I said to her,
"Look, it's been twenty or thirty years now.
Lenny's not coming back here."

You should have seen the place:
scraps of cardboard,
old shoes,
a shopping cart full of beer cans;
a real rag and bone shop.
And her,
sitting in the middle of it all
staring like a deaf mute
in a rainstorm. It was enough to give a guy a headache.
You know?
A real pain.

Brothers, Friends, Mentors, and Rivals

Having you beside me feels okay.
—Lyubomir Levchev

Brothers, friends, mentors, and rivals—each of these categories bespeaks a multitude of relationships and emotional levels. The relationships of men can range from the unconditional love of one brother for another to the sickening betrayal of a former friend. Remembering his brother at a grave site, the Icelandic poet Gudmundur Bödvarsson recalls "how loving and kind / was the wordless reticent gift" of his brother's presence, underscoring how for many men overt demonstrations of emotion are not necessarily a requirement for feeling love and connectedness. On the other hand, for Malawian poet Frank Chipasula, even the almost sacred rite of blood brotherhood, enacted in youth at a time when two friends joined arms against a mutual foe, can be foresworn when the politics of one friend changes and the two can no longer see eye to eye on passionate issues. For Chipasula, "A silent man hides war in his heart," and the estrangement of his former blood brother only brings sadness and grief.

In recent years, much has been said and written about "male bonding" and how it differs from the female equivalent. Men, for example, seem to grow close to each other more through shared activities than through conversing, or what Deborah Tannen has called women's "troubles talk." Thus, in a poem by Australian Les Murray, two men—strangers to one another—who have been digging a hole for a telegraph pole discover their relatedness in a brief and cryptic conversation during a meal break. Murray concludes that "Nearly everything / they say is ritual," lines which resonate in their implications about the conversations of all males. Out of their shared work, their meal, their brief conversation, they nonetheless forge a bond—at least for that brief duration. Similarly, but from an almost opposite cultural perspective, the Mexican American poet Alberto Ríos presents us with two men who, after a long day and evening spent in each other's company during a festival, "Announced to the world / Their love for each other." Here we have the stereotypical male expression of sentiment brought on by the lubricating effects of alcohol:

"For Mr. Ríos and Mr. Diaz it was an uncommon day, / And they never spoke of it again."

Mentors, of course, are usually older than those they guide and therefore more experienced and worldly. In some cultures, uncles take on this important role for men. For example, Spanish poet Rafael Pérez Estrada remembers his own uncle with great fondness and gratitude for what he demonstrated about the possibilities of manhood and humanity. His uncle's "levitation" becomes a powerful symbol for imagination and transcendence. Mexican poet Gaspar Aguilera Díaz seeks inspiration from one of his revolutionary-poet heroes, Roque Dalton. In trying to imagine Dalton's final night before his execution, Díaz asks, "for whom did he draw a map on the ground and the sign / of victory?"

Rivals can be serious or playful. Kofi Awoonor from Ghana writes about an ongoing rivalry that extends all the way back to boyhood. His rival, Stanislaus, stole his school fees and catapult. As an adult, he is an arms merchant. The poet is no longer afraid of him and has vowed to oppose him: "for every gun you buy / I shall command a thousand assegais, for every sword / a million Ashanti machetes and Masai spears."

Whatever their cultural background, the poets in this section share an interest in the relationships that men have with one another—both the connections and the disconnections. While we stereotypically think of men as highly competitive with one another, that obviously is not always the case. These poems go beyond mere competition and celebrate all forms of intimacy while they grieve over the things that can destroy that intimacy.

Asia

Nobuo Ayukawa

Nobuo Ayukawa (1920–86) was a founding member of the *Arechi* (Waste Land) group in Japan. He is a translator of Eliot's *The Waste Land* and, during the years following World War II, emerged as Japan's preeminent modernist poet. What could be more traditionally male than old soldiers getting together, the few remaining survivors of a war none will ever forget? And yet, life does go on, and the men, even in old age and infirmity, are grateful for their comradeship and the beauty of the day.

THE LAST I HEARD

Last January,
a friend I assumed
dead in the war
sent me a letter
after thirty-five years.
He wrote of how
he'd devoted himself
to farming in the South
and brought up two daughters
after a divorce.
Last winter,
I got news that an old friend
who ran an ironworks company
in a nearby town
died suddenly from liver disease.
I'd met him once just after the defeat
at a hotel near the black market
and never saw him again,
even after promising each other
we'd meet again.
I met both friends in college,
we were regulars at the same Shinjuku bar
and worked on the same magazine back then,
but after the war
we lived separate lives.
It is not an easy job
living the life of a man.
Love makes the body weak,
making a living wears you down.
There are small pleasures,
but they aren't bridges to the past,
and we don't have the luxury
of looking back with nostalgia
on the insanity of those crazy times.
Those soldiers who died
under the cold gaze of the sun
went back to the earth,

but those of us who were left alive
found ourselves gradually hunched over,
since life is defined
by forward motion—
our bones became brittle.
Even when we lift our heads unwittingly
our backs bear lonely shadows,
and that irreparable time is long gone.

An invitation from my old comrades arrived.
Thirteen men gathered at the Shojukaku Hotel
near Ichinomiya Beach.
We were all soldiers who'd been transferred together,
sent to Sumatra on the same ship.
I found out then that a group of classmates
who'd just graduated to lieutenant
were sent to Iou Island—
all of them died.
We sat around the hearth,
only men,
and talked about how we survived
back in the world
after the war,
but our discussion was limited
to our job histories and how many children we had.
Everyone had become his old age.
Someone took his medicine,
and night came so early.
By ten, the beds were ready.
In the darkness
the hands and feet of the war dead
made a circle
surrounding the territory of our dreams.
Lying side by side,
we rested peacefully,
breathing together in sleep.

On the faded lawn
in the bright sunshine

surrounded by pine trees,
we took a group picture,
counting the number of soldiers—
the only time the final roll call
would remain the same when the pictures
were developed.
We set out for Desert-Moon Beach
as if on a boyhood excursion.
The Sunday ocean welcomed us quietly.
We rested at a café called Sunshine,
visited first the botanical gardens,
then the horticulture hall crowded with young couples,
where tropical plants were grotesquely overgrown.
It reminded us of Sumatra.
We had a nice conversation
and ate lunch cheerfully—
noon is a safe time.
On a day that smelled of rock and sky,
waves, sand,
and flowers
there was no place
to mourn.

translated by Oketani Shogo with Leza Lowitz

Europe

Vytautas P. Bložė

Vytautas P. Bložė was born in 1930 in the village of Baisogala, Lithuania. He suffered under Soviet censorship and spent time as a prisoner of conscience in a "psychiatric" hospital. He has published more than a dozen books of poetry and is the recipient of the first National Prize since the restoration of Lithuanian independence. In this tribute to a dead friend, Vytautas Bložė weaves together the story of the romantic hopes of youth with the harsh realities of a generation caught up in the horrors of World War II—its camps, desperate migrations, and mass deportations to Siberia. He also touches on the redemptive possibilities of art and creation.

BENEATH THE STARS

to the memory of Vytautas Butkus

We stood before a great hill,
it was called our life
and it was so unreachable.
Its top was hidden in the clouds.
Marigolds grew around its edges.
During our mathematics lesson
a bee flew in through the open window.

Near the forests bullets cracked.
Time seeped with blood into the earth.

We published a class newsletter.
You illustrated it
with water colors.
You were the class artist,
tall and reddening quickly
around teachers and girls.

Water colors!
I did not know that art.
I looked at the small tabs of paint,
at the glass of colored water
where you soaked your brushes,
and smiled to myself
when you, caught up in inspiration,
rubbed the tip of your tongue
against the corner of your lips.
(That seemed so childish to me.)

For memorial day
I wrote a poem
about a soldier returning home.
You painted a flag,

a machine gun and scythe in the shape
of a cross, and beneath it—a helmet.

Then you decided suddenly to write a novel.
About war.
Your turned pages of notebook paper
filled with quick writing.
Your eyes burned
with the fever of fantastic marches.
The novel was titled "Battle."

Shots walked near the forests.
There was revenge. For that which was holy to us all.
We had to identify
the corpses thrown in the marketplace.

We climbed a difficult hill.
Its top was hidden in the clouds.
Necks craned we looked ever up.

But one night
a long train took you to the East.
(Your mother was a writer, your father the town mayor.)

You became suddenly
one of the innocent condemned.

The Siberian forest embraced you.
Pressed you firmly against its snow-drifted breast.
Hungry ax in hand.
Hundreds of kilometers of forests.
Sleeping at night beneath the stars.
It was completely different than it was then
in high school
as the first snowflakes fell
in the woods at home
as we gathered kindling for the classroom stove.

Lies fell like a great cut tree and crushed you.

Tossed you to the very depths.

The cold would reach fifty below.
You slept hoisted and tied in the trees,
above fires you had made.
And only the warmth of the embers
would call you forth unfrozen
each morning.

One night
you fell out of the tree.
Lay there unconscious.
The embers cooked your face.
The smell of human flesh slid through the forest.

One eye burned out.
You had no lips.

The others, awakened, untied themselves, jumped down
and pulled you from the fire.
Nursed you.
Only epileptic fits remained.

With a hungry ax you continued chopping the Siberian forest.
It is possible to chop down a forest!
Your water colors awaited you
and your unfinished "Battle."

But you knew:
in moments of inspiration
your tongue would not play childishly
in the corners of your lips.

Your lips burned.
Only your teeth remained.
Tightly clenched teeth.

And crumbling faith
that everything would turn out right.

Could the lies be so great!
Would nothing lift that fallen tree from your chest!
With open teeth you looked at life.
Light flashed in your one eye.

Your death was unexpected and simple.
There was a fragrance of spring.
A brook burbled in the forest.
Early in the morning
you breathed in a full chest of fresh forest air
and bent over by the brook to wash.
O, if only it were living water
able to give you back your face!
You smiled with your teeth
seeing the skull in the water.

You sank epileptically into the small brook in the forest.
The others were too late.

translated by Jonas Zdanys

Gudmundur Bödvarsson

Gudmundur Bödvarsson, one of Iceland's premier poets, was born in 1904. In a cold,
windswept graveyard, the poet remembers the loss of a brother and recalls his quiet dignity.

BROTHER

Flakes over grave and cairn
driving inland, solitary
wooden crosses shaking with
age. I bade the boisterous
wind lower its voice a little.

—You were the quietest of men,
my brother and friend.

It became clear to me
in the graveyard,
tracing an old acquaintance
in mind's dark crook and cranny,
how loving and kind
was the wordless reticent gift,
never remarked and never mentioned by any.

How feeble our tardy thanks
sink in the silence recited
like an excuse to a vanished
friend. How far we stand from
that hour when parting once
we pressed a stiffened hand at the end.

translated by Alan Boucher

Tony Curtis

Tony Curtis was born in Carmarthen, Wales, in 1946. He is a professor of poetry at the
University of Glamorgan and director of the M.A. program in writing. A prizewinning
poet, he has authored more than fifteen books of poetry and criticism. In this touching
elegy, Curtis remembers soldiers who died in battle fifty years before. He finds a kind of
camaraderie between men who fought in the same war the world over. Here, American sol-
diers are memorialized for their deaths in Dresden, Berlin, Cologne, or a Cambridgeshire
field.

THE EIGHTH DREAM

First he fingers wet sand into the names—
his hand traces the letters, then the numbers
of the squadron, then the boy's home state.
Sand spills into other names and numbers
above and below. He wipes the line

smooth with a sponge; then with an artist's brush
flicks away the final lodged grains.

This is the way to raise the dead
for the photograph the relatives receive.
It is fifty years and those who remembered
have phoned or faxed for flowers to be laid:
a wreath under one of the columns of the dead
where that long-lost brother holds his place
in the alphabet of the missing.

It is the end of the first week of December—
a brushing of snow highlights the grass
and softens the Portland stone walls of remembrance.
The rectangular ponds have coffin-lids of ice.
The stars and stripes is moulded to its towering pole,
the point from which the headstones radiate
their Roman Crosses and Stars of David.

These are the boys whose masks were torn apart,
whose blood froze in the high air over Berlin,
Dresden and Cologne. Whose minced bodies were hosed out
over the warm fuselage in a Cambridgeshire field.
The ones who died slowly by an open window, listening
to strange birdsong. Those who ploughed into the runway fog.
Sailors who gagged on diesel and salt in the dark
Atlantic, and were numbed out of life.
They were the numbers on the walls
behind the Enigma boffins, Christ's and King's men
unscrambling the alphabet in Bletchley's nissen huts.

Eighth Air Force fliers had a target of missions
that shifted—twenty, thirty, thirty-five—
always away from them as targets and statistics
were chalked across the wall of the hut.
Write it down, write it down.

They used their Zippos to burn into the pub's ceiling
memorials of crashed numbers and friends.

In the torn or frozen moment
they dreamed of a rusty red barn in Leverett,
the endless runway of roads across Oklahoma,
a foghorn in pain off Provincetown.
Their fiftieth winter in Heaven sees this present
dream of snow, the opaque, unreflecting ice,
and, in all the bare trees, one bright sweetgum,
that liquid amber of fall in the low, rinsed sun.

Snorri Hjartarson

Snorri Hjartarson (1906–86) was one of Iceland's most important twentieth-century poets.
His work has been translated into several languages. Here the speaker visits the Keats mu-
seum near the Spanish Steps in Rome and confirms the brotherhood of poets—through
time and space, and across cultures.

HOUSE IN ROME

Dark and silent
in the house by
Trinita dei Monti as then

the white steps up the hill
ringing with multicoloured young life

an evening sky above
and a few large stars

I look up at the window
and the harp on the wall

Bright star, would I were steadfast

here he vanished into the darkness

the earth's young lover
that sang sweetest

into the darkness

John Keats

to the stars

translated by Alan Boucher

Hédi Kaddour

Hédi Kaddour, born in 1945 in Tunisia, has lived in France since childhood. He has pub-
lished three books of poems and a collection of essays. He teaches literature in Paris. Kad-
dour sees a lot of sexual imagery in this statue of one of his poetic predecessors. Is he sug-
gesting that ordinary citizens will not be sensitive to the sexual overtones of the statue? Or
of Verlaine's work? Or of his own poetry?

VERLAINE

for Guy Goffette

Verlaine? He stands erect there on the grass,
Lyre and palm-tree behind him, a bronze bust
Of Verlaine, atop three good yards
Of cement prick around which writhe three
Unlikely Muses, panic-stricken to be
Discovered in such dubious company
By strollers so much less experienced
In amorous combat. The bitter roar
Of a motorcycle rudely interferes
With the rain's small music beneath the plane-
Trees and chestnut-trees; a ray of sun
Slices to chiaroscuro the red and green
Pillar, and sulking Verlaine still dreams
The air that will make everything cohere.

translated by Marilyn Hacker

Lyubomir Levchev

Lyubomir Levchev was born in 1935 in Troyan, Bulgaria. He is the editor and publisher of *Orpheus*. His many awards include the Golden Medal for Poetry of the French Academy and The World Award of Mystic Poetry Fernando Rielo (1993). His poem "Front Line" stands in contrast to the more typical portrayal of the deep bond formed by fellow combatants. Here comrades-at-arms are thrown together, probably reluctantly, because of a shared cause.

FRONT LINE

You've never been a pal of mine.
Cognac's never made us friends.
We just happen to occupy
the same front line
where two worlds clashed.

Each day the forces
of the gods descending
counterattack.
And blood-swift
the hours hurtle by.
Having you beside me feels okay.

So thanks.
No time for looks or words,
we know each other not at all.
That's why under the bullets crashing
we call each other brother.

And when the battle's over
we'll peer deep
into each other's eyes.
And we may be surprised, my friend,
to discover how different we are.

You'll say
"I love silence."
I'll say

"I love jazz."
Hearing our names
the first time, we'll smile
and say,
"Have a nice day!"

And it'll be neither early
nor late
to explore new winds
or follow birds in flight.
Only the dead remain, identical,
buried in one front line.

translated by Theodore Weiss

Dennis O'Driscoll

Dennis O'Driscoll was born in Tipperary, Ireland, in 1954. He has published four poetry collections and is a much admired literary critic. He lives in County Kildare. "The Lads" is a poignant account of what happens to men when their dreams have faded, when they find themselves in nine-to-five jobs, and have settled for the workaday lives that so many live. Where has life gone, they wonder, and talk about early retirement, buy lottery tickets, and recount the day's sporting events.

THE LADS

Technicians, overseers, assistant
depot managers, stock controllers.
Old fashioned nine-to-five men
who rose moderately up the line.
You can pick them out in tea-break
identity parades at the Quick Snack
café, bellies swelling under
diamond-patterned sweaters.

They tuck into a fry—it's pay day,
after all, a day of their lives
and their wives, a bit too fond

of calorie counting, restrict
fry-ups now to Christmas,
the odd holiday B & B.

The lads still flirt, as readily
as the next man, with the waitress
and break into synchronized grins
at her snappy repartee.
But it's mainly sport the talk
embraces these times, though
their playing days are over,
apart from the veteran's league,
a pre-pub Sunday game
of pitch-and-putt.

That there are worse fates
they know well enough;
and who'd want to be
among those bosses
monotonously talking shop?
Not for all the BMW's
in the world would they swap.

One of the lads takes to the idea
of early retirement with a convert's zeal.
Not that he feels old or anything—
never felt better, in fact, give or take
the back complaint, his smoker's hack . . .
It's just that the kids have gone
Their own strong-willed ways
And the wife works part-time
In the plastics factory crèche.

Before the lads pocket
their hands, stand up to go,
they check their lotto numbers,

bantering about the jet they'll charter
to Thailand when their syndicate wins.

Nibble on a bacon rind
discarded on the mopped-up plate.
Life tastes great some days.

Donny O'Rourke

Donny O'Rourke was born in Port Glasgow in 1959. He was a student at Glasgow University and is the editor of *Dream State: The New Scottish Poets*. This poem demonstrates the impact popular and literary culture have on our understanding of masculinity. The American writer Nelson Algren becomes a hero to young O'Rourke, who sees Algren as the "last of the bare-knuckle poets" and thinks of him as being more notorious for bringing a famous feminist to orgasm than for anything he wrote.

ALGREN

I picture you profiled in Film Noir tones
shirt-sleeves rolled back, cigar smoke

coiling like an unspent spring
as you type at a card table

in some Clark St. cathouse
in '48 or '49

before Korea and McCarthy
made it hard for Reds to work.

The book you're writing,
The Man with the Golden Arm

will make a movie star of Sinatra
and not one royalty cent for you

last of the bare-knuckle poets

more famous in the end

for being the first man
to make Simone de Beauvoir come

than for anything you wrote.
Travelling to Chicago

and later, here in the burg
you called a busted flush

I read *The Neon Wilderness*
and *City on the Make*

serenades to the low lives
and losers of these streets.

As well, after your hobo
wanderings, the time you did

for stealing a typewriter,
that you remained constant to Chicago

her soda jerks and crap games
pastures new then

reduced to scuffed
green baize.

Rafael Pérez Estrada

Rafael Pérez Estrada (1934–2000) was born in Malaga, Spain. A leading figure of avant-garde poetry in Spain, he published over forty books and was widely acknowledged as a master of the prose poem. Here is a poem that pays tribute to an uncle and his influence on a boy's life. It operates clearly in the tradition of magical realism. Which is more real in the poem—the uncle as transcendent levitator or as down-to-earth farmer? Or do both have equal value for the speaker?

MY UNCLE THE LEVITATOR

As a small child I would accompany my uncle the levitator from town to town, plaza to plaza. While he levitated (a rather exceptional exercise), I was content watching him rise above the brilliance of my marbles which were like eyes, like transparent looks sliding over the worn stones of the plazas.

My uncle was respectful and never rose above the apex of the towers and cathedral steeples, and for this he was adored by the public as well as by other levitators. It's true that he liked to search his pockets while in the air and toss crumbs of bread for doves to catch in flight. Sometimes when he was enveloped by the fluttering doves people would confuse him with an aerostat, a mistake he found flattering. And, when he tired of playing with the birds, he would hold still, weightlessly suspended, and recite old poetry, especially sonnets which he would renovate, adding a few syllables or simply giving them a bit of color. Sometimes he would juggle. In these moments it was amusing to see his figure against the light. He looked like a foolish, lunatic shadow that had escaped from its body to hunt cinders in the air.

My uncle wanted me to levitate also, but only succeeded in giving me some bumps and bruises. We finally had to stop trying, for the war came and we were very poor. To feed and clothe us, my uncle was forced into the heights to advertise rare and useless products. It was, he insisted, a miserable time. I still remember when, to make the business more profitable, he bought a drum and took to the air to advertise classy glass stockings, invisible stockings (like the invisible man) that shone in the dead of night, better than the movies.

When things got better again, and the war was relegated to a line in a schoolbook, my uncle stopped levitating and returned to the fields to till the earth. Even doing such simple work, he was able, by natural means, to make heliotropes and fuchsias of the rarest tonalities sprout up spontaneously in the furrows left by the oxen. And my uncle, who refused to let his life get too complicated, pretended he didn't see them.

He never again levitated in the daytime. As for the nighttime I'm not sure: my uncle was a sleepwalker, and I a deep sleeper.

I've placed a picture of him in the highest point of my room, and I still dream that he's levitating.

translated by Steven J. Stewart

Rafael Pérez Estrada

It is said that all of us have a novel in us, but here Estrada describes a man who has a novel on him, an intriguing metaphor for how much of our lives we wear on our very skin.

THE UNPUBLISHED MAN

Due to an urgent trip and a lack of foresight on my part, it became necessary one night for me to share a room with a stranger. As I watched him undress, I was greatly surprised to discover he had the chapter of a novel tattooed on his back.

I decided to abandon my trip and install myself in that boarding house. Thus, night after night, I found myself discovering a passionate work that extended its miniscule letters over the chest, hands, and even the wrists of that wondrous being.

I knew that this writer (or this book, as the case may be) was a suspicious man. He had few relatives and was afraid that someone would plagiarize the work that had cost him so much effort and so many years.

One day I couldn't hold back and asked, "And the tattoo artist? Aren't you afraid of him? Aren't you worried he might be a crook, that he might recopy your story letter by letter?"

He immediately told me not to worry. Though he did it in such a way that, while he was explaining the precautions he had taken, it was clear he was also trying to reassure himself one more time.

"I chose someone who was eminently artistic, an illiterate who was, paradoxically, an expert at drawing, especially copying. He could have been a high-level forger, but he found a curious pleasure in marking up bodies. It was like he made them his own that way. He could replicate symbols, but he didn't know their meaning."

My friendship with that man, with that living book, grew to the point that I wasn't just reading the passionate, fantastic chronicle written on his skin, I was rereading it and taking notes whenever I liked.

At one point, I was not only his sole reader, but I began to share his worries.

"Aren't you afraid," I asked, "that when you and your body die your work will be lost also?"

Then he took out his will and showed it to me. It directed for his remains to be preserved in the occasion of his death. Thus he would achieve (these were his words, tragic yet refined) an exclusive edition . . . printed on skin. His answer created such tension between us that he graciously tried to make the afternoon lose some of its bitterness:

"Would you mind reading me the chapter on my back? My memory isn't so good, and I'm afraid I've forgotten it."

translated by Steven J. Stewart

James Simmons

James Simmons (1933–2001) was born in Derry, Ireland. He published a half-dozen volumes of poetry and was the founding editor of *The Honest Ulsterman*. In this poem, he offers a wry and sad commentary on the great abstraction "brotherhood." He takes a safe and perhaps—given the bloody history of his part of the world—rational view of how to celebrate it.

THE PLEASANT JOYS OF BROTHERHOOD

To the tune of "My Lagan Love"

I love the small hours of the night
when I sit up alone.
I love my family, wife and friends.
I love them and they're gone.
A glass of Power's, a well-slacked fire,
I wind the gramophone.
The pleasant joys of brotherhood
I savour on my own.

An instrument to play upon,
books, records on the shelf,
and albums crammed with photographs:
I *ceili* by myself.
I drink to passion, drink to peace,
the silent telephone.
The pleasant joys of brotherhood
I savour on my own.

Ivan Slamnig

Ivan Slamnig (1930–2001) was born in Metkovic, Croatia. He published prose and literary essays along with poetry. He taught comparative literature at the University of Zagreb and has translated from English, French, and Russian. In this quick sketch of a sailor ashore, we see a particular kind of male creature: one who is openhearted and childlike, his innocence making our fearful adult concerns petty and shameful.

A SAILOR

In front of the inn we saw a sailor.
He drank his beer from a particularly large mug.
He sat facing each one of us,
and the waitress liked him too.
He explained
how he always carries his house with him
and showed a purple tattooed house
baring his chest.
He laughed
and looked at all of us
ready to receive kindness, ready to pay a fine,
he set his feet firmly on the ground
(in case it began to sway).
He was still fighting the sea
and we hid with our palms
our small-flame anxiousness.

translated by Vasa D. Mihailovich and Charles David Wright

Kit Wright

Kit Wright, born in Kent in 1944, is the author of many books for children and several prizewinning collections of poetry. Wright is a keen observer of pub life—so much so that he refers to one of his favorite pubs as his "alma mater." Pub life is in some ways at the center of British manhood, a place where men tilt back a few pints and let themselves go. English restraint is tempered, and a man can be himself.

HERE COME TWO VERY OLD MEN

Here come two very old men of exquisite caution
Who handle each other like costly pieces of china
In the perilous matter of sitting down at the bar.

And you'd think it the most demanding of all operations
Ever conducted by bodies that have come this far,
That so long ago came yelling from the vagina.

That woke the world to be sitting where they are.

Africa

Kofi Awoonor

Kofi Awoonor was born in 1935 in Wheta, Ghana, and was educated at the Universities of
Ghana and London and at the University of Texas at Austin. He is currently professor of
literature at the University of Cape Coast. "Songs of Abuse" illustrates how in some male
communities one needs to choose between being a bully or being bullied.

SONGS OF ABUSE: TO STANISLAUS THE RENEGADE

This is addressed to you, Stanislaus, wherever you are.
Listen you punk, the last time we met you were selling faulty guns in Addis.
I heard you panting afterwards in a Cairo whorehouse
Before I knew you had split with my spring overcoat
a cashmere job I danced for in a bar in Kabul.
I heard you were peddling fake jewelry to Pueblo Indians
and Washington hippies. The jail you occupied in Poonaville, Tennessee
was burnt down after you escaped; they could not eradicate the smell.
Verna wrote the other day, you remember Verna
the lean assed girl whose rent money you stole in Detroit,
she wrote to say you are still running around in her underpants.
What is this I hear about you preparing to settle in the Congo

to grow hashish in the valley of the Zaire?
I will be waiting for you; for every gun you buy
I shall command a thousand assegais, for every sword
a million Ashanti machetes and Masai spears.
I am not afraid of you any more. Those days are past
when you stole my school fees and my catapult
and fled into the cove beyond bird island.
I too came of age.

Frank Chipasula

Frank Chipasula was born in Malawi in 1949. He studied in Zambia and the United States, receiving an M.A. in creative writing and a Ph.D. in English from Brown University. He has published two collections of poetry and has edited a number of collections including, with his wife, *The Heinemann Book of African Women's Poetry*. Through a kind of timeless male ritual, blood brotherhood becomes literal in this poem, but even this deep connection between men can be breached by politics, as the last stanza suggests.

MY BLOOD BROTHER

First we locked our fingers, wove them
round each other, and murmured our brother-
hood promises: To protect each other
in time of attack and to love each other as
if from the same womb and share everything equally.

Then, with a razor sharpened with love
You cut your wrist and I mine incised.
I kissed your arm and sucked your blood
And you drank mine, sealing the bond.
We squeezed our blood into the baobab fruit,
stirred it together with the baobab milk
And together, under the mango tree, drank
the concoction, and shared our first fish.

Do you remember, Blood Brother, 1959
and the hailstorm of colonial bullets we braved

through, marching our arms locked tightly together
our hearts, almost fused into one, beating to each
other through the gun-smoke and bursting flames?
Remember, my blood flows through your veins
And your precious blood is mine, I will not
break the invisible knot.

Brother, though you came from the mountains
And I from the depths of the lake, sea-weed
in my eyes and the sun on my mouth, and the smell
of fish all over my body, that love that bound
you to me erased all that could differentiate us.
But today the Party has come between us like a wizard
and it is planting the seeds of hatred in our
different paths; you have gathered your mouth
into terrible tucks and sewn it and you know my fear
of silent men: A silent man hides war in his heart.
Today, you point a dagger at my heart, the Party armed you.
Remember the vow we took and remember the blood
That flows through me to you in a continuous path.

Chirikure Chirikure

Chirikure Chirikure was born in 1962 in Gutu, Zimbabwe. He is a graduate of the University of Zimbabwe and an Honorary Fellow of the University of Iowa. His three volumes of poetry are written in the Shona language, but the third has been translated into English. The death of a comrade in battle is an event that haunts many men who have experienced it for the rest of their lives. Here even an unknown fellow warrior inspires a dignified elegy.

THIS IS WHERE WE LAID HIM TO REST

This is where we laid him to rest
Right here on this rocky, bare ground
Surrounded by thorny bushes

Here he lies like a wild beast
A brute no one cares about

This is where he lies buried
After he had blazed the trail
Protesting with gunfire
Paving an escape route
For his besieged comrades

This is where we laid him to rest
After the enemy had cut him down
His chest riddled with bullets
The soil red and supple with his blood
Leaving us in tears

This is where he lies buried
After spending three days and nights
Writhing like a worm on fire
Quenching thirst with tears of pain
And hunger with his blood

This is where we laid him to rest
A man we knew nothing about
His name, family or totem
One thing we knew
He was a patriot

This is where he was buried
Without a farewell dance or song
Prayer or eulogy
Without a tombstone

This is where he rests
A fighter who was married to his gun
A hero whose grave we dug with bayonets
Covering it with soil
Scooped with the butts of our guns

A fighter who was mourned.
Even by animals of the wild.

translated by Haba Musengezi

South America

Gonzalo Rojas

Gonzalo Rojas was born in 1917 in Chile. Over a long writing life, he has published more
than twenty poetry volumes and has received numerous international prizes, such as the
Queen Sofia Prize of Spain, the Octavio Peace Prize of Mexico, and the National Prize of
Literature of Chile in 1992. The poet sees himself and the human predicament in the sur-
realistic image of his dead uncle flying by before he's able to get answers to important ques-
tions. He ends up as the breathless rower of a wave-tossed boat, carrying on despite the
seeming futility of his actions.

THE COAST

An uncle of mine who died of resurrection (Borges)
is who I see most in the air; he appears to me
when least expected
with a letter in his hand; what could there be
in that letter?

What's cruel is how he's flying by. I'm going
to speak to him, to
ask him something and good-bye;
what's left is only the hollow of him without an aura
in all this cold.

So then I touch my heart and the old box
huffs and puffs; buck up,
I tell myself, nothing that can't be fixed,

and rage against the waves,
keep on rowing.

What I see most on this coast is water,
the reverse of what I'm feeling,
waves and water, a few rocks
here and there, two or three boats
with dead men aboard.

translated by John Oliver Simon

Central America and the Caribbean

Gaspar Aguilera Díaz

Gaspar Aguilera Díaz lives in Uruapan, Mexico. He is the author of *Pinnic* and *Los ritos del obseso*. Roque Dalton was a Latin American revolutionary who was born in El Salvador and lived in Mexico, Cuba, and Prague. His book *Taberna y ostros lugares*, describing his experience in Prague, won the Casa de las Américas poetry prize in 1969 and established him, at the age of thirty-four, as one of the best young poets in Latin America. In 1975, a military faction of the Ejército Revolucionario del Pueblo (ERP) accused him of trying to divide their organization and condemned him to death. He was executed on May 10, 1975, four days before his fortieth birthday. Here Díaz identifies with his Latin American "brother" and imagines how Dalton spent the night he was executed.

DOES ANYONE KNOW WHERE ROQUE DALTON SPENT HIS FINAL NIGHT?

what wings of a wild bird covered his back?
who kindled the flame to incinerate his heart
    forever?
can anyone tell me what person or persons went along
    behind him erasing his amorous footsteps?
what hollow trunk or branch played scarecrow to dry his
    wet clothes?
whose were the triumphant kisses the soldiers found

around his head?
whose were those tears, as heavy as hot lead
    they found still running down his
    enthusiastic breast?
who blew his final poems into his mouth, disguised
    as diaries and travel journals?
for whom did he draw a map on the ground and the sign
    of victory?
which ear of the moon heard him murmuring and didn't
    know if it was a love song or a message
    in code?
who cleaned the sand and mud that night—the final
    one—from his left tit?
who shared a crust of bread with him and a swallow of
    water like warm nipples?
who lit his reflexive cigarette?
who pulled out of his old wallet the family photo and
    a sepia poem by vallejo?
who helped him take off his shoes knotted by the cold?
who drew his spoken portrait and gave it to death?
who said in his ear:
        let's go quickly
            the day is coming
                the dawn
                    is still ours?

translated by John Oliver Simon

Antonio Deltoro

Antonio Deltoro was born in 1947 in Mexico City, where he studied economics and where he has lived most of his life. Sometimes, despite a latent homophobia, men can become very close with other men—so close that the world around them no longer seems to exist. That's the state of affairs in this poem of male intimacy.

SUBMARINE

for Eduardo Hurtado

In the depths of the courtyard
in a hidden corner
where nobody thinks to look,
here I am again with my best friend.
Far from sordid prizes and punishments,
we submerge ourselves in conversation
inventing silent countries.
Out of planks and rubbish
under all disorder we have constructed
a submarine unknown to everyone.

translated by John Oliver Simon

Francisco Hernandez

Francisco Hernandez lives in Mexico City, where he works in a marketing firm. He received a National Poetry Prize for his book *Mar de Fundo.* We can't be sure if this is a "real" or imagined encounter with Juan Rulfo, the great Mexican novelist who was one of the inventors of "magical realism." We can be sure, however, that the younger writer is paying homage to one of his literary ancestors.

AUTOGRAPH

The man is seated before me, and there
is no one else in the room. I hand him a
small book with a black cover, and ask him
to sign it. Then the man draws himself up,
takes up his pen and the book, now huge
and opening to the size of the wall, and begins
to leaf through it with a nervous hand.
Trees surge forth with clouds instead
of leaves, wild beasts devouring the earth,
buzzards motionless in the silent air and
rusted railways leading to the horizon line.

Juan Rulfo closes the book, puts away his pen
and quietly tells me:
"Stop dreaming. This is my name."

translated by John Oliver Simon

North America

Charles Bukowski

Charles Bukowski was born in 1920 in Germany. The wild old man of American poetry, he died in 1994, but his prolific and energetic poetic output survives him. His many books are published by Black Sparrow Press. In "3 old men at separate tables," he captures both the isolation of old age and an unspoken brotherhood among solitary old men.

3 OLD MEN AT SEPARATE TABLES

I am
one of them.
how did we get here?
where are our ladies?
what happened to
our lives and years?

this appears to be a calm Sunday
evening.
the waiters move among us.
we are poured water, coffee, wine.
bread arrives, armless, eyeless bread.
peaceful bread.
we order.
we await our orders.

where have the wars gone?
where have, even, the tiny agonies

gone?
this place has found us.
the white table cloths are placid ponds,
the utensils glimmer for our
fingers.

such calm is ungodly but
fair.
for in a moment we still remember the
hard years and those to come.
nothing is forgotten, it is merely put
aside.
like a glove, a gun, a
nightmare.

Cyril Dabydeen

Cyril Dabydeen was born in Guyana and completed his formal education at Queen's University in Canada. He has published more than a dozen books of prose and poetry in the United Kingdom and Canada. He lives in Ottawa, where he was appointed Ottawa's poet laureate in the mid-1980s and granted the first Award of Excellence for Writing and Publishing. Dabydeen is one of many writers who have written tributes to Ernest Hemingway, who has symbolized what some would call the core masculine values of living a tough, adventurous, and stoic life. This poem follows Hemingway's footsteps in Havana.

HEMINGWAY

With you, I sip one *mojito* after another.
    I too write my name on the wall
Of this restaurant, eating hot Spanish rice
    And enjoying it as never before.

With you, at the Havana Libre (the former Hilton),
    I listen to the plump, light-skinned

Woman operating the elevator,
    Who hasn't yet left for Miami,

Who now asks for American dollars;
    With you, I walk the streets this night
Watching healthy young Cubans saunter about
    By the seawalls, hand in hand, much in love;

And I enter the well-lit narrow streets
Close to the harbour, where I am accosted
    By two seductive-looking girls
Who explain their need for clothes

    And other amenities (*treinta dolarés,
Por favor!*). With you, too, I drink of the spectacle
    Of *La Tropicana* and later reminisce

Over Afro-Cubano rhythms and workers' rights
    To such incentives in a proletarian state—
All eloquence to a revolution: here where
    I breathe fully of the old Spanish town

And linger by La Universidad de Habana,
    Entering a hall uninvited, where for the first time
I see posters of Castro outdo those of Marti,

And as I am about to leave (you never really did,
    Hemingway), I wonder about Batista's island-paradise,
Transformed; maybe I too belong here, your

Marlin's sea reaches up to me in the sun's sweep
    On this bone of an island—
As my blood is also on the rise.

Al Pittman

Al Pittman (1940–2001) was born in Newfoundland. He was known internationally for his poetry, plays, and radio and television scripts. Listed among his many awards are the Canada Council Arts Award and the Writer's Alliance Book Award for Poetry. Whether the central event of this poem is real or fantasized, its Cain and Abel undertones point to a certain kind of male recklessness and impulsivity capable of causing a world of regret.

THE ECHO OF THE AX

My father tells me of the time
he put his hand
on the chopping block
and dared his brother
to cut it off

and whack
just like that
he did it
and my father remembers
the blood on the steel blade
and his mangled hand
hanging barely
by a thread of skin
and he remembers too
how his brother looked
after he'd done it
in that moment
when the whack of the ax
still echoed about the yard

and he recalls
with a heavy breath
how he felt inside
having made his brother
a most amazed victim
of his weird and private fantasies

Alberto Ríos

Alberto Ríos was born in 1952 on the American side of Nogales. A prizewinning poet, he is the author of a dozen books, including eight volumes of poetry. He is Regents' Professor of English at Arizona State University. Ríos shows in this poem how little it takes for males to forge a bond: some time spent together, food and drink, conversation—all creating a special day when the world seems beauteous. With stereotypical male reticence about expressing feelings directly, the two men never speak of their special day again.

A CHANCE MEETING OF TWO MEN

Mr. Clemente Ríos and Mr. Lamberto Diaz
In a combined music
Raised to as loud as they could make their voices be
Announced to the world
Their love for each other.
Then after hugging they kissed each other on the cheek
And meant it.
There was no mistake
Though it was neither scandalous nor revelatory.
They made their announcement
After a crisp morning, a long afternoon,
And a spinning evening made of beer, blue
Wine, membrillo-flavored tequila, and cognac,
But a day made just as much
From the chili and smoke of conversation,
The butter of a pause and the chewing of agreement.
The curious thing is that they talked
About nothing in particular,
And nothing they said was news:
The feel of an old rope in the hand
On a good morning, sturdy pants that fit,
the smell of creosote after rain in the hills
So strong even the rabbits come out
To feel it in the air.
For Mr. Ríos and Mr. Diaz it was an uncommon day,
And they never spoke of it again.
But for an afternoon and an evening,
They were in each other's company
And in love with the world.

Len Roberts

Len Roberts has published nine collections of poetry. He is a professor of English at Northampton Community College, Bethlehem, Pennsylvania. Often callous and insensitive, "guy talk" may grow out of men's difficulty dealing with painful feelings. Laughter is sometimes a way of avoiding facing the hard truths, as this poem demonstrates.

MEN'S TALK

It was fuck this, fuck that,
lousy sonofabitch and stupid shit,
heads bowed in whispers
or thrown back to show
Adam's apple, jugular vein,
night when the women
drifted away from the howling
at the other end of the yard,
one yanking it out to piss in the hedges,
another throwing stones at the moon,
the guest of honor the worst
with his gratuitous belches and farts
all of us quieting down a bit
when he started to tell a joke
because of the tumor
spreading in his brain
that was slowly erasing
each address, each name,
six of us so drunk we could hardly stand,
reeling, leaning into shoulders
till he came to the punch line
and we slapped backs, arms,
threw our hands at each other's bodies
as tears filled our eyes and
we laughed so hard it hurt.

Oceania, Australia, and New Zealand

Les Murray

Les Murray was born in 1938 in Bunyah, New South Wales, Australia, where he continues
to live today with his wife, Valerie, and two youngest children. The author of a dozen books
of verse, he is Australia's foremost living poet. In "The Mitchells," he captures an emblem-
atic moment in Australian male culture, a moment of ritualized "mateship"—so foreign to
other cultures—born of the hardships of a colonial, penal past. Among other things, the
poem points to the male kinship of shared work, its power to transcend even class differ-
ences.

THE MITCHELLS

I am seeing this: two men are sitting on a pole
they have dug a hole for and will, after dinner, raise
I think for wires. Water boils in a prune tin.
Bees hum their shift in unthinning mists of white

bursaria blossom, under the noon of wattles.
The men eat big meat sandwiches out of a Styrofoam
box with a handle. One is overheard saying:
drought that year. Yes. Like trying to farm the road.

The first man, if asked, would say *I'm one of the Mitchells.*
The other would gaze for a while, dried leaves in his palm,
and looking up, with pain and subtle amusement,

say *I'm one of the Mitchells.* Of the pair, one has been rich
but never stopped wearing his oil-stained felt hat. Nearly everything
they say is ritual. Sometimes the scene is an avenue.

Work, Sports, and Games

The man in the blue smock,
going home, his hoe on his shoulder
—Günter Eich

This was loneliness
with noise
—William Matthews

Cultures with their myriad traditions, histories, and values condition us to be who we are. They give us identities that we often accept unthinkingly. Cultures, therefore, have a lot to say about what work we do, what leisure activities we engage in— in short, how we spend our precious time. Of course, we have choices, but our cultures limit the range and types of available choices.

Unless we belong to the world's small minority of the super wealthy, we are workers, engaging in activity for the better part of the day for which we receive some recompense. Traditionally, men have tended to work in the public sphere, women in the domestic, though, of course, that has changed considerably in the West and is increasingly changing throughout the world.

Because a man's work has usually provided for his family, that work is often a large part of his identity. He has been conditioned to accept that what he does is what he is. And what he does has been assessed a value—either monetarily or in terms of status—by his culture. He, too, then is seen as more or less valuable—and most men feel this judgment keenly. A man's identification with his work will affect him positively or negatively depending on a host of factors such as class, wealth, prestige, and satisfaction.

It's no wonder, then, that we came across poems in which men articulated a range of complicated responses and feelings toward work. António Jacinto, an Angolan poet, writes from the point of view of a contract worker, one who has had to leave his home for long periods of time in order to have work. In a letter to his woman, he bemoans the resulting separation and loneliness. In a similar vein, Evan Jones laments his speaker's condition as an exiled worker in England far from his native Jamaica. Men who work with tools, who are skilled craftsmen, often take pride in their work, their craftsmanship, their tools. Such is the case in American poet Andrew Hudgins's celebration of the grace and beauty of tools well kept and well used.

Whether their culture has given them baseball, cricket, soccer, or hockey, many men take an active interest in the dominant sports—sometimes as participants but especially as fans. William Matthews, an American poet, recalls sitting with his girlfriend in the cheap seats watching professional basketball and feeling a striking sense of "loneliness with noise." Many men's sense of triumph and failure, of transcendence and doom, are intimately connected to the ups and downs of their chosen teams. Of course, where there are teams, there are also those who didn't quite make the team. Iftikhar Arif, an Indian Pakistani poet, describes the feelings of the "twelfth man" on a cricket team, destined to be on the sidelines, held in reserve but never quite used. And Christopher Merrill, an American poet, describes the intense dedication of a boy practicing the ball-handling skills that are required in the game of soccer. Merrill alternates longer and shorter lines to mimic the rapid motion of soccer, depicting it as a kind of acrobatic dance.

Men's work as well as the games and sports they participate in remain central to their experience and understanding of who they are as men. A man's work may change with the seasons of his life, but nearly always that work fundamentally informs his sense of self. That identity is often strengthened by loyalties to particular teams and sports that can last a lifetime, providing a sense of continuity in a world of change.

Asia

Iftikhar Arif

Iftikhar Arif was born in 1943 in Lucknow, India, a city renowned for its Urdu literature. His first collection of Urdu poems was published in 1983. Arif, an Indian Pakistani, takes the metaphor of "fan or athlete," which suggests that most of us are destined to spend our lives cheering on the few who make it to the playing field of life, and carries it one step further. He tells us what it's like being the twelfth man on an eleven-man athletic team, so close to the playing field and yet so far.

THE TWELFTH MAN

In the season of brightness
Countless spectators
Come to spur on
Their favourite teams,
Gather to inspire
Their own idols.

I stand aside
Alienated from it all
Deriding the twelfth player.

How different he is,
That twelfth man!
Amid the game,
The noise,
The roar of acclaim
He sits alone
And waits—
For the moment to come,
For the time to come,
For that incident to happen
When he too can play
With shouts of praise,
Tumultuous applause,
Words of support
Just for him,
And he'll be one of them
Respected like the rest of them.

But that rarely happens.
People still say
The bond between game and player
Is for life.
But even lifelong bonds can snap,
And the heart that sinks
With the last whistle
Can also break.

And you, Iftikhar,
You too are a twelfth player,
You wait for a moment,
For a time,
For an incident . . .

You too Iftikhar
Will sink—
Will break.

translated by Brenda Walker

Moeen Faruqi

Moeen Faruqi was born in Karachi, Pakistan, and educated in the United States and the United Kingdom. He is currently an administrator of a private school in Karachi. The relationship of Pakistan to England is complex and often troubling. Here the speaker, having returned to his native land, reflects on the underclass life both he and his father led in London.

THE RETURN

After washing Paddington loos
and scrubbing Hampstead streets
I returned to my piece of the Punjab
bought the 26 acres they took
from my father,
dry, hot land
that stopped giving birth to dreams the day
he died in a London hospital, his lungi
covering up his bony face till eternity

Now the land is giving birth again
it cries every season
with new voices, and the stars
rain down white light again
        but the men still come

looking for Kafirs,
                    unbelievers

Two days ago another died
they called Kafir
(My old man said to me:
"I can see, but I am willing to be blind")

On nights when the air is choking with dust
and heat
I close my eyes and place
my hand on the soft, pregnant
belly next to me
and I remember the green hills
of Inglistan
        and the boot steps that
        one dark night followed me
        in a dark and sour London alley
        calling

Kafir! Kafir!
(And my old man said to me:
"I can see, but I am willing to be blind")

Alamgir Hashmi

Alamgir Hashmi writes in English, although his poems have been translated into many of
the world's languages. He has been a professor of English and comparative literature in
Pakistan, the United States, and Switzerland, and has lectured widely throughout Europe
and the Americas. In "Pro Bono Publico," he satirizes the intersection of business, politics,
and religion in an increasingly growing and bewildering global economy. What is the mean-
ing of work to a businessman and father when half that work seems to consist of cooking the
books?

PRO BONO PUBLICO

in Pakistani English

Sirji, do you recall that
I have submitted myself
on this subject before. It is now after,
but I can submit my submission
again in your respect.
Our cottage industry is in boom:
five babies are produced per minute;
they come crying for international
brands of powder milk,
which is requiring canal water. They will
hopefully compete and complete with Brooke Shields
one day in the 21st century.
Veil has really come down this time
—as the poet said, on men's wits;
and enlighten the nation
during loadshedding.
The paddy is now standing foot
deep in sulphur, hot liquid exhausts
of the tanneries. While the politicians
are making flowery multilingual & maiden speeches,
we folk are busy
clapping for them, and catching
the content later on BBC,
Voice of America, AIR,
Doordarshan, or maybe
PTV, PBC, and BBG.
I must say that my middle-young bevy
is pulling out a special antenna to watch national tv.
I used to burn the midnight's oil before.
No charm in working any more.
Everybody here is eating money
half the week, and making the books
on the other days, looking over shoulder,
pleasing the boss but cheating Allah.
In any case, deficit is not a problem

because, INTER ALIA, SUE MOTO, and SUB JUDITH,
we can always show expense as saving
from German, Swiss, and U.S. AIDS, respectively,
verily at some physical and emotional cost to us.
Every Friday, I am praying a prayer
after namaz at durbar of Data Sahib,
two nawafil for personal help with balance sheet.
May Allah show us the right path with his own Flashlight
and ever pull us out of the straight and narrow
by a wide margin.

Europe

Kashyap Bhattacharya

Kashyap Bhattacharya was born in 1979 in the United Kingdom but lived most of his
school years in Calcutta. He now lives in Dundee, where he studies economics and Euro-
pean studies. The situation described in "The Cricketer" could apply to any boy playing
any national sport in any country. The cockiness and energy of the boy's fantasy runs up
against the disappointments of actual life.

THE CRICKETER

Under a gentle blue sky,
the towering shadows of the houses
kissing the streets,
a young boy walks out—
willow tucked under his armpits,
a pair of tattered gloves in hand.

He strolls down the street—
baggy cap adjusted,

nods solemnly at his invisible audience
hiding under the thick bushes and palm trees,

inspects the nature of the wicket,
notices the familiar potholes,
clogged drains,
the weeds growing out of it.
The newly laid tar is sticky, crying
from a day of severe heat.

He notices the ant colony,
making their evening march
towards the fruit seller's makeshift shop
on the corner, scattered
with rotten mangoes and lichis,

Confident, he marks his stance,
stares into the weakening eye of the day,
rests the bat firmly onto hard concrete,
closing one eye.
He dreams of magical elegance,
raises his arms replaying the moment.

A crack.

The bat falls from his hands.
He sees the startled eyes
of the cyclist lying on the street.
The front wheel spins madly.

He stares up
at the balcony on the third floor
to meet the angry glare
of his grandfather. Smoke
billows from his pipe.

Head lowered,
knobbly knees on the warm concrete,

he gathers broken dreams
and slowly rises.

Mumbles a soft apology
then walks into the shadow of a ten storey apartment.

When he looks
from the bedroom window
the street wears a deserted look—
only a stray dog
whining in the bushes.

He hears the bell of the sandhyarati,
spots the evening star, high and lonesome
in the fading western horizon.

He turns away from the vision,
staring silently at the incomprehensible numbers
taunting him under the candle's flickering light.

John Burnside

John Burnside was born in 1955 and resides in Fife in the United Kingdom. His most recent collection of poems, *The Asylum Dance,* won the Whitbread Prize for Poetry in 2000. The subject of this carefully observed poem is the simple dignity of men—men who usually work for others—engaged in their own work on Sunday and "wanting a life that stays untraceable." This work is connected to their dreams, desires, and hopes, the work they would like to pass on to their sons, a wish they can't quite articulate.

THE MEN'S HARBOUR

Late November, Anstruther

The eider are back
                Formal as decoys
they sit at the end of the quay
in the day's first warmth;
Sunday: when the townsmen bring their sons

to fish the dock,
their rods propped by the wall, the tensed lines
streaming with light;
the boys in hats and scarves and brightly-coloured
anoraks; the men
sober, reflective; wrapped in the quiet of work
that is theirs, for once, and unaccountable

and I can't help but think
there is something they want to pass on:
a knowledge they can't quite voice though it has to do
with the grace that distinguished strength
from power.
         Beyond the quay,
a crew of gulls is shredding refuse sacks
for morsels of fishbone, choice
oozings of yoghurt or mango.
They half co-operate, half
vie with one another, butting in
for fatter scraps, then fluttering away,
tracking the tarmac with newsprint and crusted grease.

There's nothing elegant in this, no special skill,
nothing save luck and speed and the odd
flutter of threat: a clownish, loud
bravado.
         Further upshore,
the sun finds the white on white
of the caravan park:
blisters of paint and distemper flaking away
from brickwork and metal;
alleys of half-kept garden between the stands;
the scalped grass dusted with frost; a single blackbird
scratching for grubs in the dirt of the island bed.

Someone has set a flag above the dock;
a thin old man in a jerkin and fingerless gloves
mending a hull, his tight lips crammed with nails,
his eyes like shells,

and others here are working on their dreams
of water: men in overalls or coats,
or muddled sweaters, scabbed with paint and rust.
Their hands are dark with oil or coiled in rope;
their bodies subtle, verging on the edge
of weightlessness; no law to hold them here,
no harboured rage.

This is the life they want, their chosen craft,
working with hooks and chains through the sea-water-cold.
Each of them knows what it is
to have been refused,
to feel the silence swelling in their throats
and nothing to be said, lest they admit
how little they care for anything but this,
wanting a life that stays
untraceable.
                    Each of them knows
and each of them makes his peace:
the burden of a given name and place
discarded in a moment's self-forgetting.

They're out at the rim of navigable space
and ready for something no one could explain,
a mystery to fathom when it comes
like starlight, or a music in the tide,
or some new vessel, coming in to land,
one cold, bright afternoon: some unknown craft
with snow on the deck, or a phantom of morning lamplight
sealed in the hull's bright paint
like the spirit of tungsten.

Günter Eich

Günter Eich (1907–72) was a German soldier in the Second World War and spent time as a
prisoner of war in an American camp. He was awarded the Buchner Prize. In the following
poem, the simile in the last line creates a revolutionary undercurrent. Men carrying hoes

are workers—whether in the Middle East or in the French vineyards or in the American West. And the workers of the world, as a famous revolutionary once said, can unite.

THE MAN IN THE BLUE SMOCK

The man in the blue smock,
going home, his hoe on his shoulder—
I see him behind the garden fence.

Thus they went at nightfall in Canaan,
thus they go home from Myanmar's rice paddies,
Mecklenburg's vast potato fields,
from the vineyards of Burgundy and the Californian orchards.

When the lamp lights up behind clouded panes,
I start envying them their bliss that I don't have to share,
their patriarchal evenings
with the smoldering hearth, with children's wash, with modesty.

The man in the blue smock on his way home:
the hoe he is carrying on his shoulder
looks, as dusk is falling, like a gun.

translated by Reinhold Grimm

Hédi Kaddour

Hédi Kaddour was born in 1945 in Tunisia but has lived in France since childhood. He has published three books of poems and a collection of essays. He teaches literature in Paris. This poem recognizes that people we take for granted in our daily activities have their own inner lives and suffer in their own distinctive ways.

THE BUS DRIVER

What has gotten into the bus driver
Who has left his bus, who has sat down
On a curb on the Place de l'Opéra

Where he slips into the ease of being
Nothing more than his own tears? The passers-by
Who bend over such a shared and
Presentable sorrow would like him
To tell them that the wind used to know
How to come out of the woods towards a woman's dress,
Or that one day his brother said to him
Even your shadow wants nothing to do with you.
His feet in a puddle, the bus driver
Can only repeat *This work is hard*
And people aren't kind.

   translated by Marilyn Hacker

Donny O'Rourke

Donny O'Rourke was born in Port Glasgow in 1959. He was a student at Glasgow University and is the editor of *Dream State: The New Scottish Poets.* "Clockwork" reminds us literally how our relationships with our fathers are bound up with time and how painful it can be to watch them age.

CLOCKWORK

Broken clocks and watches were my father's hobby,
Killing time, he'd say, no irony intended,—
So grandfathers loitered dumbstruck in our lobby,
Hands salaaming as if begging to be mended.

Testimonial tokens of lifetimes on the job
Added to his pile their grateful mollusk gape.
Stammering snuff-stain waistcoat fob—
Tick corrected by pug and scrape.

Eyeglass squinched, he'd read the auguries
Pronounce and whistle, arrange his tiny tools,

Wind the watch until we'd hear it wheeze,
Teaching me to prod among the cogs and spools.

Though my cack-handedness loomed larger through his glass
He didn't mind the knack not passing on.
It's a stoic's pastime, letting time pass,
He knew with quartz and plastic his day had gone.

Now Dad's hands are slow and he's lost his spring
His face is scuffed by the emery-paper years
But he can value a clock by its pendulum swing
Or a watch, by the tact, of the tick, that he hears

And on Sundays sometimes we still repair
To smile at every bang on mantel chime
So many hunched gloamings unwinding there
My father and I keeping perfect time.

Africa

António Jacinto

António Jacinto (1924–91) was born in Luanda, Angola. He was active in the struggle for national independence and was imprisoned for fourteen years by the Portuguese. He is the author of two collections of poetry and was awarded the Noma Prize and the National Prize for Literature. Here Jacinto seems to enter the mind of an illiterate man who longs to express his feelings in words he knows his lover will be unable to read. In this poem, as in many, the poet serves as a voice for the voiceless.

LETTER FROM A CONTRACT WORKER

I wanted to write you a letter
my love
a letter to tell
of this longing

to see you
and this fear
of losing you
of this thing which deeper than I want, I feel
a nameless pain which pursues me
a sorrow wrapped about my life.

I wanted to write you a letter
my love
a letter of intimate secrets
a letter of memories of you
of you
your lips as red as the tacula fruit
your hair black as the dark diloa fish
your eyes gentle as the macongue
your breasts hard as young maboque fruit
your light walk
your caresses
better than any that I find down here.

I wanted to write you a letter
my love
to bring back our days together in our secret haunts
nights lost in the long grass
to bring back the shadow of your legs
and the moonlight filtering through the endless
palms,
to bring back the madness of our passion
and the bitterness of separation.

I wanted to write you a letter
my love
which you could not read without crying
which you would hide from your father Bombo
and conceal from your mother Kieza
which you would read without the indifference
of forgetfulness,

a letter which would make any other
in all Kilombo worthless.

I wanted to write you a letter
my love
a letter which the passing wind would take
a letter which the cashew and the coffee trees
the hyenas and the buffalo,
the caymens and the river fish
could hear
the plants and the animals
pitying our sharp sorrow
from song to song
lament to lament
breath to caught breath
would leave to you, pure and hot,
the burning
the sorrowful words of the letter
I wanted to write you

I wanted to write you a letter
But my love, I don't know why it is,
why, why, why it is, my love,
but you can't read
and I—oh the hopelessness—I can't write.

translated by Margaret Dickinson

Central America and the Caribbean

Luis Miguel Aguilar

Luis Miguel Aguilar lives in Mexico City, where he works as an editor of *Nexos*, a review of art, culture, and politics. The narrator of this poem twice asks ". . . what else could you do in Chetumal?" a phrase that evokes the boredom of life in a small Mexican village. The question underscores the exoticism of the motorcycles that, despite—or perhaps because of—their inherent danger, appeal to the masculine sensibility of Memo, who orders a used Harley the day the catalog arrives from California.

MEMO, WHO LOVED MOTORCYCLES

This is where my recklessness has gotten me.
But what else could you do in Chetumal?
About the rest, I don't know. I climbed,
Every afternoon, onto the most beautiful and fastest Honda
Motorcycle this town had ever seen. It wasn't
That I ignored the horrible way
Jornis, Asar, Ignacio, Pato and Tebo died
—My best friends since forever—
All of them on their bikes. After each of those deaths
I was afraid; they were like a series of warnings
From a superior something, God or fate.
But no one who's ever felt
How the machine demands speed
And then more speed as its only sustenance
Will ignore why it was that we all decided,
In the end, to run the risk.
I ran into a truck full of construction materials
at the corner of Heroes and Hidalgo Street.
I was forewarned; but even so
The day the catalogue of motorcycles for sale
Arrived from California,
Its cover showing off that thing of beauty
Which is the Harley-Davidson/1200,
I sent off the order, telling myself
That when my hand shut the mailbox door,
It might as well have signed my death sentence.
What else could you do in Chetumal?

translated by Robert L. Jones

Evan Jones

Evan Jones was born in Jamaica in 1927. He was educated in the United States and at Oxford University. He has lived in England since 1956, writing full-time, primarily for films and television. In this "nation language" poem, he deals touchingly with the plight of the migrant/immigrant worker: he doesn't exactly like being in England, though the money is adequate; he'd like to go home to his woman in Jamaica, but not quite yet.

THE LAMENT OF THE BANANA MAN

Gal, I'm tellin you, I'm tired fo true,
Tired of Englan, tired o' you.
But I can't go back to Jamaica now . . .

I'm here in Englan, I'm drawin pay,
I go to de underground every day—
Eight hours is all, half-hour fo lunch,
M'uniform's free, an m'ticket punch—
Punchin tickets not hard to do,
When I'm tired o punchin, I let dem through.

I get a paid holiday once a year.
Ol' age an sickness can't touch me here.
I have a room of m'own, an a iron bed,
Dunlopillo under m'head,
A Morphy-Richards to warm de air,
A formica table, an easy chair.
I have summer clothes, an winter clothes,
An paper kerchiefs to blow m'nose.

My yoke is easy, my burden is light,
I know a place I can go to, any night.
Dis place Englan! I'm not complainin,
If it col', it col', if it rainin, it rainin.
I don't mind if it's mostly night,
Dere's always inside, or de sodium light.
I don't mind white people starin at me,
Dey don'want me here? Don't is deir country?

You won' catch me bawlin any homesick tears
If I don' see Jamaica for a t'ousan years!

. . . Gal, I m tellin you, I'm tired fo true,
Tired of Englan, tired o' you
I can't go back to Jamaica now
But I'd want to die there, anyhow.

North America

Robert Francis

Robert Francis (1901–87) was a master of the short lyric. His collected poems have been published by the University of Massachusetts Press. Here he applies his singular talent to the cat and mouse dance between a base runner and a pitcher.

THE BASE STEALER

Poised between going on and back, pulled
Both ways taut like a tightrope-walker,
Fingertips pointing the opposites,
Now bouncing tiptoe like a dropped ball
Or a kid skipping rope, come on, come on,
Running a scattering of steps sidewise,
How he teeters, skitters, tingles, teases,
Taunts them, hovers like an ecstatic bird,
He's only flirting, crowd him, crowd him,
Delicate, delicate, delicate, delicate—now!

Andrew Hudgins

Andrew Hudgins was born in Killeen, Texas, in 1951. He has published four volumes of poetry and has been awarded the Witter Byner Award. He teaches at the University of Cincinnati. The passing of tools from father to son is an initiation ritual that many men have experienced. In this ode to the metallic companions to manhood, Hudgins clarifies the difference between working with the right tools and working with the wrong ones.

TOOLS: AN ODE

The cheap
        screwdriver reams the cheap
                        screwhead,
and the dull blade burns white oak and splinters cherry.
The loose wrench
           torques the bolt on crookedly
and strips the thread. But guided by good tools,
the screw bites freely to its full length,
                    the board
rips cleanly,
        and the hex nut weds its bolt.
Thin shavings rise in long unbroken curls,
each lovely in itself.
           The good tool
                smoothes
rough lumber underneath the unforced hand,
unwarps
        the warped board, trues
               the untrue edge
before it chops the mortise, cuts the tenon,
and taps them home
           in happy marriage. With good tools
the edge falls
        plumb and all
             four corners square.
The house holds snug against the crashing wind,
and there
        is order in the polity
and pleasure in the handmade marriage bed.

William Matthews

William Matthews (1942–97) was a much honored American poet during his lifetime. He was director of the creative writing program at New York's City College. This sonnet captures something of the complete devotion of the young sports fan.

CHEAP SEATS, THE CINCINNATI GARDENS, PROFESSIONAL BASKETBALL, 1959

The less we paid, the more we climbed. Tendrils
of smoke lazed just as high and hung there, blue,
particulate, the opposite of dew.
We saw the whole court from up there. Few girls
had come, few wives, numerous boys in molt
like me. Our heroes leapt and surged and looped
and two nights out of three, like us, they'd lose.
But "like us" is wrong: we had no result
three nights out of three: so we had heroes.
And "we" is wrong, for I knew none by name
among that hazy company unless
I brought her with me. This was loneliness
with noise, unlike the kind I had at home
with no clock running down, and mirrors.

Christopher Merrill

Christopher Merrill is director of the International Writing Program at the University of Iowa. He is a translator and nonfiction writer as well as a poet. "A Boy Juggling a Soccer Ball" is a happy instance of form following function as the lines mimic the boy's every nimble move.

A BOY JUGGLING A SOCCER BALL

    after practice: right foot
to left foot, stepping forward and back,
    to right foot and left foot,
and left foot up to his thigh, holding

it on his thigh as he twists
around in a circle, until it rolls
        down the inside of his leg,
like a tickle of sweat, not catching
        and tapping on the soft
side of his foot, and juggling
        once, twice, three times,
hopping on one foot like a jump-roper
        in the gym, now trapping
and holding the ball in midair,
        balancing it on the instep
of his weak left foot, stepping forward
        and forward and back, then
lifting it overhead until it hangs there;
        and squaring off his body,
he keeps the ball aloft with a nudge
        of his neck, heading it
from side to side, softer and softer,
        like a dying refrain,
until the ball, slowing, balances
        itself on his hairline,
the hot sun and sweat filling his eyes
        as he jiggles this way
and that, then flicking it up gently,
        hunching his shoulders
and tilting his head back, he traps it
        in the hollow of his neck,
and bending at the waist, sees his shadow,
        his dangling T-shirt, the bent
blades of brown grass in summer heat;
        and relaxing, the ball slipping
down his back . . . and missing his foot.

        He wheels around, he marches
over the ball, as if it were a rock
        he stumbled into, and pressing
his left foot against it, he pushes it
        against the inside of his right
until it pops into the air, is heeled

over his head—the rainbow!—
and settles on his extended thigh before
        rolling over his knee and down
his shin, so he can juggle it again
        from his left foot to his right foot
—and right foot to left foot to thigh—
        as he wanders, on the last day
of summer, around the empty field.

Len Roberts

Len Roberts has published eight books of poetry, the most recent being *The Silent Singer: New and Selected Poems* (University of Illinois, 2001). He is a professor of English at Northampton Community College, Bethlehem, Pennsylvania. In this poem, blame, miscommunication, booze, and silence characterize the father-son relationship. These negative interactions nonetheless mask a deep hunger for love that seems to emanate palpably from both ends of that table on Olmstead Street described at the end of the poem.

I BLAME IT ON HIM

when I'm a quarter-inch off
and the molding won't fit
no matter how hard I hammer it,
and when the outlet goes dead,
it's his fumbling hands
trying to sort green from white from black
while I shout at my wife
to call an electrician
even as the wires spark and short,
and it's him when I won't talk
for days after an argument,
his small fists pounding the dust
from the bag in the barn,
left jab to get it moving,
right cocked to knock it out, my old man
drinking with my hand on the patio after,
his lips singing my songs

till 2 a.m. and every neighbor's light off
but I'm still looking for more of something
like him those nights in Boney's Bar,
the red neon bull charging down
while he bought for the house
and came home with nothing, the two of us
sitting silent then at either end
of that table back on Olmstead Street,
our skin blue-cold as his heart-struck death within a few months,
neither willing to go get a coat,
trying not to blink, tapping our fingers, our feet,
waiting for the other one to start.

Aging, Illness, and Death

The world
is gradually slipping away from him
—Alain Bosquet

Take your time choosing a gravesite;
you'll be there a long while
—Duo Duo

Aging, illness, and death—the three conditions that Buddha encountered as a youth when he first stepped out of his father's palatial estate—mark, more than any other, the essence of human suffering. Poets—both men and women—in all cultures and in all times have dwelt on these three conditions, expressing the gamut of human emotions, from rage and despair to joy and acceptance. The poems in this section capture distinctly male responses to these universal human conditions. For example, in most cultures men have been trained to be strong, independent, and ambitious. As men age, the waning of their physical powers can trigger a host of anxieties from the trivial to the serious. The Swedish poet Kjell Hjern bemoans the fact that as he loses hair on his head, his nose hair increases. In a more serious vein, the Iraqi poet Buland al-Haydari confronts the loneliness of old age, "dreaming that a woman might dream of me," as he spends yet another winter alone, huddled by his stove.

Despite a miraculous number of scientific advances, illness remains one of the greatest sources of human suffering. For gay men around the world, AIDS, of course, has been nothing less than a scourge. Sky Gilbert from Canada imagines the possibility that gay men's tears transmit the disease and, in a touching twist, proposes an Island of Lost Tears where grief over the deaths caused by AIDS can be collectively expressed. Vikram Seth, the Indian poet and novelist, creates a persona who, ill with AIDS, helplessly appeals to his lover to "not let me die." The American poet and famed short-story writer Raymond Carver, in what is surely an autobiographical poem, experiences a momentary blessing in nature on a clear morning, even in the middle of his terminal condition.

Whatever men's beliefs and values are about death, the Great Leveler brings each to a condition of fear and awe at some point. The Nicaraguan Juan Sobalvarro creates a graphic picture of a dead body "attacked by flies" but also surrounded by "barefoot angels." Duo Duo from China imagines he has already died and can look at things from the point of view of a dead man, which gives him a fresh appreciation of his life—and those who have gone before him. Anthony Lawrence, an Australian, re-creates an encounter with a large lizard that allows him to feel empathy and compassion for the animals we slaughter for our food.

When men write about these experiences, they reveal a vulnerability otherwise frequently unacknowledged and unexpressed. The "poetry of men's lives" explores deeper levels of the male psyche, and nowhere is this more apparent than in poems that deal with men's primordial fears and anxieties.

Asia

Duo Duo

Duo Duo was born in Peking in 1951. He witnessed the Tienanmen Square Massacre in 1989 and since then has lived in exile in either the United States or England. This is a new translation of the title poem of his volume *Looking Out from Death*. The speaker reflects a consciousness born of a heightened awareness of suffering and oppression. The paradoxical bitterness and stoicism displayed here create a distinctive male voice coming to terms with the actualities of contemporary existence.

LOOKING OUT FROM DEATH

Looking out from death you see
things a little differently.
Things you missed completely
while living come into focus.
Take your time choosing a gravesite;
you'll be there a long while—
the view could be tedious.

When they shovel dirt in your face,
be sure to thank them

for blanking out the faces
of your enemies forever.

Looking out from death you will
hear a silent scream
from the chorus of voices
you will never hear again.
If you listen hard,
you can hear that scream now.

adapted from the Chinese by Fred Moramarco

Nissim Ezekiel

Nissim Ezekiel was born in Bombay in 1924 of Jewish parents and educated in London. For
many years he was a professor of English at the University of Bombay. He is the author of
several books of poetry and an award winner. He has been called "India's first genuine poet
in English." In "Case Study," Ezekiel reviews the high and low points of a man's life from
the perspective of a detached observer. For men, as for women, the cultural messages about
success and failure are mixed and contradictory: to care too much about success makes one
a sellout; to care too little makes one a rationalizing slacker.

CASE STUDY

Whatever he had done was not quite right,
The Masters never failed, however weak,
To know when they had sinned against the light.
Can their example purify his sight?
Ought he to practise Yoga, study Greek,
Or bluff his way throughout with brazen cheek?

Beginning with a foolish love affair
After common school and rotten college,
He had the patient will but not the flair
To climb with quick assault the envied stair;

Messed around instead with useless knowledge,
And staked on politics a fatal pledge.

His marriage was the worst mistake of all.
Although he loved his children when they came,
He spoilt them too with just that extra doll,
Or discipline which drove them to the wall.
His wife and changing servants did the same—
A man is damned in that domestic game.

He worked at various jobs and then he stopped
For reasons never clear or quite approved
By those who knew; some almost said he shopped
Around for dreams and projects later dropped
(Though this was quite untrue); he never moved
Unless he found something he might have loved.

He came to me and this is what I said:
"The pattern will remain, unless you break
It with a sudden jerk; but use your head.
Not all returned as heroes who had fled
In wanting both to have and eat the cake.
Not all who fail are counted with the fake."

Huan Fu

Huan Fu (b. 1922) is the senior member of the generation of so-called Bamboo Hat poets in Taiwan. He is also a translator of modern Japanese poetry. The speaker in this playfully serious poem rejects the perks of senior citizenship because they rob him of his dignity and self-sufficiency—and because he did nothing to earn them.

DON'T, DON'T

You don't have to give me your seat, lady:
The bus runs me rapidly and
Soon to my destination.
In this crowd

Think you that I, an old man,
Cannot hold on to his feet?

Don't, you don't have to pity,
Although I have arrived at old age,
I didn't earn it with effort;
Doing nothing
I could still come to be old and ugly.
Old age doesn't deserve respectable privilege.

My wrinkles do not request pity;
I have eaten history
And spit out conventions and morality,
To the degree of my wrinkles
I appear respectable,
But I know
That I am a debaucher
Who has not written a modern Red Chamber Dream.

Don't, don't tax me with your support;
In this crowd,
Within this rickety, public bus
Only if I can stand on my feet
Will contentment come.
Needing no other one to help me walking down,
I will soon reach my destination.

translated by Dominic Cheung

Kuan Kuan

Kuan Kuan (b. 1930) describes himself as "a Chinese man, a Shangtung man, a Chiao-hsien man, a Ch'ing-tao man, and a Taipei man." He has been described as the "e. e. cummings of Chinese poetry." Here he reviews the events of his life from the perspective of age sixty and finds them ridiculous, but wonderfully so. After all, it's the only life he has.

AUTOBIOGRAPHY OF A SLOPPY SLUGGARD

Elementary school for six years,
Three years in junior high, three in senior high,
Four years college,
Two years each: M.A. and Ph.D.
Thank heavens I didn't endure all these.
Five times in love,
Two lovers, one wife, and three kids.
A few foes, two or three buddies, a handful of relatives.
A soldier for some years, on payroll for a few, but never fought a war.
In battlefields of life
A few times won little, a few times made truces.
I have a long gown, several suits, and several pairs of jeans.
I smoke a pipe, drink two cups of tea, eat three bowls of rice, and sleep on a
    wooden bed;
I am a born vegetarian.
I don't gamble, nor play chess;
A few torn books by my pillow side, I play silly.
I went through a few shocks, a few changes, and sickness.
In the sunset, I hold on to my knees and ponder:
Is this nonsense how I spent my sixty years?
My life seems colorful, but it's goddamned ridiculous,
It's ridiculous, but it's goddamned wonderful.
When I look back at my unfinished works,
Ridiculous! Ridiculously wonderful!
Even a sword hanging on the wall
Wavers ridiculously in the evening breeze.
Even if as tasteless as the quintuply diluted tea in my hand,
I would like another cup,
Wonderfully or ridiculously.

translated by Dominic Cheung

Vikram Seth

Vikram Seth was born in 1952 in Calcutta. Educated at Oxford, Seth was also a creative writing fellow at Stanford. He is a widely published poet and novelist and a recipient of the Commonwealth Poetry Prize of Asia. Sometimes, as in "Soon," the most painful subjects gain a quiet dignity from their treatment in poems of a deceptively simple, restrained, and formal arrangement.

SOON

I shall die soon, I know.
This thing is in my blood.
It will not let me go.
It saps my cells for food.

It soaks my nights in sweat
And breaks my days in pain.
No hand or drug can treat
These limbs for love or gain.

Love was the strange first cause
That bred grief in its seed,
And gain knew its own laws—
To fix its place and breed.

He whom I love, thank God,
Won't speak of hope or cure.
It would not do me good.
He sees that I am sure.

He knows what I have read
And will not bring me lies.
He sees that I am dead.
I read it in his eyes.

How am I to go on—
How will I bear this taste,

My throat cased in white spawn—
These hands that shake and waste?

Stay by my steel ward bed
And hold me where I lie.
Love me when I am dead
And do not let me die.

The Middle East

Buland al-Haydari

Buland al-Haydari was born in Iraq in 1926 of a Kurdish family. As a political activist, he was forced into exile and is now living in Lebanon, where he edits a literary journal. "Old Age" captures the loneliness and isolation of an old man as he dreams of a woman who might be dreaming of him.

OLD AGE

Another winter,
And here am I,
By the side of the stove,
Dreaming that a woman might dream of me,
That I might bury in her breast
A secret she would not mock;
Dreaming that in my fading years
I might spring forth as light,
And she would say:
This light is mine;
Let no woman draw near it.
Here, by the side of the stove,
Another winter,
And here am I,
Spinning my dreams and fearing them,
Afraid her eyes would mock

My bald, idiotic head,
My greying, aged soul,
Afraid her feet would kick
My love,
And here, by the side of the stove,
I would be lightly mocked by woman.

Alone,
Without love, or dreams, or a woman,
And tomorrow I shall die of the cold within,
Here, by the side of the stove.

translated by Mounah A. Khouri and Hamid Algar

Ahmad Shamlu

Amhad Shamlu (1925–2000) was born in Tehran, Iran. He spent time living in exile in Princeton, New Jersey, and in England. He authored numerous books of poetry and was an active translator from French into Persian. In "Somber Song," the raw physical energy of a horse and the erotic energy of a young woman are juxtaposed against the fading hopes of aging men, who often want a last chance to make a mark in the world.

SOMBER SONG

In a leaden dawn
the horseman stands silent, and
the long mane of his horse is disheveled in the wind.

Oh God, God,
horsemen should not stand still
when things are imminent.

By the burnt hedge
the girl stands silent, and
her thin skirt moves in the wind.

Oh God, God,

girls should not remain silent
when the men, hopeless and weary, grow old.

translated by anonymous

Europe

Alain Bosquet

Alain Bosquet (1919–98) was born in Odessa, Russia. He was enlisted in the U.S. Army and taught for a few years in the United States before settling in France, where he was literary editor of *Le Monde* for many years. In "An Old Gentleman," Alain Bosquet writes in both the first and third person, simultaneously experiencing and observing the phenomenon of aging.

AN OLD GENTLEMAN

I am an old gentleman who, in his bath,
knows that the world
is gradually slipping away from him.
He washes, pinches himself,
not caring if it's raining outside
or if the sky comes in through the window
to converse briefly with him.
He wonders what his shoulder is for.
He loses his mind, bit by bit,
certain that his soul
will soon no longer function.
Water strokes him.
The century still has a sweet smell.
I am an old gentleman,
a towel around his neck,
who, looking for his glasses,
has lost his life deep within the mirror.

translated by William Jay Smith

Alain Bosquet

An old man, the speaker of Bosquet's poem, finally bids good-bye to his literary and artistic ancestors, those great names of the past that now only oppress him and keep him from "hearing the music of silence."

CELEBRITIES

I took the train to Rome.
I said to Michelangelo:
"I won't be back, old man,
you'll have to make do with all those Japanese."
I took the train to Bruges
and spat
on all the Memlings, one after the other:
"I no longer admire anything;
all that once was sweet is now a torture."
I took the ferry to London.
On the crumbling stage, during the first act
of Richard the Second, I shouted:
"Stop it, William!
All tragedies now take place here inside me."
Then I stayed home
with Mozart on the tape-deck,
Corelli on the record-player.
"Stop," I cried, "you keep me
from hearing the music of silence."
Finally I burned
my two Matisses and the complete works
of Gogol, Balzac, and Kafka.

translated by William Jay Smith

Kjell Hjern

Kjell Hjern (1916–84) was a native of Gothenburg, Sweden, a life-long freelance writer, art magazine editor, theater and art critic, local historian, and translator and anthologist. In this poem, the poet deals with a minor cross to be borne by aging males: the increased growth of nose hair.

ON THE GROWTH OF HAIR IN MIDDLE AGE

No poem has yet been written
except possibly in Chinese
about the growth of hair that occurs
during a man's best years
when the hair on his head has begun to thin.

The hair then growing from the nose
can more readily be tolerated
when a man sports a full beard,
but even then it gets in the way
if the cathedral of the nose
has delicate walls.

For this is not just innocent fluff
as on a bald pate
when it tries to deny the aging process.
No, these hairs are like lances,
unfavorably disposed one toward the other.

And when you wish to remove them,
they stick together;
and you are left cursing those miserable tools,
tweezers with warped shanks.

There are, to be sure, bold blades
that seize the nose hairs by the end
and quickly yank them out,
blades that may be compared to those
that operate farther down to snip out the appendix,

which, incidentally, needs to be done but once,
while nose hair returns again and again.

Here Science,
which otherwise horses about,
asking in that self-important way,
"What can I do for you?
May I help you?"
has shamefully failed;
and Poetry,
the pompous winged mare,
patronizingly turns her rump on us
when we attempt to re-create
these wretched scenes of everyday life.

translated by William Jay Smith and Leif Sjöberg

Michael Longley

Michael Longley was born in Belfast in 1939 and educated at the Royal Belfast Academical
Institution and Trinity College, Dublin, where he studied the classics. He is the recipient of
many poetry awards, including the prestigious Whitbread Prize for Poetry. He currently
lives and works in Belfast. "A Flowering" describes aging as a kind of Ovidian metamor-
phosis that allows the poet to see the beauty of men's bodies in their youth and wholeness,
in their fleeting moment in the sun.

A FLOWERING

Now that my body grows woman-like I look at men
As two or three women have looked at me, then hide
Among Ovid's lovely casualties—all that blood
Colouring the grass and changing into flowers, purple
Lily-shaped, wild hyacinth upon whose petals
We doodled our lugubrious initials, they and I,
Blood dosed with honey, tumescent, effervescent—
Clean bubbles in yellow mud—creating in an hour
My own son's beauty, the truthfulness of my nipples,

Petals that will not last long, that hand on and no more,
Youth and its flower named after the wind, anemone.

Henrik Nordbrandt

Henrik Nordbrandt was born in 1945. He studied at Copenhagen University, where he specialized in Asian languages. He has traveled widely and lived in Turkey, Greece, and Spain. He has written more than twenty books of poetry, stories, and a novel, and won a host of awards as the most accomplished poet of his time in Denmark. Beginning with a quiet sense of objectivity and detachment, "Old Man in Meditation" ends with the speaker's recognition of the reality of his own aging.

OLD MAN IN MEDITATION

I think of a man in a forest
an old man with a storm lantern
quite alone in a huge forest.

I think of what he is staring at
which demands his attention so much
that he doesn't even blink when a leaf
whirls into his face.

In the circle of lantern light
you see that what he stares at
only he can see.

I think of his shadow,
the shadow of an old man
falling among tree trunks.

The wind blows through his beard

and through his wide sleeves;
the shadow of his figure sways in the wind

the wind that now sounds everywhere
and increases until the lantern goes out.

Then I think of the darkness;
I think of the man,
of the wind, of the darkness
and of the empty place in the forest.

Then I think of myself.

translated by Ann Born

Central America and the Caribbean

Juan Sobalvarro

Juan Sobalvarro was born in 1966 in Nicaragua. He is the author of a book of poems and a book of short stories and is a cofounder and editor of the literary magazine *400 Elephants*. In facing the mystery of death, poets often resort to metaphor. In "I've Seen a Dead Man," Juan Sobalvarro uses a pair of winged creatures, flies and angels, to suggest the despair and hope that exist in a revolutionary culture.

I'VE SEEN A DEAD MAN

I've seen a dead man
attacked by flies
and barefoot angels in the mud.
How silent this dead man is! This death
has no speech prepared,
here in what's lost
where the family of fear and confusion
is born.

I want to scream for him.
I don't want his death to make me cry.

Where was his guilt hatched?

I see his death blurring,
something like night coming down,
in this deep green of the mountain.

translated by John Oliver Simon

North America

Raymond Carver

Raymond Carver (1938–88) was born in Washington State and is best known for his influential short stories. His collected poems, *All of Us,* were posthumously published in 2000. The narrator of "This Morning" will not let thoughts of death, divorce, and financial woes crowd out the simple beauty and calm of a lovely morning. He has "trampled on stuff" in order to stay alive, and his past weighs heavily on him, but Nature helps to bring him back to the mystery of the present.

THIS MORNING

This morning was something. A little snow
lay on the ground. The sun floated in a clear
blue sky. The sea was blue, and blue-green,
as far as the eye could see.
Scarcely a ripple. Calm. I dressed and went
for a walk—determined not to return
until I took in what Nature had to offer.
I passed close to some old, bent-over trees.
Crossed a field strewn with rocks
where snow had drifted. Kept going
until I reached the bluff.
Where I gazed at the sea, and the sky, and

the gulls wheeling over the white beach
far below. All lovely. All bathed in a pure
cold light. But, as usual, my thoughts
began to wander. I had to will
myself to see what I was seeing
and nothing else. I had to tell myself this is what
mattered, not the other. (And I did see it,
for a minute or two!) For a minute or two
it crowded out the usual musings on
what was right, and what was wrong—duty,
tender memories, thoughts of death, how I should treat
with my former wife. All the things
I hoped would go away this morning.
The stuff I live with every day. What
I've trampled on in order to stay alive.
But for a minute or two I did forget
myself and everything else. I know I did.
For when I turned back I didn't know
where I was. Until some birds rose up
from the gnarled trees. And flew
in the direction I needed to be going.

Peter Cooley

Peter Cooley teaches in the creative writing program at Tulane University. His most recent books of poetry are *The Astonished Hours* (1993), *Sacred Conversations* (1998), and *A Place Made of Starlight* (2001). In "The Language of Departure," a man searches for words to express his true feelings as he realizes the brevity of life in a midafternoon, midlife epiphany. But the language of feeling does not come easily to most men, even in the midst of crisis.

LANGUAGE OF DEPARTURE

Late afternoon and the man finds himself,
his face in his hands at his desk,
nodding, about to drop off a few minutes.
He'd better wake up, shake himself with coffee.
It's past the middle of middle age:

soon he'll be asleep for the next millennia
and the gods may or may not wake him.
There are only a few decades left if he's lucky
to tell his wife, his children, all he feels
they've given him, and already he knows
his language of departure comes from that other country.
He must learn a new alphabet, open his mouth farther
to form vowels. Where he is going there are no words
except those given as they enter to the chosen.

Sky Gilbert

Sky Gilbert is one of Canada's most controversial artistic forces. In his earlier years, his work was mainly theatrical, with such hits as *Drag Queens on Trail* and *Drag Queens in Outer Space*. Gilbert is among the many gay male writers who feel an imperative to continue speaking out about the AIDS epidemic. In this poignant poem he takes off on the possibility that AIDS can be transmitted by tears.

THE ISLAND OF LOST TEARS

Haven't you heard the latest news about AIDS?
You can get it from tears
O yes
You mustn't let anyone cry on you or
cry near you, in fact it's a very good idea not to let anyone cry in the same
room as you
We have received notice that at the moment authorities are considering
taking all the weepers (all the wettest people in the world)—shipping them
off, and putting them on a small island off Southern England where they
can all weep on each other to their heart's content and it rains there all the
time anyway so they won't know the difference
And all those great movies
the tearjerkers:
*The Heiress, Now Voyager, Madame X, Love Is a Many Splendored Thing,
The Rainmaker, The Rains of Ranchipur* and even for you really sappy
ones, parts of *The Music Man*
will no longer be allowed on TV

And if you know someone who's a sentimental type you'd better warn them, you'd better have a heart to heart or safer yet, a mind to mind and say "In the past you were wont to get emotional at the slightest provocation. Though there's nothing really wrong with being emotional—everyone, in the past, got emotional from time to time—now, because of what we know about tears, it's better that you try to control yourself and not get into situations where you might be moved. You know . . . one thing leads to another and just taking casual notice of an impoverished beggar woman or watching a sunset for an extended length of time, for many, could lead to such minor yet dangerous feelings as sadness, love, pity, affection, and from these it is but a short step to the dreaded tears. For some even the old fashioned notion of warmth will become a thing of the past. Certainly old habits die hard, many will be unwilling to give up their emotional lives. But the danger to human health is too great. Do yourself a favour. Stop feeling deeply. Your partner, your lover, your husband, wife, or significant other will thank you for your consideration in repressing your deepest most profound emotions."

But me

I will go

To the Island of Lost Tears

No boat will take you there

No plane will fly you there

You must find your own way

Some swim, some walk on the water

Some claim they fly there

And as you approach

you can hear the faint sounds of sobbing

and you see nothing

but a lush greenery shrouded in mist

And when you reach the shore

they rush to you

and hold you

in their strong arms

arms made so much stronger warmer by being caressed with tears

And they take you to their

wet little houses

and sit you down by their

wet little fires

and they say to you

"Cry
my sweet boy
my inscrutable girl
cry until you have no more tears
until the very well that is your sadness and your joy is dry
and when you think that you can cry no more
you find that you can cry still!"
No one dies there
in the Island of Lost Tears
they simply fade into the mist
But late at night through the trees
(they have none but weeping willows)
the voices whisper the forbidden words
"Weep . . . cry . . . feel . . . let yourself go!"
These are the ghosts of those who dared
to cry when all others had forgotten how, and they will not be silenced

Steve Kowit

Steve Kowit was born in Brooklyn in 1938 and lives in Potrero, California. He has published many books of poetry and is the editor of *The Maverick Poets*, an anthology of alternative American verse. In "Snapshot," the aging writer ties visual imagery, music, memory, and solitude together in a poignant moment of both reminiscence and presence.

SNAPSHOT

At night, a man is sitting at his desk in pain,
aging, full of dreams & fears, till Jessie
barges in & nuzzles his left leg & says, *Hey,*
you know that open box of Milk-Bones in the kitchen?
Well, I've been thinking . . .
The man washes down another Vicodin,
scratches the dog's head, & the two of them
get up & leave the room. When he returns,
he sees how dark it is outside, & late.
He types & stops, looking for a phrase he can't
quite find, some gesture that the past

388

had given him & taken back.
Above his desk, that ancient snapshot of his folks,
two Lower East Side kids, their lives together
just beginning, who will never understand
that everything the future holds for them
has passed. Dexter Gordon's lush & melancholic
take on "Don't Explain" drifts quietly
across the room, as if that saxophone knew,
somehow, that the fellow staring at that photo
had been weeping, stupidly
& over nothing. At the keyboard, Sonny
Clark looks over once at Dex & nods, & shuts
his eyes, & listens to himself—to both of them.
Staring out the window at the dark,
the man finds, he thinks,
at last, what he's been looking for, & goes on typing.

Oceania, Australia, and New Zealand

Anthony Lawrence

Anthony Lawrence was born in 1957 in Tamworth, New South Wales. He has published five volumes of poetry and has won prizes including the Kenneth Slessor Poetry Prize and the Gwen Harwood Memorial Prize. In "Goanna," a bizarre encounter with a large lizard causes the speaker to reflect on his primal fear of dying and to feel momentarily some empathy for the animals we sacrifice for our own sustenance.

GOANNA

I was standing outside the killing shed,
ankle deep in skulls that knock and roll when you kick them.
I was thinking about the way a sheep dies,
the knife in behind the wind-pipe, the head
snapped back over the knee
when a black goanna ran up my back

and fixed its claws into my neck.
Its tongue was flicking in my ear.
I screamed and reached behind me,
trying to lift its claws from my skin.
The sharp pain, the fear, the way a sheep dies.

THE TRANSLATORS

Sanda Agalidi
Hamid Algar
Radu Andriescu
Anonymous
Brother Anthony
Harry Aveling
David Ball
Lois Bar-yaacov
E. Bell
Adria Bernardi
Sadhu Binning
Liviu Bleoca
Chana Bloch
Ann Born
Alan Boucher
Steve Bradbury
Robert Brady
Inara Cedrins
Vitaly Chernetsky
Dominic Cheung
Nancy Coleman
Martha Collins
Diana Der Hovanessian
Margaret Dickinson
Afia Dil
Melvin Dixon
Charles Doria
Vivian Eden
Richard Ellman
Sharif Elmusa
Thomas G. Ezzy
Ruth Feldman
Bassam Khalil Frangieh
Gary G. Gach
Antonela Glavinic

Margaret Greer
Aniela Gregorek
Jerzy Gregorek
Reinhold Grimm
Olav Grinde
Nandini Gupta
Marilyn Hacker
Talat Sait Halman
Robert Hass
Patrick Henry
James Hoggard
Michael James Hutt
Kathleen Jamie
Lena Jayyusi
Sakna Khadra Jayyusi
Robert L. Jones
J. Kates
Lisa Katz
Mounah A. Khouri
Young-Moo Kim
James Kirup
Carol A. Klee
Lyudmila Kolechkova
Herbert Kuhner
Issam A. Lakkis
Renate Latimer
Paul Lawton
Naomi Lazard
Herbert Lomas
Leza Lowitz
Marzbed Margossian
Narlan Matos-Teixeira
William Matthews
Ken McCullough
W. S. Merwin

Vasa D. Mihailovich
Ian Miher
Jarmila Miher
Czeslaw Milosz
Stephen Mitchell
Gerald Moore
Fred Moramarco
Marco Morelli
Leith Morton
Haba Musengezi
Michio Nakano
Leonard Nathan
Mark Nowak
Naomi Shihab Nye
Ewald Osers
Ron Padgett
Marcus Perryman
Jerzy Peterkiewicz
Wang Ping
Delia Poey
Gilbert Wesley Purdy
G. J. Racz
Burton Raffel
Kathryn Rhett
Peter Robinson
Stephen A. Sadow
Ucha Sakhltkhutsishvili
Minas Savvas
Suchart Sawadsri
Julian Semilian
Oketani Shogo
Richard Sieburth
Charles Simic
John Oliver Simon
Luke Icarus Simon

Leif Sjöberg	Mihai Ursachi	Beth Wellington
William Jay Smith	Muna Asali van Engen	Richard Wilbur
Judith Sonnabend	Ernst van Heerden	John Hartley Williams
Adam J. Sorkin	Marilya Veteto-Conrad	Charles David Wright
Herlinde Spahr	Lidia Vianu	Harold Wright
Steven J. Stewart	Jan Erik Vold	Michelle Yeh
Mark Strand	Keith Waldrop	Jonas Zdanys
Oonagh Stransky	Brenda Walker	Richard Zenith
Brian Swann	Susanne Akemi Wegmüller	Mustafa Ziyalin
Peter Tyran	Mark Weiss	Al Zolynas
Abdulla al-Udhari	Theodore Weiss	

CREDITS

Chinua Achebe: "Love Cycle" from *New Poetry from Africa,* edited by R. Johnson, D. Ker, C. Maduka, and O. Obafemi, University Press, Ibadan, Nigeria, 1996.

Adonis: "A Woman and a Man" from *Victims of a Map: A Bilingual Anthology of Arabic,* translated by Abdulla al-Udhari, Al Saqi Books, London, © Abdulla al-Udhari, 1984.

Luis Miguel Aguilar: "Memo, Who Loved Motorcycles," translated by Robert L. Jones, from *Light from a Nearby Window: Contemporary Mexican Poetry,* edited by Juvenal Acosta, City Lights Books, San Francisco, 1993.

Risto Ahti: "The Beloved's Face," translated by Herbert Lomas, from *Contemporary Finnish Poetry,* edited by Herbert Lomas, Bloodaxe Books, Northumberland, U.K., 1991.

Frank Aig-Imoukhuede: "One Wife for One Man" from *The Penguin Book of Modern African Poetry, 1984,* © Gerald Moore and Ulli Beier, 1963, 1968, 1984. Penguin Books Ltd., Harmondsworth, Middlesex, England.

Agha Shahid Ali: "Ghazal" from *Country without a Post Office,* W. W. Norton and Co., New York, 1997.

Yehuda Amichai: "A Flock of Sheep near the Airport" and "An Ideal Woman," translated by Chana Bloch, from *Literary Olympians, 1992: An International Anthology,* edited by Elizabeth Bartlett, Ford-Brown and Co. Publishers, Boston.

Radu Andriescu: "The Apple" by permission of the translator, Adam J. Sorkin.

Chairil Anwar: "At the Mosque" and "Heaven" from *The Voice of the Night: Complete Poetry and Prose of Chairil Anwar,* 1993, translated by Burton Raffel. Reprinted with the permission of Ohio University Press, Athens, Ohio.

Kofi Anyidoho: "Desert Storm" from the Web site Africaresource.com, http://www.africaresource.com/poe/kofi.htm.

Iftikhar Arif: "The Twelfth Man" from *The Twelfth Man,* translated from Urdu by Brenda Walker, Forest Books, London, 1989.

Peter Armstrong: "Sunderland Nights" from *The Red-Funnelled Boat,* Picador Books, an Imprint of Macmillan Publishers Ltd., London, 1998.

Hector Avellán: "Declaration of Love to Kurt Cobain" from *Rubén's Orphans: Anthology of Contemporary Nicaraguan Poetry,* translated by Marco Morelli, Painted Rooster Press, New Hyde Park, N.Y., 2001.

Kofi Awoonor: "Songs of Abuse: To Stanislaus the Renegade" from *The Heritage of African Poetry: An Anthology of Oral and Written Poetry,* edited by Isidore Okpewho, Longman, U.K., 1985.

Nobuo Ayukawa: "Love," "Sister, I'm Sorry," and "The Last I Heard" translated by Shogo Oketani with Leza Lowitz.

Rafiq Azad: "Woman: The Eternal" translated by Afia Dil.

Wolfgang Bächler: "A Revolt in the Mirror," translated by Reinhold Gromm, from *German 20th Century Poetry* (vol. 69, The German Library), edited by Reinhold Gromm and Irmgard Hunt, Continuum, New York and London, 2001. Reprinted by permission of the Continuum International Publishing Group.

Abdul Wahab al-Bayati: "Secret of Fire" from *Love, Death, and Exile: Poems*, translated from Arabic by Bassam K. Frangieh, Georgetown University Press, 1991.

Mario Benedetti: "The Magnet," translated by Richard Zenith, from *Literary Olympians, 1992: An International Anthology*, edited by Elizabeth Bartlett, Ford-Brown and Co. Publishers, Boston.

Ciaran Berry: "Uascán" from *Poetry Ireland Review* 67 (winter 2000). Reprinted by permission of *Poetry Ireland Review*.

Kashyap Bhattacharya: "The Cricketer" by permission of the poet.

Sadhu Binning: "Revenge" from *Literary Olympians, 1992: An International Anthology*, edited by Elizabeth Bartlett, Ford-Brown and Co. Publishers, Boston.

Vytautas P. Bložė: "Beneath the Stars" from *Four Poets of Lithuania*, selected and translated by Jonas Zdanys, Vaga Publishers, Vilnius, Lithuania, 1995.

Michael Blumenthal: "The Forces" from Dusty Angel, BOA Editions Limited, Rochester, N.Y., 1999.

Robert Bly: "The Man Who Didn't Know What Was His" from *Morning Poems*, HarperCollins, New York, April 1998.

Gudmundur Bödvarsson: "Brother" from *Twenty-Five Modern Icelandic Poets*, selected and translated by Alan Boucher, Icelandic Review Library.

Alain Bosquet: "The Lovers," "An Old Gentleman," and "Celebrities" from *No More Me and Other Poems*, edited by Roger Little, The Dedalus Press, Dublin.

David Bottoms: "Bronchitis" from *Vagrant Grace.* Copyright 1999 by David Bottoms. Reprinted with the permission of Copper Canyon Press.

Breyten Breytenbach: "Eavesdropper," translated by Ernst van Heerden from *The Vintage Book of Contemporary World Poetry*, edited by J. D. McClatchy, Vintage, New York, 1996.

Rofel G. Brion: "Love Song" from *Literary Olympians, 1992: An International Anthology*, edited by Elizabeth Bartlett, Ford-Brown and Co. Publishers, Boston, 1992.

Alan Brownjohn: "Sonnet of a Gentleman" from *In the Cruel Arcade,* Sinclair-Stevenson, London, 1994.

Dennis Brutus: "I Am Alien in Africa and Everywhere" from *Echoes of the Sunbird: An Anthology of Contemporary African Poetry,* compiled by Don Burness, Ohio University Center for International Studies Monographs in International Studies, Africa Series Number 62, Athens, Ohio, 1993.

Charles Bukowski: "3 old men at separate tables" by Charles Bukowski, © 1999 by Linda Lee Bukowski. Reprinted from *What Matters Most Is How Well You Walk through the Fire* with the permission of Black Sparrow Press.

Evgeny Bunimovich: "Excuse and Explanation," translated by Patrick Henry, from *Crossing*

Centuries: The New Generation in Russian Poetry, edited by John High et al., Talisman House Publishers, Jersey City, N.J., 2000.

John Burnside: "The Men's Harbour" from *The Asylum Dance* by John Burnside, published by Jonathan Cape. Reprinted by permission of The Random House Group Ltd.

Roberto Carifi: "Things don't forget . . . ," translated by Oonagh Stransky, from *Amore d'autunno* by Roberto Carifi, Guanda, Milan, Italy, 1998.

Mircea Cartarescu: "A happy day in my life," translated by Julian Semilian and Sanda Agalidi, from www.durationpress.com/kenning/Cartarescu.html.

Raymond Carver: "This Morning" from *All of Us* by Raymond Carver, Knopf, 1996. Permission granted by Tess Gallagher.

Ricardo Castillo: "Ode to the Urge," translated by Robert L. Jones, from *Light from a Nearby Window: Contemporary Mexican Poetry,* edited by Juvenal Acosta, City Lights Books, San Francisco, 1993.

Yi Cha: "Neighbors" from *New Generation: Poems from China Today,* © 1999 by Wang Ping (ed.), by permission of Hanging Loose Press.

Frank Chipasula: "My Blood Brother" from *The Heinemann Book of African Poetry in English,* selected by Adewale Maja-Pearce, Heinemann International, a division of Heinemann Educational Books Ltd. "Manifesto on *Ars Poetica*" from *The New African Poetry: An Anthology,* edited by Ojaide, Tanure, and Tijan M. Sallah, Lynne Rienner Publishers, Boulder and London, 2000.

Chirikure Chirikure: "This Is Where We Laid Him to Rest," College Press, Harare, Zimbabwe.

Antonio Cisneros: "Dedicatory (to My Wife)" from *Coleccion Poiesis, The Newest Peruvian Poetry in Translation,* edited by Luis A. Ramos and Edgar O'Hara, © 1979 by Studia Hispanica, University of Texas, Austin.

Leonard Cohen: "Suzanne" from *Book of Mercy,* Villard Books, New York, 1984; McClelland and Stewart, Toronto, 1984.

Peter Cooley: "Language of Departure" from *Triquarterly* 105 (spring/summer 1999). By permission of Peter Cooley.

Robert Crawford: "Masculinity" from *Masculinity* by Robert Crawford, published by Jonathan Cape. Reprinted by permission of The Random House Group Ltd.

Martin Crucefix: "Pietà" from *A Madder Ghost,* Enitharmon Press, London, 1997. By permission of Enitharmon Press, London.

Tony Curtis: "The Eighth Dream" from *Cimarron Review* 126/127 (winter/spring 1999). By permission of *Cimarron Review.*

Cyril Dabydeen: "Hemingway" from *Discussing Columbus,* Dabydeen, Cyril, Peepal, 1997. Guyana, Canada. Peepal Tree Press Ltd., Leeds U.K.

Philip Dacey: "Four Men in a Car" from *The Deathbed Playboy,* Eastern Washington University Press, 1999. By Permission of Philip Dacey.

Jim Daniels: "Falling Bricks" from *Show and Tell: New and Selected Poems,* University of Wisconsin Press, 2003. By permission of Jim Daniels.

Mahmud Darwish: "Give Birth to Me Again That I May Know" from *Victims of a Map: A Bilingual Anthology of Arabic*, translated by Abdulla al-Udhari, Al Saqj Books, London. © Abdulla al-Udhari, 1984. "On a Canaanite Stone in the Dead Sea," translated by Muna Asali van Engen, from *American Journal of Cultural Exchange, Present and Future* 7/8 (1996).

Jose Manuel del Pino: "Doré V" translated by G. J. Racz.

Antonio Deltoro: "Submarine," translated by John Oliver Simon, from *Light from a Nearby Window: Contemporary Mexican Poetry*, edited by Juvenal Acosta, City Lights Books, 1993.

Carlos Edmundo de Ory: "Silence" from *Atlanta Review* 9, no. 2 (spring 2003). By permission of Steven J. Stewart.

Xue Di: "Nostalgia" from *New Generation: Poems from China Today*, © 1999 by Wang Ping (ed.), by permission of Hanging Loose Press.

Gaspar Aguilera Díaz: "Does Anyone Know Where Roque Dalton Spent His Final Night?" translated by John Oliver Simon, from *Light from a Nearby Window: Contemporary Mexican Poetry*, edited by Juvenal Acosta, City Lights Books, San Francisco, 1993.

Pier G. Di Cicco: "Male Rage Poem" from *The New Canadian Poets, 1970–1985*, edited by Dennis Lee, McClelland and Stewart, Toronto, 1985.

Sa 'di Yusuf: "A Woman," translated by Lena Jayyusi and Naomi Shihab Nye, from *Modern Arabic Poetry*, edited by Salma Khadra Jayyusi, Columbia University Press, New York, 1987.

Stephen Dobyns: "Why Fool Around" from *Pallbearers Envying the One Who Rides*, © 1999 by Stephen Dobyns. Used by permission of Penguin, a division of Penguin Group (USA) Inc.

Michael Donaghy: "Inheritance" from *Dances Learned Last Night: Poems 1975–1995*, Picador, London, 2000. Used with permission of Picador, an Imprint of Macmillan Publishers Ltd.

Theo Dorgan: "The Choice" from *Poetry Ireland Review* 67 (winter 2000). By permission of *Poetry Ireland Review*.

Carlos Drummond de Andrade: "Ballad of Love through the Ages" and "Boy Crying in the Night" from *Looking for Poetry / Songs from the Quechua*, Knopf, 2002.

Stephen Dunn: "Odysseus's Secret" from *Different Hours: Poems* by Stephen Dunn, W. W. Norton and Co., New York, 2000.

Amal Dunqul: "Corner" from *Modern Arabic Poetry: An Anthology*, edited by Salma Khadra Jayyusi, Columbia University Press, New York, 1987.

Duo Duo: "Looking Out from Death" translated and adapted by Fred Moramarco.

Arnljot Eggen: "He called her his willow," translated by Nancy Coleman, from *20 Contemporary Norwegian Poets: A Bilingual Anthology*, edited by Terje Johanssen. Copyright © ed. Johanssen, Terje. St. Martin's Press, Inc., 1984. Reprinted with permission of Palgrave Macmillan.

David Eggleton: "Bouquet of Dead Flowers" from *Poetry NZ* 21 (November 2001). By permission of Alistair Paterson, editor, *Poetry NZ*.

Günter Eich: "The Man in the Blue Smock," translated by Reinhold Gromm, from *German*

20th Century Poetry (vol. 69, The Gemian Library), edited by Reinhold Gromm and Imigard Hunt, Continuum, New York and London, 2001.

Jorge Esquinca: "Fable of the Hunter," translated by Robert L. Jones, from *Light from a Nearby Window: Contemporary Mexican Poetry*, edited by Juvenal Acosta, City Lights Books, 1993.

Rafael Pérez Estrada: "My Uncle the Levitator" and "The Unpublished Man" from *Devoured by the Moon: Selected Poems of Rafael Pérez Estrada*, edited and translated by Steven J. Stewart, Hanging Loose Press, Brooklyn, 2004. By permission of Steven J. Stewart.

Nissim Ezekiel: "Case Study" from http://www.indiaworld.com.

Faiz Ahmed Faiz: "Before You Came" translated by Naomi Lazard. (Widely published on the Internet.)

Moeen Faruqi: "The Return" from *A Dragonfly in the Sun: An Anthology of Pakistani Writing in English*, selected and edited by Muneeza Shamsie, © Oxford University Press 1997, Oxford, New York, Delhi.

Ricardo Feierstein: "Sex," translated by J. Kates and Stephen A. Sadow, from *We, the Generation in the Wilderness*, Ford-Brown and Co. Publishers, Boston, 1989.

Jonathan Fisher: "Six Part Lust Story" from *Poetry NZ 21*. By permission of Alistair Paterson, editor, *Poetry NZ*.

Franco Fortini: "The Seed" from *Summer Is Not All: Selected Poems*, translated by Paul Lawton, Carcanet, Manchester, 1992. By permission of Carcanet Press Ltd.

Robert Francis: "The Base Stealer" from *Collected Poems 1936–76*, University of Massachusetts Press, 1985.

Huan Fu: "Don't, Don't" and "Flower" from *The Isle Full of Noises: Modern Chinese Poetry from Taiwan*, edited and translated by Dominic Cheung. By permission of Columbia University Press, New York.

Juan Carlos Galeano: "Eraser" and "Tree" by permission of the translator, Delia Poey.

Sunil Gangopadhyay: "Blindfold" and "From Athens to Cairo" by permission of the poet.

Herbert Gassner: "Fear" from *Hawks and Nightingales: Current Burgenland Croatian Poetry*, edited by Peter Tyran, Wilhelm Braumüller, Vienna, 1983.

Sky Gilbert: "The Island of Lost Tears" from *Plush: Selected Poems of Sky Gilbert, Courtnay McFarlane, Jeffery Conway, R. M. Vaughan and David Trinidad*, edited by Lynn Crosbie and Michael Holmes, Coach House, Toronto, 1995.

Douglas Goetsch: "Bachelor Song" from *Nobody's Hell*, © 1999 by Douglas Goetsch, by permission of Hanging Loose Press.

Tonino Guerra: "Canto Three" and "Canto Twenty-Four" from *Abandoned Places*, translated by Adria Bernardi, Guernica, Toronto–Buffalo–Lancaster (U.K.), 1999.

Oscar Hahn: "Candlelight Dinner," "Good Night Dear," and "Little Phantoms," from *Love Breaks*, translated by James Hoggard, Latin American Literary Review Press, Pittsburgh, 1991.

Alamgir Hashmi: "Pro Bono Publico" from *A Choice of Hashmi's Verse*, Oxford University Press, Pakistan, copyright Alamgir Hashmi, 1997.

Buland al-Haydari: "Old Age" from *An Anthology of Modern Arabic Poetry*, selected, edited, and translated by Mounah A. Khouri and Hamid Algar, University of California Press, Berkeley, Los Angeles, London, 1974.

Seamus Heaney: "In Memoriam M. K. H." from "Clearances" from *Opened Ground: Selected Poems 1966–1996* by Seamus Heaney. Copyright © 1998 by Seamus Heaney. Reprinted by permission of Farrar, Straus and Giroux.

A. L. Hendriks: "Will the Real Me Please Stand Up?" from *The Penguin Book of Caribbean Verse in English,* selected and edited by Paula Burnett. © Paula Burnett, 1986. Penguin Books Ltd.

Zbigniew Herbert: "Rosy Ear," translated by Czeslaw Milosz, from *Selected Poems,* Ecco Press, 1986.

Francisco Hernandez: "Autograph," translated by John Oliver Simon, from *Light from a Nearby Window: Contemporary Mexican Poetry,* edited by Juvenal Acosta, City Lights Books, 1993.

Anzai Hitoshi: "New Blade" from *An Anthology of Contemporary Japanese Poetry,* edited and translated by Leith Morton, Garland Publishing, Inc., New York and London, 1993.

Snorri Hjartarson: "House in Rome" from *Poems of Today from Twenty-Five Icelandic Poets,* selected and translated by Alan Boucher, Iceland Review Library, 1971.

Kjell Hjern: "On the Growth of Hair in Middle Age" and "To My Love" from *The Forest of Childhood: Poems from Sweden,* edited and translated by William Jay Smith and Leif Sjöberg, New Rivers Abroad Book, New Rivers Press, 1996.

Vladimir Holan: "Meeting in a Lift" and "She Asked You" from *Erotic Poems,* selected and edited by Peter Washington, Everyman's Library Pocket Books, Alfred A. Knopf, New York, 1994.

Andrew Hudgins: "Tools: An Ode" from *Babylon in a Jar* by Andrew Hudgins. Copyright © 1998 by Andrew Hudgins. Reprinted by permission of Houghton Mifflin Company. All rights reserved.

Michael Hulse: "Concentrating" from *Eating Strawberries in the Necropolis,* Harvill, London, 1991.

Hung Hung: "A Hymn to Hualien" and "Helas!" from *Chinese Pen* (Taiwan); "A Hymn to Hualien" reprinted in *Manoa: A Pacific Journal of International Writing.* By permission of the translator, Steve Bradbury.

Ismael Hurreh: "Pardon Me" from *Poems of Black Africa,* edited by Wole Soyinka, Hill and Wang, a division of Farrar, Straus and Giroux, New York, 1975.

Yair Hurvitz: "An Autobiographical Moment" translated by Lois Bar-Yaacov.

Nadir Hussein: "A Wedding" from *A Dragonfly in the Sun: An Anthology of Pakistani Writing in English,* selected and edited by Muneeza Shamsie, Oxford University Press, Oxford, New York, Delhi, 1997.

Evan X Hyde: "Super High" by Evan X. Hyde from *Of Words: An Anthology of Belizean Poetry* (Belizean Writers Series Number Three), 1997.

Igor Irtenev: "At the Pavelets radial-line station . . .," translated by Mark Nowak and Patrick Henry, from *Crossing Centuries: The New Generation in Russian Poetry,* edited by John High et al., Talisman House Publishers, Jersey City, N.J., 2000.

Jayanta Mahapatra: "Shadows" from *Literary Olympians, 1992: An International Anthology,* edited by Elizabeth Bartlett, Ford-Brown and Co. Publishers, Boston, 1992.

Nicholás Maré: "You can say that the bird as the saying goes" by permission of the translator, Gilbert Wesley Purdy.

Harry Martinson: "Santa Claus" from *The Forest of Childhoood: Poems from Sweden,* edited and translated by William Jay Smith and Leif Sjöberg, New Rivers Abroad Book, New Rivers Press, 1996.

Marco Martos: "Casti Connubi" from *Colección Poiesis: The Newest Peruvian Poetry in Translation,* edited by Luis A. Ramos and Edgar O'Hara, © 1979 by the authors. Studia Hispanica Editors, University of Texas, Austin.

Salman Masalha: "Cage" and "On Artistic Freedom in the Nationalist Era" by permission of the poet.

Ivan Matanov: "Still I see in front of me" from *Young Poets of a New Bulgaria: An Anthology,* edited by Belin Tonchev, Forest Books, London and Boston, 1990. Original work © *Bulgarian poets do Jusautor,* Sofia 1990.

Narlan Matos-Teixera: "My Father's House" by permission of the poet.

William Matthews: "Cheap Seats, the Cincinnati Gardens, Professional Basketball, 1959," from *Time and Money,* Houghton Mifflin, 1995.

Walt McDonald: "Crossing the Road" from *Blessings the Body Gave,* Ohio State University Press, Columbus, Ohio, 1998.

Semezdin Mehmedinovic: "An Essay" and "The Only Dream" from *Scar on the Stone: Contemporary Poetry from Bosnia,* edited by Chris Agee, Bloodaxe Books.

Stein Mehren: "Mother, we were a heavy burden," translated by Olav Grinde, from *20 Contemporary Norwegian Poets: A Bilingual Anthology,* edited by Terje Johanssen. Copyright © ed. Johanssen, Terje. St. Martin's Press, Inc., 1984. Reprinted with permission of Palgrave Macmillan.

Orlando Ricardo Menes: "Sodomy" by permission of the poet.

Christopher Merrill: "A Boy Juggling a Soccer Ball," from *Watch Fire,* White Pine Press, 1994.

W. S. Merwin: "Yesterday" from *Flower and Hand: Poems 1977–1983: The Compass Flower: Opening the Hand: Feathers from the Hill,* Copper Canyon Press.

Henri Michaux: "Simplicity," translated by Richard Ellmann, from *99 Poems in Translation: An Anthology,* edited by Harold Pinter, Anthony Astbury, and Geoffrey Godbert, Faber and Faber and Greville Press, 1994.

Virgil Mihaiu: "The Ultimate Luxury Woman" from *The Café Review* 7 (spring 1996). By permission of the translator, Adam J. Sorkin.

Czeslaw Milosz: "After Paradise" from *The Collected Poems, 1931–1987,* translated by Robert Hass. Copyright © 1988 by Czeslaw Milosz Royalties, Inc. Reprinted by permission of HarperCollins Publishers Inc.

Fabio Morabito: "Master of an Expanse," translated by E. Bell, from *Light from a Nearby Window: Contemporary Mexican Poetry,* edited by Juvenal Acosta, City Lights Books, 1993.

Fred Moramarco: "Clark Kent, Naked" by permission of the poet.

Marco Morelli: "A Volunteer's Fairy Tale" by permission of the poet.

Mervyn Morris: "The Pond" from *The Pond,* New Beacon Books, London, 1973.

Lupenga Mphande: "I Was Sent For" by permission of the poet.

Oswald Mbuyiseni Mtshali: "A Voice from the Dead" from *New Poetry from Africa,* edited by R. Johnson, D. Ker, C. Maduka, and O. Obafemi, University Press PLC, Ibadan, 1996.

Yang Mu: "Let the Wind Recite" from *The Isle Full of Noises: Modern Chinese Poetry from Taiwan,* edited and translated by Dominic Cheung. © Columbia University Press. Reprinted with the permission of the publisher.

Les Murray: "Folklore," "Performance," and "The Mitchells" by permission of the poet.

Leonard Nathan: "Circlings" from *Circlings,* Orchises Press, by permission of the poet.

Shuja Nawaz: "The Initiation" from *A Dragonfly in the Sun: An Anthology of Pakistani Writing in English,* selected and edited by Muneeza Shamsie, © Oxford University Press 1997, Oxford, New York, Delhi.

Luis Rogelio Nogueras: "A Poem," translated by Mark Weiss, from *Poetry International* 6 (2002).

Cees Nooteboom: "Midday," translated by Herlinde Spahr and Leonard Nathan, from *Literary Olympians, 1992: An International Anthology,* edited by Elizabeth Bartlett, Ford-Brown and Co. Publishers, Boston.

Henrik Nordbrandt: "Old Man in Meditation," translated by Ann Born, from *Literary Olympians, 1992: An International Anthology,* edited by Elizabeth Bartlett, Ford-Brown and Co. Publishers, Boston.

Dennis O'Driscoll: "The Lads" from *Poetry Ireland Review* 67 (winter 2000). By permission of Dennis O'Driscoll and *Poetry Ireland Review.*

U Sam Oeur: "The Loss of My Twins," translated by Ken McCullough, from *Sacred Vows* by U Sam Oeur, Coffee House Press, 1998.

Tanure Ojaide: "State Executive" from *The Heinemann Book of African Poetry in English,* Heinemann, Portsmouth, N.H., 1990.

George Oommen: "A Private Sorrow" by permission of the poet.

Donny O'Rourke: "Clockwork" and "Algren" from *The Waistband* by Donny O'Rourke, Polygon, Edinburgh, 1997.

Valeri Petrov: "A Cry from Childhood" from *Window on the Black Sea: Bulgarian Poetry in Translation,* by permission of Carnegie Mellon University Press, Pittsburgh, © 1992 by Richard Harteis.

Al Pittman: "The Echo of the Ax" from *The New Canadian Poets, 1970–1985,* edited by Dennis Lee, McClelland and Stewart, Toronto, 1985.

Nizar Qabbani: "The Fortune Teller" from http://aqaffaf.hypermart.net/fortune.htm, adapted by the editors.

Taufiq Rafat: "Circumcision" from *A Dragonfly in the Sun: An Anthology of Pakistani Writing in English,* selected and edited by Muneeza Shamsie, © Oxford University Press, Pakistan 1997.

Cecil Rajendra: "Prince of the Dance" from *Child of the Sun and Other Poems,* by permission of Bogle-L'Ouverture Publications, London.

Vikram Seth: "Unclaimed" and "Soon" from *The Oxford India Anthology of Twelve Modern Indian Poets*, chosen and edited by Arvind Krishna Merrotra, Oxford University Press, Calcutta, 1993.

Ahmad Shamlu: "Somber Song" from *Literature East and West: Major Voices in Contemporary Persian Literature*, vol. 20, 1976, edited by Michael Hillman. "Poetry That Is Life" from *Manoocheer Aryanpour, A History of Persian Literature*, Tehran, 1973. Poems found at http://www.shamlu.com/index.htm.

Aleksandr Shatalov: "I love bathing in the river . . . ," translated by Vitaly Chernetsky, from *Crossing Centuries: The New Generation in Russian Poetry*, edited by John High et al., Talisman House Publishers, Jersey City, N.J., 2000.

Aleksey Shelvakh: "Veterans" translated by J. Kates.

Bishwabimohan Shreshtha: "Should I Earn My Daily Bread, or Should I Write a Poem?" from *Himalayan Voices: An Introduction to Modern Nepali Literature*, translated and edited by Michael James Hutt, University of California Press, Berkeley and Los Angeles, California, University of California Press Ltd., Oxford, England, © 1991 by The Regents of the University of California.

Alexander Shurbanov: "Attractions," translated by Ewald Osers, from *Literary Olympians, 1992: An International Anthology*, edited by Elizabeth Bartlett, Ford-Brown and Co. Publishers, Boston.

Charles Simic: "At the Cookout" from *Walking the Black Cat: Poems*, Harcourt Brace and Company, 1996.

James Simmons: "The Pleasant Joys of Brotherhood" from *Poems 1956–1986*, by permission of the poet and The Gallery Press, Loughcrew, Oldcastle, County Meath, Ireland.

Luke Icarus Simon: "Measuring Apollo" and "Ravine," translated from the Greek by Luke Icarus Simon, by permission of the poet.

Peter Skrzynecki: "Buddha, Birdbath, Hanging Plant," from *Time's Revenge*, 1999, by permission of the poet and Brandl and Schlesinger Pty. Ltd., Rose Bay, New South Wales, Australia.

Ivan Slamnig: "A Sailor" from *Contemporary Yugoslav Poetry*, edited by Vasa D. Mihailovich, University of Iowa Press, Iowa City, 1977.

Russell Soaba: "Looking thru Those Eyeholes" from *Through Melanesian Eyes: An Anthology of Papua New Guinean Writing*, compiled by Ganga Powell, Macmillan, Melbourne, 1987.

Juan Sobalvarro: "I've Seen a Dead Man" by permission of the translator.

Marin Sorescu: "Balls and Hoops" from *Midday Moon* 2 (winter 2001), and "Don Juan (after he'd consumed tons of lipstick . . .)" from *Poetry International* 3 (1999), by permission of the translator, Adam J. Sorkin.

Gary Soto: "Mexicans Begin Jogging," © 1981 by Gary Soto, by permission of the poet.

Jon Stallworthy: "The Source" from *Rounding the Horn: Collected Poems* by Jon Stallworthy, Carcanet, 1998.

Olafs Stumbrs: "Song at a Late Hour" from *Contemporary Latvian Poetry*, edited by Inara Cedrins, University of Iowa Press, Iowa City, 1984.

Virgil Suarez: "Duende" by permission of the poet.

Husein Tahmiščić: "You're Not a Man If You Don't Die" from *Scar on the Stone: Contemporary Poetry from Bosnia*, edited by Chris Agee, Bloodaxe Books, Newcastle upon Tyne, U.K., 1998.

Tsujii Takashi: "Woman Singing" from *Disappearance of the Butterfly* by Tsujii Takashi, translated by Robert Brady and Susanne Akemi Wegmuller. Permissions from Katydid Books, Rochester, Mich.

Ulku Tamer: "The Dagger," translated by Talat Sait Halman, from *Literature East and West* (March 1973), from http://www.cs.rpi.edu/~sibel/poetry/poems/ulku_tamer/english/the_dagger.

Shuntarō Tanikawa: "Kiss" from *The Selected Poems of Shuntarō Tanikawa*, translated by Harold Wright, North Point Press, Berkeley, 1983.

Bahadur Tejani: "Lines for a Hindi Poet" from *Poems of Black Africa*, edited by Wole Soyinka, Hill and Wang, a division of Farrar, Straus and Giroux, New York, 1975.

Nguyen Quang Thieu: "Eleven Parts of Feeling" from *Poetry International* 5 (2001).

Simon Thompson: "All Apologies to L. Cohen" from *A Web Journal of Contemporary Canadian Poetry and Poetics* 2, no. 1 (fall 1997), by permission of the poet.

Edwin Thumboo: "The Exile" from *The Second Tongue: An Anthology of Poetry from Malaysia and Singapore*, selected and with an introduction by Edwin Thumboo, Heinemann Educational Books (Asia) Ltd., Singapore, Kuala Lumpur, Hong Kong, 1097.

Ahmed Tidjani-Cissé: "Home News," translated by Gerald Moore, from *The Penguin Book of Modern African Poetry*, edited by Gerald Moore and Ulli Beier, Third Edition, Penguin Books Ltd., Harmondsworth, Middlesex, England.

Quincy Troupe: "Change" from *Weather Reports: New and Selected Poems*, Harlem River Press, 1991.

Dimitris Tsaloumas: "Epilogue," "A Song for My Father," and "Old Snapshot" from *Stoneland Harvest: New and Selected Poems by Dimitris Tsaloumas*, Shoestring Press, 1999.

Tenzin Tsundue: "My Tibetanness" from *Crossing the Border*, by permission of poet.

Ko Un: "Headmaster Abe" from *The Sound of My Waves: Poems by Ko Un*, translated by Brother Anthony, Young-Moo Kim, and Gary G. Gach, © 1993 Brother Anthony. Cornell East Asia Series, Cornell University, Ithaca, N.Y., 1993.

Mihai Ursachi: "A Monologue" by permission of the translator, Adam J. Sorkin.

Jan Erik Vold: "Hokusai the old master who painted a wave like nobody ever painted a wave before him" and "Thor Heyerdahl's mother" from *20 Contemporary Norwegian Poets: A Bilingual Anthology*, edited by Terje Johanssen. Copyright © ed. Johanssen, Terje. St. Martin's Press, Inc., 1984. Reprinted with permission of Palgrave Macmillan.

Al-Munsif al-Wahaybi: "The Desert" from *Modern Arabic Poetry*, edited by Salma Khadra Jayyusi and translated by Salma Khadra Jayyusi and Naomi Shihab Nye, Columbia University Press, New York, 1987.

Derek Walcott: "Love after Love" from *Collected Poems 1948–1984*, Noonday Press. By permission of Derek Walcott.

John Powell Ward: "In the Box" from *A Certain Marvelous Thing* (Bridgend, Wales: Seren Books, 1993). By permission of Seren Books, Poetry Wales Press.

Andrew Waterman: "Birth Day" from *In the Planetarium*, Carcanet Press, Manchester, U.K., 1990.

Howard White: "The Men There Were Then" by permission of the poet.

Hugo Williams: "Making Friends with Ties" from *Selected Poems*, Oxford University Press, 1989.

Karol Wojtyla: "Sister" from *Karol Wojtyla, Collected Poems*, translated by Jerzy Peterkiewicz, Hutchinson, London, 1982. Reprinted with permission of the publisher.

Kit Wright: "Here Come Two Very Old Men" from *Hoping It Might Be So*, Leviathan, Oxford, 2000. Permission from Leviathan.

Liang Xiaobin: "China, I've Lost My Key" from *Anthology of Modern Chinese Poetry*, edited and translated by Michelle Yeh, Yale University Press, New Haven and London, 1992.

Wang Xiaolong: "In Memoriam: Dedicated to My Father" from *Anthology of Modern Chinese Poetry*, edited and translated by Michelle Yeh, Yale University Press, New Haven and London, 1992.

Zahrad: "The Woman Cleaning Lentils" from *Anthology of Armenian Poetry*, translated and edited by Diana Der Hovanessian and Marzbed Margossian, New York. © 1978 Columbia University Press. Reprinted with permission of the publisher.

Andrea Zanzotto: "From a New Height" from *Selected Poetry of Andrea Zanzotto*, edited and translated by Ruth Feldman and Brian Swann, Princeton University Press, Princeton, N.J., 1975.

Tawfiq Zayyad: "Here We Will Stay," translated by Sharif Elmusa and Charles Doria, from *Modern Arabic Poetry*, edited by Salma Khadra Jayyusi, Columbia University Press, New York, 1987. By permission of Columbia University Press, N.Y.

Jonas Zdanys: "The Angels of Wine" from *Lithuanian Crossing*, The White Birch Press, Mt. Carmel, Conn., 1999, and by permission of the poet.

Adam Ziemianin: "Heart Attack" by permission of the translators.

Péter Zilahy: "Dictators" by permission of the poet.

Mustafa Ziyalan: "Night Ride on 21" by permission of the poet.

Al Zolynas: "Whistling Woman" by permission of the poet.

Every effort has been made to acknowledge and gain permission for all of the previously published poems included in this anthology. The editors and the University of Georgia Press apologize for any errors or omissions in the above list. Any corrections or emendations to these acknowledgements should be directed to the University of Georgia Press.

INDEX OF POETS

INDEX OF TITLES